Social Studies Alive!®
Regions of Our Country

Chief Executive Officer
Bert Bower

Chief Operating Officer
Amy Larson

Director of Product Development
Maria Favata

Strategic Product Manager
Nathan Wellborne

Content Developer
Ginger Wu

Senior Strategic Editor
Kim Merlino

Program Editors and Writers
Mikaila Garfinkel
Sally Isaacs
Glenda Stewart
Kelly Stewart
Alex White
Ginger Wu

Production Manager
Jodi Forrest

Operations & Software Manager
Marsha Ifurung

Designer
Sarah Osentowski

Art Direction
Julia Foug

Teachers' Curriculum Institute
PO Box 1327
Rancho Cordova, CA 95741

Customer Service: 800-497-6138
www.teachtci.com

ISBN 978-1-58371-743-1
2 3 4 5 6 7 8 9 10 -WC- 21 20 19 18 17

Manufactured by Webcrafters, Inc., Madison, WI
United States of America, June 2017, Job #130620

English Language Arts & Literacy and *Social Studies Alive!*

Social Studies Alive! is aligned with the Common Core State Standards for English Language Arts & Literacy[1] (CCELA) to ensure that students develop literacy skills through learning social studies. The K–5 CCELA are organized around four college and career readiness strands: reading, writing, speaking and listening, and language.

Key Points from the ELA Common Core	*Social Studies Alive!*
Reading	
Informational and literary texts should be balanced, with at least 50 percent of reading time devoted to expository texts.	*Social Studies Alive!* reflects this balance in the Student Text. Each lesson has several sections of purely informational text that explain the content of that lesson, followed by a Reading Further article that blends literary and informational style text to engage students.
There is a "staircase" of increasing complexity in what students must be able to read as they move throughout the grades.	*Social Studies Alive!* is written with close attention paid to the text complexity, with increasingly sophisticated text as students progress through the grades. However, within each grade's text, there is variation in the complexity to ensure that there is challenging text for all students.
Close reading of text is used to identify main ideas, supporting details, and evidence.	*Social Studies Alive!* Reading Notes in the Interactive Student Notebook require students to answer questions using evidence from the text and require a clear understanding of the main ideas and other details provided in the section.
Writing	
Routine production of writing appropriate for a range of tasks, purposes, and audiences is emphasized.	From the earliest grades, *Social Studies Alive!* students practice three types of writing—writing to persuade, writing to inform or explain, and writing to convey experience. For example, when they record Reading Notes, students enjoy the challenges of writing about a personal experience related to the lesson, creating timelines, and writing song lyrics.
Effective use of evidence is central throughout the writing standards.	*Social Studies Alive!* students are expected to use evidence appropriately to support their analysis, reflections, and research. They are given support in identifying key details, which will serve most effectively as evidence. They also reflect on the role evidence plays in the social sciences and argument in general.

[1]National Governors Association Center for Best Practices, Council of Chief State School Officers. *Common Core State Standards for English Language Arts & Literacy in History/Social Studies, Science, and Technical Subjects.* National Governors Association Center for Best Practices, Council of Chief State School Officers, Washington D.C. Date: 2010.

Key Points from the ELA Common Core	*Social Studies Alive!*
Speaking and Listening	
Participation in rich, structured academic conversations in one-on-one, small-group, and whole class situations is emphasized.	The teaching strategies in *Social Studies Alive!* provide varied grouping techniques, resulting in a balance of paired, small group, and whole class discussions in which students reflect on their experiences and understanding of the activities. These discussions are designed to build clear communication skills that are critical to success in social studies and for college and career readiness.
Contributing accurate, relevant information; responding to and building on what others have said; and making comparisons and contrasts are important skills for productive conversations.	The cooperative tolerant classroom conventions emphasized throughout all of TCI's curricula encourage students to respond to and build on ideas and arguments presented by other students. During discussions, *Social Studies Alive!* guides students to compare and contrast relevant experiences across the four disciplines of social studies.
Language	
Students should acquire and use general academic and domain-specific words.	*Social Studies Alive!* has a progression of increasingly sophisticated vocabulary built into it. Key terms are used throughout a lesson or the year without overwhelming students with too many unfamiliar words. Every component of *Social Studies Alive!* makes use of the vocabulary and includes activities to help solidify comprehension.
Skills to determine or clarify the meaning of unknown words or phrases are essential.	*Social Studies Alive!* vocabulary terms are previewed at the beginning of the lesson and students complete vocabulary development assignments, such as a Word Parts Log, that trains students to parse words to infer meaning.
Students should demonstrate command of standard English, including grammar, punctuation, and spelling.	Throughout all components of *Social Studies Alive!*, students are expected to demonstrate command of the conventions of written and spoken English. An Editing and Proofreading Checklist is included to help students write with minimal errors.

Considerate Text

Social Studies Alive! is both engaging and helps students read text that is more complex and at a higher level. That's because our authors wrote it as a "considerate text," which is another way of saying that it makes readers want to read it. Here are some ways this book is considerate for all levels of readers.

Thoughtfully selected large images illustrate the main idea and support visual learners.

Short sections, each with an informative title, make it easier for readers to understand and remember the main ideas.

New York City has more than 27,000 people per square mile. Small towns in the Northeast are much less crowded.

population density a measure of the average number of people living in one unit of area

Important new social studies words are in bold type. These words are defined in the margin and in the glossary.

Section conclusions summarize the main ideas of the section and prepare readers for the next section.

1. Living in the Northeast

Where do you live? Do you live in a big city? Maybe you live in a medium-sized suburb. Maybe you even live in a small town or rural area. Each of these places has a different **population density**. Population density is a measure of how many people live in a given amount of land. It is often shown as the number of people per square mile of land. The word *per* means "for each." A square mile is a square piece of land measuring one mile on each side.

Population density affects how people live. Many rural areas often have fewer than 1,000 people per square mile. This means that there are, on average, fewer than 1,000 people living on each square mile of land. Larger areas have more than 1,000 people per square mile. Some urban areas can have over 25,000 people per square mile.

There are good things about living in both rural and urban areas. In small towns, people can get to know each other more easily, and neighbors often help each other. Life can be quiet and peaceful there.

Cities may not seem as friendly as small towns, but cities offer people more choices. There are many places to shop, and restaurants serve food from many places around the world. There are many exciting things to do in a city.

Each lesson is carefully
constructed so that each section
builds on the previous one.

2. Reading a Population Density Map

Some maps show the population density of places in
the United States. They often show how many people per
square mile live in different parts of the nation. Population
maps have map keys. Some population maps use colors to
represent different numbers of people per square mile.

In the Northeast, population density is very high along
the coast. This area is a **megalopolis**. The word megalopolis
means "great city." The megalopolis of Boswash stretches
from Massachusetts south through parts of Rhode Island,
Connecticut, New York, New Jersey, Pennsylvania,
Delaware, and Maryland.

Look at this population density map of the Northeast.
What do you notice about the population density of
Boswash? Now look at the states of Vermont, New
Hampshire, and Maine on the map. How is the population
density of these states different from that of Boswash?

megalopolis a "great
city" consisting of a string of
towns and cities where many
people live

This map shows the population
density of the Northeast. The
map key shows what areas have
more people per square mile.

Section introductions help
link the new section to the
last section.

Captions for photos,
illustrations, and maps
reinforce the main idea of
the section and provide
details about the picture.

Single-column text makes it
easier to read. Paragraphs
end at the bottom of the
page instead of continuing
on the next page.

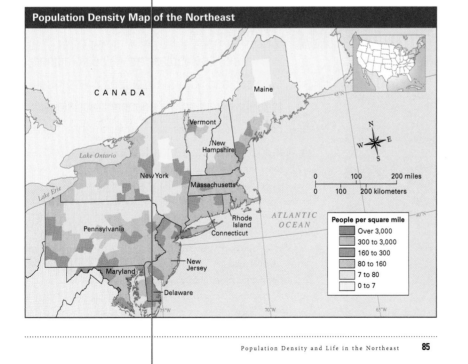

Population Density Map of the Northeast

CANADA

Maine

Vermont

New
Hampshire

Lake Ontario

New York

Lake Erie

Massachusetts

Rhode
Island

Connecticut

ATLANTIC
OCEAN

Pennsylvania

New
Jersey

Maryland

Delaware

N
W   E
S

0   100   200 miles
0   100   200 kilometers

People per square mile
- Over 3,000
- 300 to 3,000
- 160 to 300
- 80 to 160
- 7 to 80
- 0 to 7

Population Density and Life in the Northeast **85**

The Four Core Disciplines of Social Studies

Each of the four core disciplines identified by the National Council for the Social Studies in its C3 Framework[2] has a unique set of ideas, tools, and ways of thinking. Each lesson of *Social Studies Alive!* is aligned to one or more of these disciplines.

 Civics

Important ideas of civics are based on understanding government at various levels, the political system, rules and laws, civic engagement, and democratic principles.

 Economics

The idea of "resources" as including human, physical, and natural resources is essential for understanding the economic decisions people, businesses, and governments make in local, national, and global markets.

[2]National Council for the Social Studies (NCSS), *The College, Career, and Civic Life (C3) Framework for Social Studies State Standards: Guidance for Enhancing the Rigor of K–12 Civics, Economics, Geography, and History* (Silver Spring, MD: NCSS, 2013).

Geography

Using maps and other representations of Earth, understanding the relationship between culture and the environment, analyzing how human populations change, and learning that some environmental changes occur on a global scale are all essential aspects of geography.

 History

Reasoning about chronological patterns, explaining how people's perspectives can change, working with historical sources, identifying causes and effects, and developing claims from evidence are some of the skills students develop as they study history.

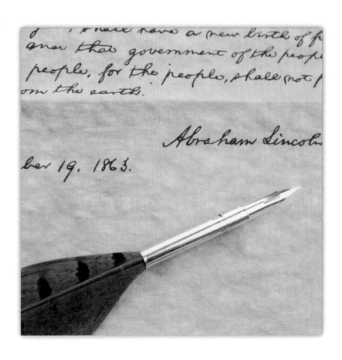

Look for the discipline icons at the beginning of each lesson and Reading Further.

Study Your State

Every lesson of the *Social Studies Alive! Regions of Our Country* Student Text includes a section called Study Your State. Here students learn skills aligned with the National Council for the Social Studies' C3 Framework for Social Studies Standards. This framework is organized into four dimensions.

Dimension 1: Developing Questions and Planning Inquiries

The Student Text models the kinds of questions students may ask when investigating their own state. Students learn to identify sources that will help them answer their questions.

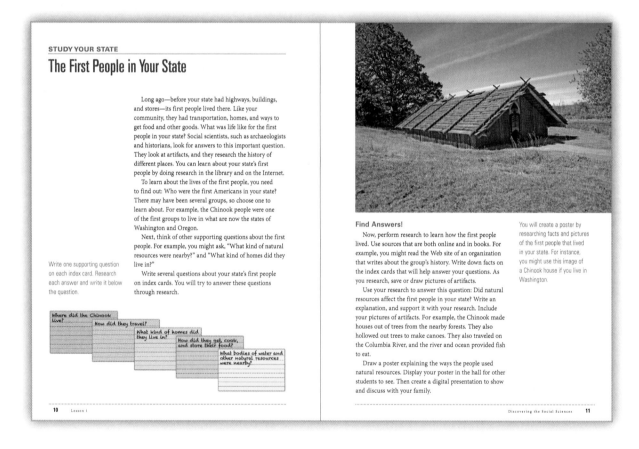

The First People in Your State

Long ago—before your state had highways, buildings, and stores—its first people lived there. Like your community, they had transportation, homes, and ways to get food and other goods. What was life like for the first people in your state? Social scientists, such as archaeologists and historians, look for answers to this important question. They look at artifacts, and they research the history of different places. You can learn about your state's first people by doing research in the library and on the Internet.

To learn about the lives of the first people, you need to find out: Who were the first Americans in your state? There may have been several groups, so choose one to learn about. For example, the Chinook people were one of the first groups to live in what are now the states of Washington and Oregon.

Next, think of other supporting questions about the first people. For example, you might ask, "What kind of natural resources were nearby?" and "What kind of homes did they live in?"

Write several questions about your state's first people on index cards. You will try to answer these questions through research.

Write one supporting question on each index card. Research each answer and write it below the question.

Where did the Chinook live?
How did they travel?
What kind of homes did they live in?
How did they get, cook, and store their food?
What bodies of water and other natural resources were nearby?

Find Answers!

Now, perform research to learn how the first people lived. Use sources that are both online and in books. For example, you might read the Web site of an organization that writes about the group's history. Write down facts on the index cards that will help answer your questions. As you research, save or draw pictures of artifacts.

Use your research to answer this question: Did natural resources affect the first people in your state? Write an explanation, and support it with your research. Include your pictures of artifacts. For example, the Chinook made houses out of trees from the nearby forests. They also hollowed out trees to make canoes. They also traveled on the Columbia River, and the river and ocean provided fish to eat.

Draw a poster explaining the ways the people used natural resources. Display your poster in the hall for other students to see. Then create a digital presentation to show and discuss with your family.

You will create a poster by researching facts and pictures of the first people that lived in your state. For instance, you might use this image of a Chinook house if you live in Washington.

Dimension 2: Applying Disciplinary Tools and Concepts

Skill instruction focuses on the tools of the lesson discipline: civics, economics, geography, or history.

Dimension 3: Evaluating Sources and Using Evidence

After reading the text, students carry out corresponding activities located in the online lesson Presentation and in their Interactive Student Notebooks. They collect data about their own state, make decisions about the resources they use, record their sources, and organize the information they collect.

Dimension 4: Communicating Conclusions and Taking Informed Action

The activity procedure guides students in using evidence to construct arguments and explanations and in summarizing them for others. For example, students may present their conclusions as maps, scripts, drawings, graphs, timelines, or songs.

As your class uses Study Your State, students learn to think and act like social scientists—historians, geographers, economists, and political scientists—challenge themselves to learn about your state, and develop insights that they will want to share with others in the school community.

"Study Your State" Skills

✓ Asking compelling questions that can be answered with inquiry

✓ Identifying content from the core disciplines (geography, civics, history, and economics) needed to carry out inquiry

✓ Identifying and evaluating research resources

✓ Distinguishing fact from opinion

✓ Gathering evidence from multiple sources, including maps, photos, and other graphics

✓ Constructing maps and other graphic representations

✓ Using evidence to develop claims

✓ Constructing and critiquing explanations and arguments

✓ Applying democratic procedures and identifying strategies for civic action

✓ Presenting summaries of the results of inquiry to others outside the classroom using print, oral, or digital technologies

How to Use this Program

Welcome to *Social Studies Alive! Regions of Our Country,* where students discover how the skills of the social sciences are used to explore the United States.

1 The teacher begins each lesson with a **Presentation** that previews the lesson and facilitates one or more minds-on or hands-on activities.

2 In the Presentations, students participate in an interactive **activity** that connects to English Language Arts literacy by using the tools of social studies inquiry: asking questions, using sources and other evidence to develop claims, and communicating conclusions.

3a In the online **Student Subscription,** students expand their knowledge through reading the Student Text and processing what they have learned in the **Interactive Student Notebook.** Students can also play a game-like **Reading Challenge** activity.

3b Alternatively, students can read from the **Student Edition** and complete a consumable Interactive Student Notebook.

4 The lesson ends with students demonstrating their knowledge of the core ideas and essential social studies skills of the lesson through a variety of paper and online **assessments.**

How to Read the Table of Contents

The table of contents is your guide to *Social Studies Alive! Regions of Our Country*. It lists all the lessons in your text as well as additional resources, such as an in-depth look at the ideas that unite us as Americans.

The **lesson title** tells you the overall topic of the lesson.

Every lesson emphasizes one or more of the four **core disciplines** of social studies: Civics, Economics, Geography, and History.

A **summary** of the lesson tells you what you will read about and discover.

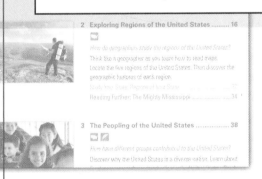

Every lesson includes a **Study Your State** section, which helps you develop the skills you need to research information about your state.

Every lesson begins with an **essential question** to prepare you for inquiry—asking your own questions and proposing answers and solutions.

Every lesson includes a **Reading Further**—an interesting in-depth article that promotes literacy and helps you engage with the content even further.

Contents

What attracts people to the cities of the West?

Explore seven cities of the West region. Read about each city's geography, history, population, and economy. Then discover some fun things to do there.

How has geography influenced life in your state?

Think like a geographer. Discover tools a geographer might use. Follow the suggestions to find out more about your state's geography.

How can you learn about your state's history?

Think like a historian. Discover how states were settled. Follow the suggestions to find out how your state grew.

16 Researching Your State's Economy............... 284

What do you need to know to understand your state's economy?

Think like an economist. Read about how states' economies grow. Then use the suggestions to find out which industries helped your state develop.

17 Researching Your State's Government.......... 298

How does your state's government work?

Think like a political scientist. Explore how state governments work. Then learn how ideas become laws.

Ideas That Unite Us as Americans...................... 312

Read about the shared ideals of Americans. Discover how American ideals are expressed in the written documents of our country.

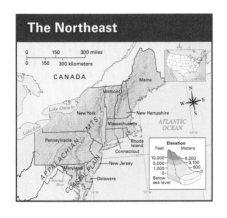

The Northeast

Maps

Primary Sources

Primary sources are created by people who have seen or taken part in the events described. See for yourself what you can learn about history from old photos, advertisements, and artifacts.

Discovering the Social Sciences

What do social scientists do?

Introduction

Why are some people rich and others poor? How can studying the past help us live better today? These are the kinds of questions that social scientists ask.

Social scientists study the ways people live in groups. Their field is called social science. Some social scientists study small groups, such as families, and others study large groups, such as nations. Think about some other examples of groups that a social scientist could study. Your class is an example of a small group, and your school is a larger group. Some social scientists may study the groups in schools.

How do people spend their money? What physical features lie around us? How do political leaders use their power? What happened in the past? By asking and answering these questions, social scientists learn about the economy, geography, politics, and history of the groups they study. Social scientists want to understand why people behave as they do. To find out, they watch people, ask questions, and study written records, such as legal documents, letters, and news stories.

They also study other artifacts, which are things people have made. Your clothes are a kind of artifact, and so are all the things you carry in your backpack. Items in your classroom like a globe, pencil, and desk are artifacts, too. What would a social scientist learn about you by studying these artifacts? You might be surprised by the answer!

> **Social Studies Vocabulary**
>
> **economy**
>
> **geography**
>
> **history**
>
> **political science**

◀ Social scientists study how people live in society. They do so by searching for clues and asking questions.

 Civics   Economics   Geography   History

Analyzing prices is one way to study an economy. An economist might examine a shopping receipt to learn about spending habits.

1. The Social Science of Economics

You find a dollar in your pocket. Should you spend it on a snack or save it for a new comic book? You might think that no one cares about how you choose to spend your money, but that is not true! Some social scientists are economists. They are very interested in the choices people make about money every day.

Economists study the **economy** of a city, state, or country. An economy is the way people in a community use resources to meet their needs and wants. We all need food, clothing, and shelter, and we all want things that we don't really need. You may want a new game, and your parents may want a new car. In the economy of the United States, a variety of resources meets people's needs and wants.

Economics is the study of how people make, buy, and sell things. Economists want to know how people decide what to make and what to buy.

Think of yourself as an economist. You are studying how families decide what to buy. What artifacts might help you? Here are a few ideas:

- price tags
- receipts
- coupons
- advertisements
- items your family bought recently

economy the way people in a community use resources to meet their needs and wants

2. The Social Science of Geography

You are on a trip somewhere new. Nothing looks familiar. You don't recognize the countryside, the buildings, or even the people. You begin to feel a little lost. Finally, you ask yourself, "Where am I?"

You could use some help from another social scientist called a geographer. Geographers study **geography**. Geography is the study of Earth.

Geographers like to know where places are on a map. They study Earth's surface to find out what physical features lie around them. They also study climate and plant and animal life.

Geographers use maps and globes to show the features of our planet's surface. Land, water, plants, and animals are part of nature, so they are called natural features. Towns, roads, bridges, and dams are built by people, so they are called human features.

The United States has a great range of natural and human features. It has mountains, deserts, rivers, and lakes. Our nation has large cities filled with people and buildings. It has tiny towns, miles of highways and roads, and vast empty spaces.

Think of yourself as a geographer. You are studying the natural and human features of your community. These artifacts and natural objects might help you in your studies:

- maps
- weather records
- newspaper articles
- buildings
- wildflowers
- birds' nests

geography the study of the natural and human features of Earth's surface, and its climate and life-forms

Learning to use maps is an important part of thinking like a geographer. Geographers also study how humans impact and are impacted by Earth.

3. The Social Science of Political Science

You are riding your bike down the street when—*bam!*—your front wheel hits a pothole and you fall to the ground. As you pick yourself up, you grumble, "This is dangerous! Who's in charge of fixing the streets, anyway?"

This is just the type of question a political scientist might ask. Political scientists are interested in who is in charge. They want to know how people get the power to run a city, state, or nation. They also look at how the people in charge use their power.

Political science is the study of governments. All groups—even families—have some sort of government. A government is a system for deciding what is best for the group. Its main job is to make and carry out rules and laws.

These rules help people live together in peace. Governments also supply things that people need. Your local government provides things that you need, such as schools and safe streets.

Suppose a political scientist is visiting your town. What artifacts might interest him or her? Here are a few ideas:

- election advertisements
- stories about government
- information about how and where to vote
- newspaper articles about laws

political science the study of governments and how they work

Political scientists study all types of government. City councils like this one are an example of local government.

This old school photograph is an artifact that might interest a historian. What do you think a historian could learn from this photo?

4. The Social Science of History

Your class takes a field trip to the cemetery. Your assignment is to make a rubbing of a tombstone and report on it to the class. When you read the tombstone, you think, "I wonder how many people buried here were related to this person." Now you are thinking like a historian.

History is the study of the past. Human beings have been around a very long time so we have a lot of past to study. Historians, however, are most interested in the last few thousand years, which is when people began leaving written records.

The first question historians ask is *What happened in the past?* To find out, they study all kinds of artifacts, including records made by people in the past. Once historians know what happened, they ask other questions to help them interpret or understand the past, such as *Who took part in these events? How did these things happen?* and *Why did they happen this way?*

Suppose you have been asked to write a history of your family. What artifacts would help you? Here are some suggestions:

- birth certificates
- baby books
- family photos
- letters
- diaries
- family treasures

history the study of the past

The objects in your backpack are artifacts. What kinds of questions would a social scientist ask about them?

5. Thinking Like a Social Scientist

Now that you know more about social scientists, can you start thinking like one? In order to think like a social scientist, you must first ask questions about what you are studying.

Try this experiment: choose one object from your desk or backpack to study, and ask yourself, *What kind of social scientist would be most interested in this artifact? An economist, a geographer, a political scientist, or a historian? What would that person want to know about this artifact— who made it, how much it cost, where it came from, or something else?*

One class of fourth graders tried this experiment with a pair of shoes. To their surprise, the shoes turned out to be a rather interesting artifact.

The students found out that all four types of social scientists could study the shoes that the class chose. The class broke up into four different groups, and each group came up with questions that one type of social scientist would ask about the pair of shoes. Read each group's results.

Social Scientist Questions

An economist might ask these questions:

1. How much did the shoes cost to make?
2. How much did you pay for them?
3. Why did you choose to buy these shoes instead of another pair of shoes?

A geographer might ask these questions:

1. Where were these shoes made?
2. What route did the shoes travel from the factory to your shoe store?

A political scientist might ask these questions:

1. Are there any laws about making these shoes, and did the maker follow them?
2. Who was in charge of buying this pair of shoes?

A historian might ask these questions:

1. How have shoes changed over time?
2. What is the history of these shoes? Who made them and when, and why? What has happened to these shoes since they were made?

Lesson Summary

As you have learned, the social sciences are the study of how people live in groups. Some social scientists study small groups like families, and others study large groups like nations.

Social scientists want to understand why people behave as they do. To find out, they watch people, ask questions, and look at written records and other artifacts.

Economists are interested in the choices people make about money, so they look at what people make, buy, and sell. Geographers want to know what lies around them, so they examine human and natural features. Political scientists study governments, so they explore political power. Historians study the past, so they analyze items like old letters and photographs to learn what happened in the past.

Social scientists help us understand society, past and present. There is a lot more to learn.

The First People in Your State

Long ago—before your state had highways, buildings, and stores—its first people lived there. Like your community, they had transportation, homes, and ways to get food and other goods. What was life like for the first people in your state? Social scientists, such as archaeologists and historians, look for answers to this important question. They look at artifacts, and they research the history of different places. You can learn about your state's first people by doing research in the library and on the Internet.

To learn about the lives of the first people, you need to find out: Who were the first Americans in your state? There may have been several groups, so choose one to learn about. For example, the Chinook people were one of the first groups to live in what are now the states of Washington and Oregon.

Next, think of other supporting questions about the first people. For example, you might ask, "What kind of natural resources were nearby?" and "What kind of homes did they live in?"

Write several questions about your state's first people on index cards. You will try to answer these questions through research.

Write one supporting question on each index card. Research each answer and write it below the question.

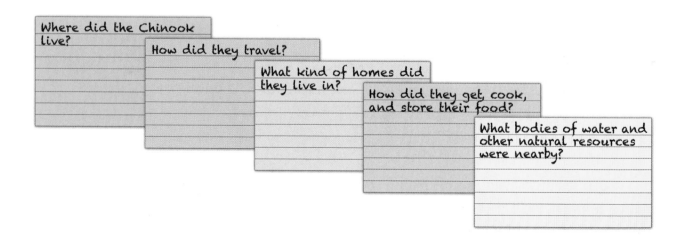

Where did the Chinook live?

How did they travel?

What kind of homes did they live in?

How did they get, cook, and store their food?

What bodies of water and other natural resources were nearby?

Find Answers!

Now, perform research to learn how the first people lived. Use sources that are both online and in books. For example, you might read the Web site of an organization that writes about the group's history. Write down facts on the index cards that will help answer your questions. As you research, save or draw pictures of artifacts.

Use your research to answer this question: Did natural resources affect the first people in your state? Write an explanation, and support it with your research. Include your pictures of artifacts. For example, the Chinook made houses out of trees from the nearby forests. They also hollowed out trees to make canoes. They also traveled on the Columbia River, and the river and ocean provided fish to eat.

Draw a poster explaining the ways the people used natural resources. Display your poster in the hall for other students to see. Then create a digital presentation to show and discuss with your family.

You will create a poster by researching facts and pictures of the first people that lived in your state. For instance, you might use this image of a Chinook house if you live in Washington.

Clues from Cahokia

In southern Illinois, a large mound rises from the ground, but it is not a natural hill. People built it long ago. Who? Why? How? These are questions social scientists ask. How do social scientists help us learn about life long ago?

"What a strange looking hill!" you might think as you walk toward the mound. "It's squared off instead of round. Look, the top is flat and it has different levels. Is it really a hill?"

These questions and observations show that you are thinking like an **archaeologist**. Archaeologists are a special kind of social scientist. Like historians, they study the past, but they don't study people's written records. To find clues about the past, they hunt for and examine objects that people have left behind.

archaeologist a social scientist who studies the past by looking at artifacts people have left behind

This huge mound, called Monks Mound, is one *giant* artifact! It is about as tall as a ten-story building, and it is the largest of several mounds in the area. Archaeologists have learned that the mounds were part of a long-lost American Indian city called Cahokia.

The Monks Mound is located in the state of Illinois. It might just look like a hill, but it is actually a huge artifact!

How did archaeologists begin their explorations at Cahokia? What did they find?

Monks Mound at Cahokia

Illinois

Mississippi River

•Cahokia

N W E S

0   100   200 miles
0 100 200 kilometers

An archaeologist carefully sifts the soil in search of clues about the past. Geographers help archaeologists figure out where to look.

Help from Geography

The people who built Monks Mound left the area more than 600 years ago. Why did they build these mounds? The people left no written language. So how can we know?

Luckily, there are archaeologists eager to search for clues. Modern-day archaeologists use high-tech tools to look in the ground and underneath the soil that has collected on top of these very old structures over time. They also dig into the soil for clues—slowly and very carefully.

Before they start investigating, archaeologists need to figure out where to focus their attention, so they turn to geography for help. They look at the land and think about where people might have lived. Are there places where it is easy to get water? Are there fertile places to grow food? They also study areas that appear to have been changed by the people who lived there. This helps archaeologists choose the likeliest places to search for more clues.

Archaeologists have made many discoveries at Cahokia since the 1920s. One of the most exciting was at the top of Monks Mound, where they discovered the remains of a large wooden building. It stood on top of the hill about 850 years ago and was probably the biggest building in the city. Here was a wonderful clue about life long ago.

Archaeologists teamed up with political scientists to reconstruct what life was like in Cahokia one thousand years ago. An artist based this drawing on the findings of these social scientists.

Help from Political Science

Archaeologists now knew that a building once stood at the top of the great mound. But what was it for?

Nothing they found on the mound explained it, so they turned to political science for help. Political scientists study how people organize into governments. To make such a large mound, thousands of people would have had to work together. These people must have had leaders. Could this explain the building atop the mound?

Picture the scene a thousand years ago. Everywhere you look, people are at work. Some are in the vast fields beyond the city, raising corn for food, while others dig soil from pits and place it in baskets. People carry the heavy baskets to the foot of the mound. Up and up they climb, until at last, exhausted, they drop their loads. Slowly, very slowly, the mound grows taller. Who is in charge of all this work?

Convincing thousands of people to move more than 22 million cubic feet of soil takes powerful leadership! Political scientists say that a group of high-ranking nobles may have ruled Cahokia. They may have lived on top of this mound, while the people lived in the city below.

Help from Economics

Archaeologists now knew that nobles ruled the large, rich city, but how had the city grown so large and become so wealthy? Archaeologists turned to economics for help. Economists ask questions about resources. What resources did Cahokia have?

One of the resources they had was the rich soil along the Mississippi River that allowed people to grow as much food as they needed. This also meant that more people could live in one place and that not everyone had to work in the fields or hunt for food. Some people could work on building a great city.

Rivers were another resource because they served as water highways for trade. Traders brought salt to Cahokia in canoes. They also carried shells from the Gulf of Mexico and copper from the Great Lakes. People used these things to make objects of great beauty. Archaeologists have found carved-shell jewelry, copper ornaments, and stone figures.

Why did people leave? Nobody knows exactly, but part of the answer may be that people *used up* the resources. Archaeologists believe that the Cahokia cut down trees and farmed the same fields until the land could no longer support so many people. Today, the mounds at Cahokia are an important monument. Thanks to the work of social scientists, we now know that, long ago, a large, lively city existed in this place. ◆

Artifacts similar to this Cahokia head pot tell us something about culture. The pot shows what early American Indian tattoos might have looked like.

Exploring Regions of the United States

How do geographers study the regions of the United States?

Introduction

Because Earth is so large, geographers divide it into regions to study. A region is an area with common features that set it apart from other areas. The United States can be divided into regions, too. One way to do this is by grouping states with similar features into five different regions.

In this lesson, you will learn how geographers study regions. Geographers have identified five major themes, or topics, to help them organize the study of geography. Maps are useful for understanding these five themes of geography:

Location: Where is this place located? What is it near?

Place: What is this place like?

Human-environmental interaction: How does this place affect the people living here? How do the people who live here affect this place?

Movement: How do people, goods, and ideas move to and away from this place?

Regions: What features about this place set it apart from other places?

Try answering the questions above about your school. Now you are thinking like a geographer. Keep thinking that way as you read more about the regions of the United States.

◀ You can use maps to explore different regions in this country.

Geography

North Pole

South Pole

If you face the North Pole, you are facing north. If you face the South Pole, you are facing south.

If you get lost, you can use a map and a compass to find your way. Once you know one cardinal direction, you can determine the other three.

1. Location and Direction

Every place has its own location. A location is the site where something can be found. People describe locations in many ways. You might describe the location of your home by talking about what it is near. This is the relative location of your home. Or you might use your street address. This is the exact location of your home.

Geographers use globes and maps to show the locations of places on Earth. Globes are round like Earth. They are useful when you want to know where places are on the planet. When you need to see where many places are all at once, maps can be more useful. Maps show all or part of Earth on a flat surface.

To use a map, you need to know the four cardinal directions. North is the direction toward the North Pole. When you face north, your back is facing south. East is to your right. West is to your left. On a map, the letters N, S, E, and W stand for the cardinal directions.

The intermediate directions are halfway between the cardinal directions. Northeast, for example, lies halfway between north and east. The other intermediate directions are southeast, southwest, and northwest. On a map, the letters NE, SE, SW, and NW stand for the intermediate directions.

Most maps use a compass rose to show directions. A compass rose sits on a map, with N pointing toward the North Pole. This tells you which way on the map is north. Why is it important to know your directions?

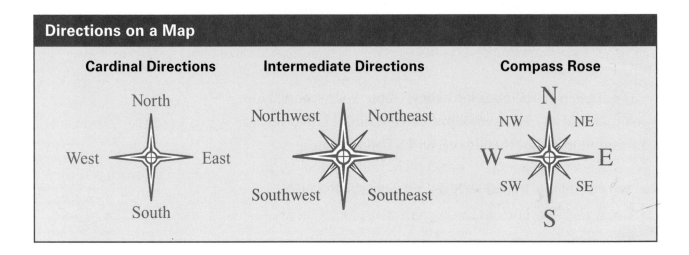

Directions on a Map

Cardinal Directions — North, West, East, South

Intermediate Directions — Northwest, Northeast, Southwest, Southeast

Compass Rose — N, NW, NE, W, E, SW, SE, S

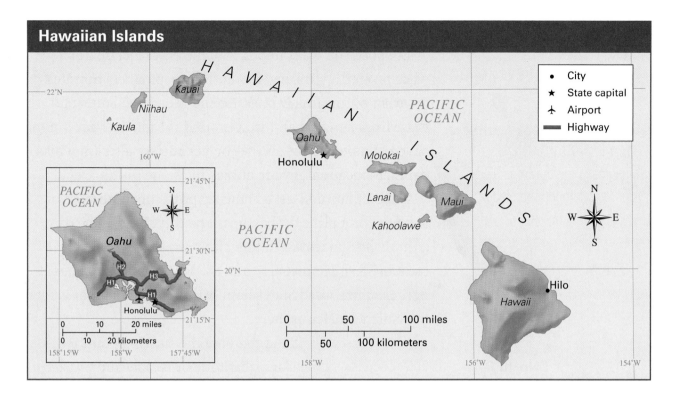

Hawaiian Islands

2. Scales and Symbols

Maps never show sizes and distances as they really are. They are always much smaller than the part of Earth they represent. A short distance on a map represents a much greater distance on Earth.

The **scale** of a map shows the relationship between map distances and real distances. A map's scale can be shown in many ways. The most common is a line scale. The scales on the Hawaiian Islands map show two measures of distance. One is for miles, the other is for kilometers.

Maps use symbols to show other kinds of information. A symbol is anything that stands for something else. Sometimes symbols look like what they stand for. For example, mapmakers often use tiny airplane symbols to stand for airports.

Color is another important map symbol. The color blue usually stands for water. Mapmakers often use different colors to show separate states or countries.

Mapmakers use a **map key** to explain their symbols. (A key is also called a legend.) The map key tells what each symbol stands for. Look at the key on this map. What does the star stand for?

Maps like this one use scales and symbols. According to the map key, where is the airport on this map?

> **scale** a diagram that shows the relationship between distances on a map and real distances on Earth
>
> **map key** an explanation of what the symbols on a map stand for

3. Lines of Latitude

Suppose you want to describe the exact location of a place on Earth. To help you do this, mapmakers invented a system of imaginary lines around the globe. Some of these lines run east and west around the globe. They are called **lines of latitude**. Lines of latitude are also known as parallels because they are always the same distance apart.

Lines of latitude tell us how far north or south of the equator a place on Earth is. The equator is a line of latitude. It divides Earth into two halves. They are called the Northern Hemisphere and the Southern Hemisphere. Because the United States lies north of the equator, it is in the Northern Hemisphere.

The equator is the starting point for measuring latitude. It is labeled 0°, or zero degrees. Parallels north of the equator are labeled N. The North Pole is 90°N. Parallels south of the equator are labeled S. The South Pole is 90°S. Lines of latitude measure between 0° and 90°N or 90°S. The closer a parallel is to the equator, the smaller its number of degrees. The closer it is to one of the poles, the greater its number of degrees. Do you live closer to the North Pole or the equator?

line of latitude an imaginary line that runs east and west around the globe; also called a parallel

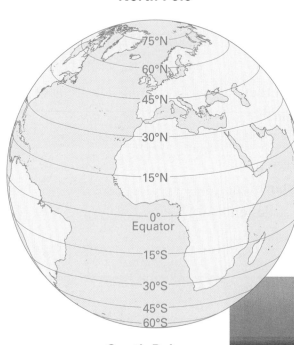

North Pole

75°N
60°N
45°N
30°N
15°N
0°
Equator
15°S
30°S
45°S
60°S

South Pole

A boat's location on the ocean can be pinpointed using imaginary lines. These are called lines of latitude and longitude.

4. Lines of Longitude

Lines of longitude tell us how far to the east or west we need to go to locate a place. Look at this map. It shows lines circling Earth. Lines of longitude run north and south between the North and South poles and are called meridians.

Unlike lines of latitude, meridians are not parallel to each other. All meridians meet at the North Pole and the South Pole. The distance between meridians is greatest at the equator. That distance shrinks as you move from the equator to the poles.

Can you find the line that is labeled *prime meridian* on the map? This imaginary line divides the world into the Eastern Hemisphere and the Western Hemisphere. Because the United States lies west of the prime meridian, it is in the Western Hemisphere.

The longitude of the prime meridian is 0°. Lines of longitude west of the prime meridian are labeled W. Lines of latitude east of the prime meridian are labeled E.

Lines of longitude measure between 0° and 180°. The closer a meridian is to the prime meridian, the smaller its number of degrees. The farther it is from the prime meridian, the greater its number of degrees.

> **line of longitude** an imaginary line that runs between the North and South Poles; also called a meridian

North Pole

South Pole

North Pole

South Pole

global grid   the grid formed
by crisscrossing lines of
latitude and longitude on
a map

Lines of latitude and longitude
help us locate places.

5. The Global Grid

Mapmakers combine lines of latitude and longitude to form a grid. A grid is a set of crisscrossing lines. The grid below is called a **global grid** because it covers all of Earth.

Using the lines of latitude and longitude on the global grid, you can locate places anywhere in the world. Let's find New Orleans on the map below. It is 30 degrees north of the equator, or 30°N. It is also 90 degrees west of the prime meridian, or 90°W. Geographers call the degrees of latitude and longitude a set of coordinates. You state latitude first, then longitude. New Orleans's coordinates are 30°N, 90°W.

The city of Uíge (weej), Angola, is located at 8°S, 15°E. To find this location, put your finger on the map where the equator and the prime meridian meet. Move your finger east to the 15°E meridian. So far, so good.

Now you have a problem. The 8°S parallel is not marked on this map. You know, though, that 8°S must lie between the equator and 15°S. If you move your finger along the 15°E meridian to the spot halfway between these two parallels, you will find the city you are looking for.

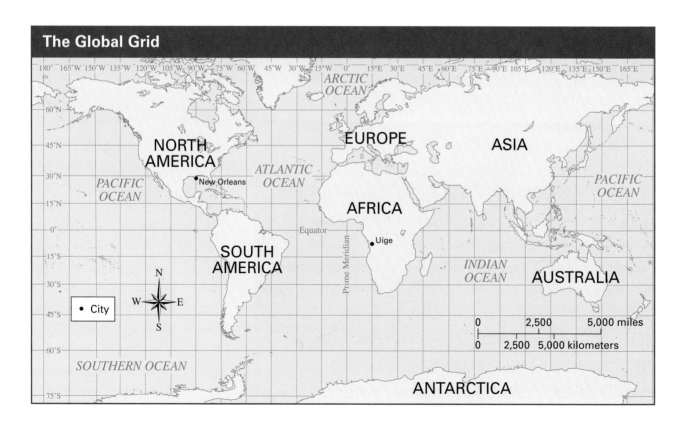

The Global Grid

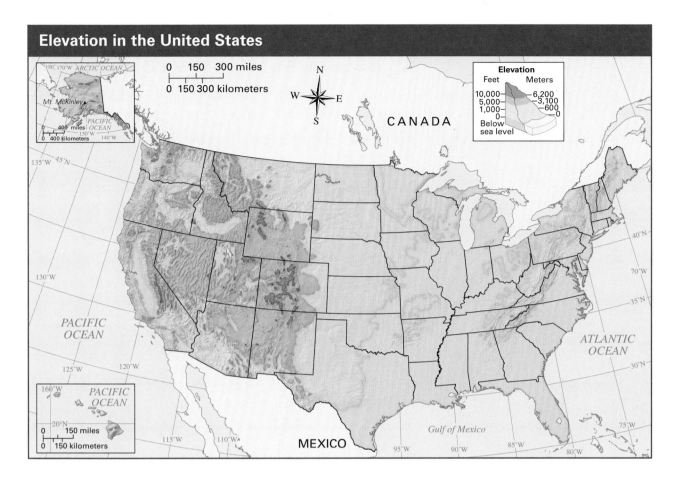

Elevation in the United States

Elevation

Feet	Meters
10,000	6,200
5,000	3,100
1,000	600
0	0
Below sea level	

6. Kinds of Maps

Geographers make different kinds of maps for different purposes. Maps that show natural features are called physical maps. Physical maps show landforms, such as mountains, valleys, and plains. They also show bodies of water, such as rivers, lakes, and oceans. Other maps show human features. For example, a political map shows cities, capitals, states, and countries.

Special-purpose maps show just one kind or type of information. Rainfall maps, for example, show how much rain falls in different parts of the world. Population maps show how many people live in different areas. Language maps show what languages people speak in different places.

One example of a special-purpose map is an elevation map of the United States. Elevation is the height of the land above the ocean. The surface of the ocean, called sea level, is at zero elevation. The highest point in North America is Denali, or Mt. McKinley, in Alaska. Its elevation is 20,320 feet. What does the map show about your state's elevation?

This special-purpose map shows the elevation of the United States. Use the elevation key to find the highest areas in the country. What is the elevation where you live?

special-purpose map a map that shows just one kind of information such as rainfall or elevation

Regional Map of the United States

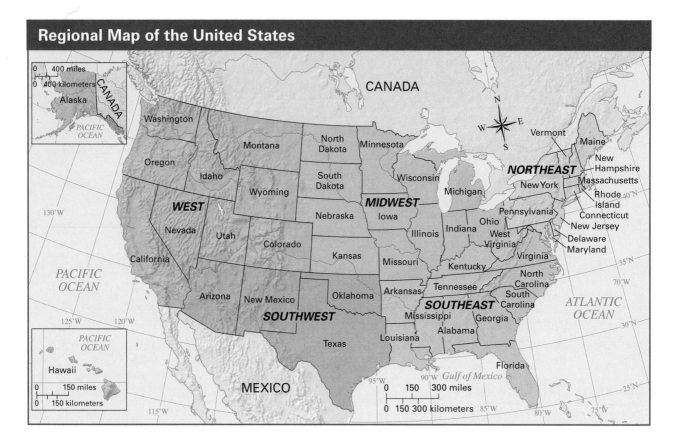

This map shows five regions in the United States. How do these regions differ?

region an area that shares similar features

7. Regions in the United States

Now that you know how to read maps, you can use them to study different areas in the United States. Certain areas may have similar characteristics. An area that shares similar features is called a **region**.

Geographers can divide the United States into many different regions. In this map, the United States has been divided into five regions. They are the Northeast, Southeast, Midwest, Southwest, and West. As you can see on the map, each region has a different group of states. In which region is your state located?

Each region is named after its location in the United States. For example, suppose you are standing in the middle of this country with a compass. In which direction can you find Florida? If you use your compass, you can see that Florida is toward the south and east. So Florida and the states around it are in the Southeast region.

The other four regions are also named after where they are found in the United States. Find the regions on the map. How would you describe their locations?

Other than location, how else do these regions differ? Often part of what makes a region special is an important natural feature, such as an ocean coast, a chain of mountains, a desert, a series of lakes, or a great river. The West region, for example, borders the Pacific Ocean, while the Northeast region borders the Atlantic Ocean.

The features in a region can affect the people living there. For example, the Midwest is mostly made up of flat plains covered with rich soil. So, many people who live there are farmers. People can also affect the environment in good ways and bad. Farmers in the Midwest, for instance, might protect the environment by growing crops on terraces to prevent erosion. But they might also use pesticides that can pollute soil.

Climate also varies from region to region. In the Southwest winters are mild, but in the Midwest and Northeast, winters are harsh and snowfall is common. Climate also affects how people live. It shapes how we dress, what we eat, and how we spend our spare time.

Each region also has its own history and way of life. People in different regions eat different foods. They celebrate different holidays. They wear different kinds of clothing. They tell particular stories and honor special heroes.

People interact with their environment. For example, there are many farmers who grow corn on the flat plains of the Midwest.

This is what fall looks like in Vermont, a state in the Northeast region.

coastal plain low, flat land that runs along a coast

8. The Northeast

The Northeast region is located close to the Atlantic Ocean. There are 11 states in this region. You can see these states on this map. Despite its many states, the Northeast region is the smallest region. With big cities such as New York City, Boston, and Philadelphia, the Northeast region is the most densely populated region in the United States.

The region includes a variety of landforms. A low, flat plain known as a **coastal plain** runs along the coast of New Jersey, Delaware, and Maryland. The Coastal Plain has sandy soil and marshy land. The Appalachian mountain range runs through the entire region. This range has many forests. Large rivers flow out of these mountains. The rivers that flow east cut across the Coastal Plain to the Atlantic Ocean.

The Northeast region has a different climate than the other regions in United States. The climate of a place is the kind of weather it has over many years. Temperature, rainfall, and wind conditions are parts of climate.

In the Northeast region, winters are long and cold. Snowstorms are common. Summers are warm and sometimes can be hot.

This map shows the Northeast region in the United States. It is the most densely populated region.

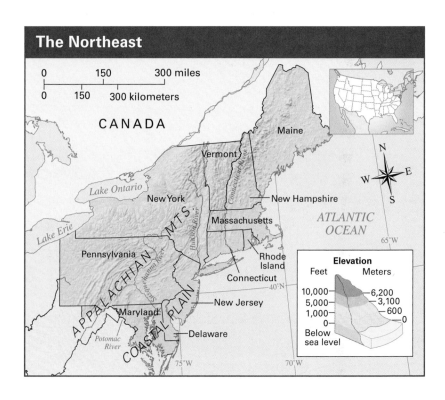

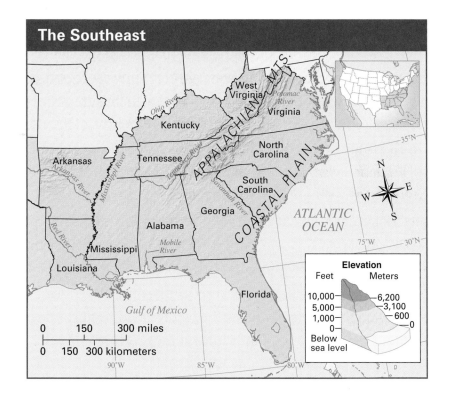

The Southeast

West Virginia
Potomac River
Virginia
Ohio River
Kentucky
APPALACHIAN MTS.
North Carolina
Arkansas
Tennessee
Tennessee River
South Carolina
Mississippi River
Arkansas River
COASTAL PLAIN
Georgia
Savannah River
Alabama
ATLANTIC OCEAN
Red River
Mississippi
Mobile River
Louisiana
Florida
Gulf of Mexico

N W E S

35°N
75°W
30°N

0 150 300 miles
0 150 300 kilometers
90°W   85°W   80°W

Elevation
Feet   Meters
10,000―   ―6,200
5,000―   ―3,100
1,000―   ―600
0―   ―0
Below
sea level

This is a map of the Southeast region of the United States. How many features do you recognize in this region?

9. The Southeast

Just south of the Northeast region is the Southeast region. This region is composed of 12 states and includes big cities like Atlanta and Miami. The Southeast does not have as many big cities as the Northeast, but the two regions do share a number of features.

Like the Northeast, the Southeast is bordered by the Atlantic Ocean on the east. The Appalachian mountain range and Coastal Plain found in the Northeast also extend into the Southeast. Which states in the Southeast region include these features?

The Southeast has other features, too. The Gulf of Mexico, for example, with its warm ocean water lies to the south of the region. The Southeast also has forests, beaches, swamps, and rivers. One of those rivers is the Mississippi River, which is one of the largest rivers in the United States. The Mississippi River starts way up north in Minnesota and flows south more than 2,300 miles before emptying into the Gulf of Mexico.

The Southeast region has a mild winter climate. Winters there are usually warmer than in the Northeast. Summers are hot and humid. Humid means damp or moist.

Wetlands and swamps are common in the Southeast region.

The Midwest region has some of the best conditions for farming in the United States.

inland not bordering an ocean or a large body of water by an ocean

10. The Midwest

The Midwest is one of the regions that lies in the center of our country. There are 12 states in the Midwest region. The largest city in the region is Chicago, which is the third largest city in the United States.

The Midwest is an **inland** region. This means it does not border any ocean. However, the Great Lakes form part of the Midwest's northern border. The five Great Lakes are Lakes Superior, Michigan, Huron, Erie, and Ontario. These lakes are so large that they hold one-fifth of all the fresh water on Earth.

Most of the Midwest region is flat plains. The Central Plains and Great Plains are covered with some of the best soil on Earth. That soil makes the Midwest an important farming region. The region is known for growing crops such as corn, soybeans, and wheat.

The Mississippi River also runs through the Central Plains. It is a busy water highway that connects to the Gulf of Mexico and the Atlantic Ocean. Many boats and barges travel on this river.

The climate varies greatly by season in the Midwest. Winters are bitter cold, and snowfall is common. However, summers are hot and humid.

This is a map of the Midwest region. What do you notice about the water features in this region?

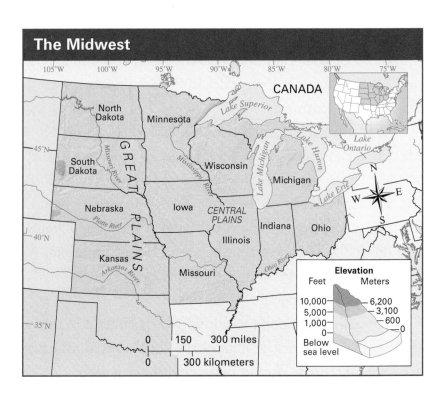

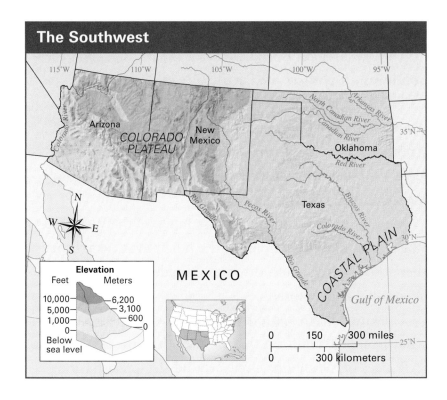

The Southwest

This is a map of the Southwest region of the United States. What features does it share with other regions?

11. The Southwest

The Southwest region is positioned just south of the Midwest region. The Southwest is made up of only four states.

One of them is Texas, the second largest state in the United States. The coastal plain extends from the Southeast into Texas, and the Gulf of Mexico borders the state. Texas also has three of the ten most populated cities in America. One of those is Houston, the largest city in the Southwest region and the fourth largest city in the country.

Plains cover the eastern part of the Southwest. Farther west, the land rises to form the Colorado Plateau. A **plateau** is a high, flat landform that rises steeply from the land around it.

Most of the Colorado Plateau is crisscrossed by many deep canyons. The largest and most famous is the Grand Canyon, which is in Arizona. The Grand Canyon is carved by the Colorado River, which is the second longest river in the region behind the Rio Grande.

The Southwest region has a dry climate with high temperatures. In the summer, it is not uncommon for the temperature to reach triple digits in some places. Winters are cooler, but snow is rare.

plateau a high, flat landform that rises steeply from the land around it

It is difficult for many plants to grow in the dry climate of the Southwest region.

12. The West

The West region is to the west of the Midwest and the Southwest. It borders the Pacific Ocean.

The West is made up of 11 states. One of the states is Alaska, which is the biggest state in the United States. Another state is California, which is the most populous state. California's biggest city, Los Angeles, is the second most populous city in the country.

Mountain ranges stretch across much of the West. The Rocky Mountains begin far to the north in Alaska. From there they stretch south through Canada, Montana, Idaho, Wyoming, and Colorado.

The Great Basin lies to the west of the Rockies. A **basin** is a bowl-shaped landform that is lower than the land around it. Ranges of mountains circle around the Great Basin.

There are several mountain ranges along the Pacific coast. The Coast Ranges are mountains that seem to rise right out of the Pacific Ocean. The Cascade Range and the Sierra Nevada are further inland. (*Sierra Nevada* means "snowy range" in Spanish.)

> **basin** a bowl-shaped landform that is lower than the surrounding land

This map shows the West region of the United States. Based on the scales, which state is the largest in the region?

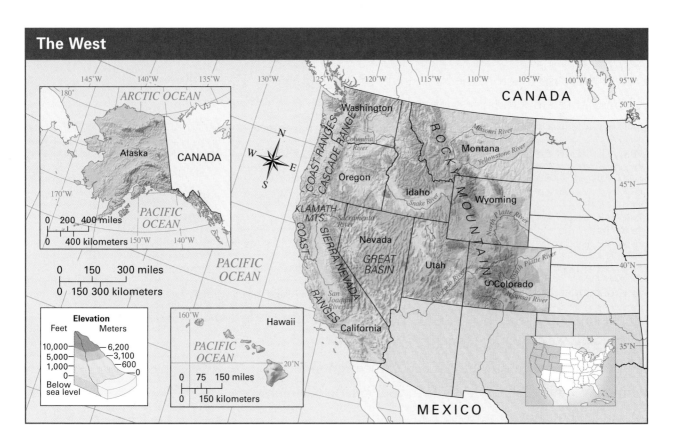

The West

Oregon's Willamette Valley lies between the Coast Range mountains and inland mountains. The soil here is rich enough to plant many crops.

Between the Coast Range mountains and the inland mountains are two rich farming valleys. One is California's Central Valley. The other is Oregon's Willamette Valley.

Hawaii is also mountainous. Volcanoes formed its islands long ago. A volcano is an opening in Earth's surface through which hot, melted rock and ash may pour out. As the liquid rock cools, it forms a cone-shaped mountain.

Lesson Summary

You now know that there are different kinds of maps. Some maps show locations of places around the world. Lines of latitude and longitude help us find exact locations of places and measure distances north to south and east to west. Map scales also help us measure distances from place to place. Did you remember to think like a geographer as you looked at the maps of each region?

As you read about each region of the United States, you considered the five themes of geography: location, place, human-environmental interaction, movement, and regions. You looked at physical maps of each region to see where a place is located and what it is like. There are many other kinds of maps, including special-purpose maps. To compare climates around the country, you might use a climate map. A product map might show what each region grows or manufactures.

Which region do you live in? How is it different from the others? Each region of the United States varies by location, natural features, climate, and way of life.

Regions of Your State

New Jersey's government hired geographers to create a map like this. It shows high and low places as well as regions. You can find similar maps on government Web sites, which are usually reliable sources.

You have read about the regions of the United States. A region is an area with common features that set it apart from other areas. In your state, there may be a region with mountains or valleys. Another region may be by an ocean or river. Knowing your state's regions can help you understand how natural features affect the people who live there.

To explore different regions of your state, first make a large outline of the state. Gather sources that can help you label your map with physical features and region names.

These sources might include maps from books or online. For example, if you live in New Jersey, you might find maps and useful photographs on New Jersey's state government Web site.

On your map, label major bodies of water, mountains, and other big landforms. Label the neighboring states. Label your community on the map. Add any additional land features that you know about.

Now label the regions on your map. In New Jersey, the regions are called: Valley and Ridge Region, Highlands, Piedmont, and Coastal Plains. The region names come from the state's landforms, such as mountains, valleys, plateaus (Piedmont), and waterways.

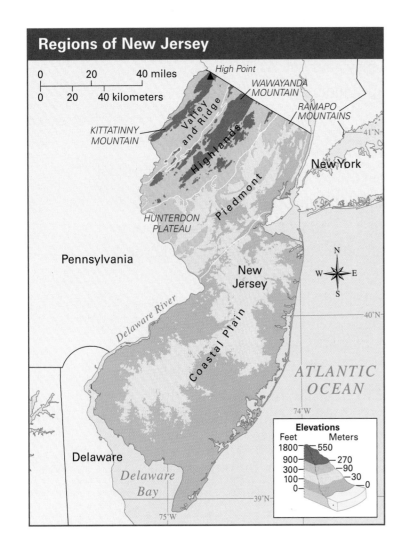

Regions of New Jersey

Regions and Their People

Now let's use your map to learn how people live in the region. Read about your state's regions in books and Internet articles. For each region, answer questions that help you understand how the region's features affect the people who live there. Are there mountains, farmland, forests, lakes, or rivers? Is it near an ocean or far inland? What do people do for a living? Do they use the land for fun activities?

In New Jersey, for example, people in the Piedmont region built highways, railways, and shipping docks by the Atlantic Ocean. Transportation near this body of water affect jobs. Many people work at jobs that move products over land and water. The Coastal Plains region includes the Jersey Shore by the Atlantic Ocean. People built boardwalks and amusement parks by the shore. They enjoy the sandy beaches.

Write a few paragraphs about your region. Tell how natural features affect how people live. Share this information with your classmates.

Every year, more than 600,000 containers arrive at Port Newark in the Piedmont Region. They travel on ships, trucks, and trains. They take products all over the world.

The Mighty Mississippi

The Mississippi River is one of the largest rivers in the United States, and it runs down the middle of the country. The famous author Mark Twain often wrote about the Mississippi and how it influenced the states and their people. Why do geographers consider it one of the most important rivers in the nation?

It was dark. Tom Sawyer and Huck Finn could hear the great river in front of them. They found their raft, untied it, and climbed on. In his book *The Adventures of Tom Sawyer*, Mark Twain tells what happens next:

"The raft drew beyond the middle of the river; the boys pointed her head right, and then lay on their oars . . . They came near letting the current drift them out of the range of the island."

The boys were off on an adventure down the great Mississippi River. Although Tom and Huck are made-up characters, the Mississippi is a real river. It is just as remarkable as the two friends in the story discovered.

Many readers enjoyed Twain's story. He followed it with *Adventures of Huckleberry Finn*. This book, too, features the Mississippi River. Twain's writings brought the river into the minds of many Americans.

Mark Twain's *Adventures of Huckleberry Finn* was published in 1884. Ever since, Americans have enjoyed reading about Huck's adventures.

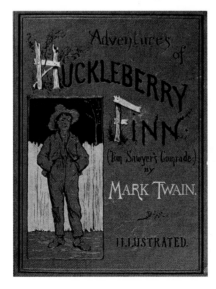

As a boy, Mark Twain loved to watch steamboats like this travel down the Mississippi River. The map in this image shows how far people could travel along the Mississippi.

Life on the Mississippi Long Ago

Mark Twain's real name was Samuel Clemens. He based Tom and Huck's adventures on his own life growing up in a small town on the Mississippi.

To the young boy, one of the most exciting sounds in the world was the cry "S-t-e-a-m-boat a-comin'!" The steamboats brought interesting people and new things—like goods for the store or letters from faraway places.

In 1859, Twain became a steamboat pilot. Standing behind the wheel of his boat, he learned to avoid dangers in the muddy waters. He took his name as a writer from the calls the boatmen made to tell the pilot how deep and safe the water was: "M-a-r-k three! . . . Half twain! . . . M-a-r-k twain!"

In Twain's time, the Mississippi was like a great highway. People could travel down smaller rivers and then into the Mississippi all the way from Minnesota to the Gulf of Mexico.

People used rafts and boats to carry goods down the Mississippi to the busy port at New Orleans. After the invention of the steamboat, people could send goods up the river, too.

This photo shows the Mississippi river overflowing in 1898. Levees have been built to stop future flooding.

levee a wall typically made of dirt, built along a river to keep it from flooding

Levees were used to prevent the river from flooding nearby areas.

Changing the River

People depended on the Mississippi River, but they could never quite rely on it to be safe for traveling or even living nearby. Travel was dangerous for boats in low water, and they could even crash into tiny islands in the river. During very rainy times, the river sometimes overflowed and flooded the surrounding settlements and farmland. In his writings, Mark Twain recalled that during one flood, the river became 70 miles wide.

With so many dangers, people began to change the river. They built **levees** to stop the river from flooding farms and towns, which worked well most of the time. People also changed the river to improve travel. They built bridges across the river. They also dug mud out of the river bottom to make it deeper so that large boats could travel more easily.

Even with these changes, the river was not always predictable. As Mark Twain once wrote, "The Mississippi River will always have its own way; no engineering skill can persuade it to do otherwise . . ." This proved true when the river still flooded in 1898, despite the levees. People had to fix the levees and build more of them. They hoped the new ones would hold better.

The River Today

The changes people made to the river have made it easier to use. If Mark Twain visited the river today, he would see huge barges that carry millions of tons of goods up and down the river each year.

But changing the river does not mean people control it. In 2005, a hurricane called Katrina hit the city of New Orleans. Huge winds and heavy rains from the storm made the Mississippi overflow. One by one, the levees failed. Most of the city was under water. Lots of people climbed onto roofs to get away from the water, but many did not get away and died. Thousands of people lost their homes and their businesses. The storm and the flood cost billions of dollars. It was one of the greatest disasters in our nation's history. Since that time, people have worked hard to rebuild New Orleans. They have looked to geographers for help.

Geographers study the Mississippi River and the ways human change influences it. And though the river might never be completely controlled, geographers' knowledge helps people who live near the Mississippi River plan well for the future. ◆

Today, the Mississippi is still a major water highway. Barges carrying goods regularly travel down the river.

The Peopling of the United States

How have different groups contributed to the United States?

Introduction

The United States is a nation with many different places and features, like mountains and rivers. But the United States is much more than the geography of the land. A nation, like the United States, is a place where people live together under one government.

People who live in the United States are very different from one another. Look around your school. Do your fellow students look the same way or eat the same types of foods? Do they all speak the same language at school or at home? Do their families all share the same way of life? For many schools, the answer is, "No."

The United States is a nation where people from many different backgrounds live together. These people come from many parts of the world. They come to the United States for many reasons.

In this lesson, you will learn about people from five parts of the world who came to our country. You will learn about how and why these different people first came to America, and you will see how each group has contributed to our country in a special way.

> **Social Studies Vocabulary**
>
> the Americas
>
> colony
>
> culture
>
> democracy
>
> diverse
>
> immigrant

◀ America has many different types of people in it. Some may speak different languages or live a different way of life.

 Geography   History

1. The First Americans Arrive

Archaeologists agree that the first Americans arrived long ago. But they have different ideas about exactly how and when people came to North America.

For many years, most scientists believed that the first people in **the Americas** came from the continent of Asia about 11,500 years ago.

At that time, Earth's climate was much colder than it is today. Much of Earth's surface was covered with ice. This long cold period is known as the ice age. During the ice age, snow piled up that created huge sheets of ice called glaciers. Because so much water was in the form of ice, the level of the oceans went down. A narrow strip of seawater between Asia and North America disappeared. This left a bridge of land between the two continents.

Scientists believed that herds of animals wandered onto this land bridge, looking for food. Hunters from Asia may have followed them and crossed the land bridge to North America. Years later, the seawater once again covered up the land bridge.

More recent discoveries have led some scientists to think that people may have arrived in the Americas even earlier. About 12,500 years ago, people with boats may have moved along the Pacific coast of Alaska and northwestern Canada and then south.

Over time, people spread throughout North and South America. American Indians are the *descendants* of these first Americans. A descendant is someone who is related to a particular person or group from the past.

the Americas the landmasses and islands of North America and South America

Many scientists believe that early American Indians crossed a land bridge into North America. Other people believe that they came by boats from Asia.

Possible Early Routes to the Americas

ASIA

NORTH AMERICA

PACIFIC OCEAN

ATLANTIC OCEAN

Equator

SOUTH AMERICA

0   1,000 2,000 miles
0   2,000 kilometers

☐ Glaciers during the last ice age
▨ Land area during the last ice age
→ Land bridge route
➡ Coastal route
— Present-day shoreline

N
W ✦ E
S

2. Contributions of American Indians

American Indians are a **diverse** people, with many different tribes and languages. They have affected American life in many ways. One important contribution has been that their **cultures,** or ways of life, respect nature. Native peoples did not harm the environment as much as people in other nations around the world.

American Indians also gave names to many of the places in our country, including major rivers, such as the Mississippi River. We still use many of these names today. Some of our states, such as Iowa and Minnesota, have American Indian names as well.

You may be able to see other contributions in your kitchen at home. American Indians were the first to grow many of the foods we eat today. One of the most popular foods they grew was corn. In the different areas where they settled, American Indians also grew fruits and vegetables like beans and squash.

There are many other contributions that American Indians have made to American life. Before the United States was created, a group of American Indian tribes worked closely together, separating power between a central government and each individual tribe. When the United States was formed, our early leaders were influenced by these American Indian tribes. You can research contributions that American Indians have made in the United States.

American Indians lived in tribes. Each tribe developed its own language and customs.

diverse made up of different groups of people

culture a way of life shared by a group of people

3. The Spanish Settle the Americas

In 1492, an explorer named Christopher Columbus set sail west across the Atlantic Ocean believing that he would reach Asia. Instead, he landed on a Caribbean island.

Columbus returned to Spain, but he left some men behind to start a **colony** for Spain. More Spanish people followed Columbus's route to the Americas. These Spaniards began colonies on islands in the Caribbean Sea and in North and South America, often near where American Indians lived.

One of the largest Spanish colonies was in Mexico. From Mexico, settlers moved into what is now the United States. They built towns, churches, and forts in the areas we know as Texas, New Mexico, Arizona, California, and Florida.

Today, Mexico, all the countries to its south, and the many islands in the Gulf of Mexico are called Latin America. Most people who were born in Latin America or whose *ancestors* were born there are called Latinos. An ancestor is a relative from a past generation.

Some Latinos have lived in the United States for many years, while others have just arrived. Many have come from Mexico, Cuba, and Puerto Rico.

colony a settlement that is ruled by another country

Spanish colonies spread north from South America through parts of the United States. They built towns, churches, and forts throughout this area.

Area of Spanish Settlement in North America

Spanish settlement by 1750
Modern-day border

140°W
40°N
30°N
60°W
20°N
California
Arizona
New Mexico
Texas
Florida
PACIFIC OCEAN
ATLANTIC OCEAN
Gulf of Mexico
Mexico
130°W
120°W
90°W
80°W
70°W
110°W

0   250   500 miles
0   250 500 kilometers

4. The Contributions of Latinos

Latinos have made many contributions to American life. In 1848, there were many experienced miners in Chile. When a sawmill worker discovered gold in California, thousands of people, including many miners from Chile, went to California hoping to become rich. Wealthy Americans hired many people from Chile to dig tunnels to help them mine for gold.

Mexican vaqueros, or cowboys, wear large-brimmed hats to protect them from the sun. Americans created the cowboy hat based on this type of hat.

Another contribution is that many Latinos have helped other Americans turn the dry Southwest into a rich farming region. Many crops, such as oranges, that are grown in this region today were first brought by Spanish settlers to Mexico and then from Mexico to the United States.

You may have seen another contribution on television: the cowboy. Cowboys came to the United States from Mexico—even the cows, which originally came from Spain. Mexican settlers brought cattle to the Southwest and built cattle ranches. And they introduced the Mexican cowboy, called a *vaquero* (vah-KEHR-oh).

Americans learned how to be cowboys from Mexican vaqueros. Their wide-brimmed cowboy hats came from Mexican *sombreros*. Their high-heeled cowboy boots came from Mexican *botas*. Mexican vaqueros taught Americans how to use *la reata*, or the lariat, to rope their cattle.

There are many other contributions that Latinos have made to American life. Many cities and towns in the West and Southwest have been heavily influenced by Latinos. Some cities are named using Spanish words. Others places have buildings, called *haciendas*, that are similar to those built by the people from Spain. What other contributions have Latinos made to American life?

The Landing on Cape Cod.

Some people came to America so they could freely practice their religion. These pilgrims from England settled in what is now Massachusetts.

5. More Europeans Come to America

The Spanish were the first Europeans to colonize North America, but other Europeans soon followed. The French started a colony in Canada. Russians began a colony in Alaska. Dutch settlers built a colony in what is now New York.

Settlers from England began colonies on the eastern shore of North America. Between 1607 and 1733, the English built 13 colonies in America. These colonies hugged the Atlantic Coast from Maine to Georgia.

The 13 English colonies attracted settlers from many parts of Europe. Many of these people were poor and came to find land or work. Others were searching for freedom to follow their religion or to gain wealth. All hoped to start new lives in a new land.

In 1776, the 13 English colonies broke away from England. Together, they formed a new nation called the United States of America.

The new nation continued to welcome immigrants from Europe. An **immigrant** is a person who comes from some other place to live in a country. European Americans are immigrants from Europe or descendants of European immigrants.

immigrant someone who comes from another place to live in a country

At first, most of the immigrants came from western Europe. Later, others came from eastern and southern Europe. Each group added to America's diversity, or mix of peoples.

6. The Contributions of European Americans

European Americans have played a large part in shaping American life. One significant contribution is the English language. Americans speak English today in part because so many English colonists settled in the English colonies. By contrast, few French colonists settled in Canada. When the British won the French and Indian War in 1763, it meant that English became the primary language spoken in the North American colonies.

European Americans also contributed to the creation of the American government. They brought ideas of **democracy,** which has its roots in the governments of ancient Greece and Rome. The colonists from Europe eventually tired of being told what to do by an English king. They wanted to govern, or rule, themselves. The colonists decided to fight for their freedom. The king of England did not want to give American colonists this freedom. He sent troops to America to keep the colonies under his control. The war they fought is known as the American Revolution.

There are many other contributions that European Americans have made to American life. A number of European Americans were also inventors. Their inventions included the telephone, the radio, and electric lights. These inventions have shaped the way Americans live today. What other contributions have European Americans made to American life?

democracy a form of government in which people vote for their leaders

European Americans come from many countries. Each group brings different languages, customs, and foods to the United States.

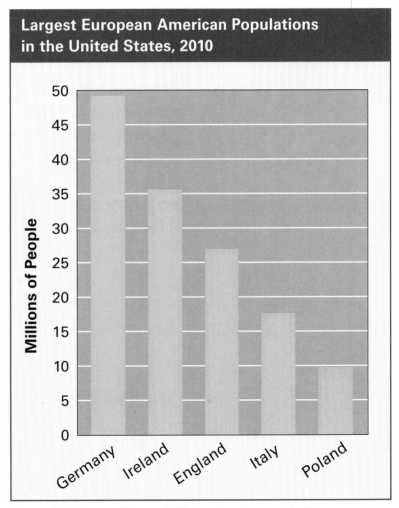

Largest European American Populations in the United States, 2010

Source: U.S. Census Bureau, 2010 American Community Survey

7. Africans Arrive in America

In 1619, a ship arrived in the colony of Virginia. The ship's captain traded 20 Africans, taken from their homes in Africa by force, for food. Within a few decades, more people brought from Africa were forced to be slaves. A slave is a person who is owned by another person.

In 1619, the practice of buying and selling people was common in much of the world. In Africa, for example, people who were captured in raids were often sold as slaves.

For almost 250 years, traders used force to bring hundreds of thousands of Africans to this country. Most Africans were sold as slaves. They worked on farms raising tobacco, rice, and cotton. For this work, slaves received no pay. Slave owners viewed their slaves as property, rather than as people who worked for them. They often treated the slaves very harshly.

Slavery became part of life in the American South. But outside the South, fewer people owned slaves and others opposed slavery. The fight over slavery finally led to the American Civil War in 1861. When the war ended in 1865, the practice of slavery was stopped. But the struggle by African Americans to be treated like other Americans was just beginning.

Most African Americans that were forced into slavery lived in the southern states. But other states had slaves as well.

Where Slaves Lived Before the Civil War

Areas without slaves
0–100,000 slaves
100,000–200,000 slaves
200,000–300,000 slaves
Over 300,000 slaves

8. The Contributions of African Americans

African Americans have made many contributions to American life. In many African countries, telling stories is often an honored art. African slaves brought that art to America. We can enjoy many of these stories today in books, plays, and poetry.

Martin Luther King, Jr. was one of the leaders of the movement for equal rights in the 1960s. He helped bring equal rights for African Americans in the United States.

Another very important contribution has been the fight for equal rights. Rights are freedoms that belong to all people. The American Civil War ended slavery in 1865, but it did not end *prejudice* against African Americans. Prejudice is the use of skin color, cultural background, or religion to form an unfair opinion about other people.

Because of prejudice, whites often denied African Americans the same rights that whites enjoyed. In some states, white people made laws to keep African Americans separate from them in restaurants and in schools. The rules to keep the two groups separate were unfair to African Americans. Separate meant, in effect, not equal.

African Americans fought long and hard for equal rights. Some Americans were killed in that struggle. Others were sent to jail. Laws were finally passed to end the unfair treatment.

Today, all Americans—no matter what their skin color— are equal under the law. We all have equal rights because African Americans refused to accept anything less.

There are many other contributions that African Americans have made to American life. In the South, the blues, a type of music, was created by African Americans who were facing injustice. Today, blues has inspired many other types of music such as jazz, rock 'n' roll, and country music. African Americans have also created music like hip hop, rap, and some types of gospel music. What other contributions have African Americans made to American life?

Many people from China came to the United States to find gold. Some of these people chose to stay and live here.

9. Asians Come to America

People from Asia came to America for many different reasons. In 1848, after the discovery of gold in California, many Chinese immigrants traveled to the United States. Not all Americans welcomed the Chinese gold-seekers. But many admired how hard they worked.

Other people from Asia came to America for work. As Americans moved west in the late 1800s, they had big dreams. They wanted railroads to cross the country. They wanted to build new farms and factories. But to make these dreams come true, Americans needed workers. So the word went out across Asia: send workers!

Between 1850 and 1882, many Chinese came to the United States to work. Some saved their money and later returned to China. But others stayed in the United States for good.

Immigrants also came from Japan, Korea, and the Philippines. Some immigrants went to Hawaii to work in the sugar fields. Others worked on farms and in factories on the West Coast. One Japanese immigrant wrote this poem about going to the United States:

Huge dreams of fortune
Go with me to foreign lands
Across the ocean.

Instead of finding fortune, however, most of the Asian immigrants found hard lives. They worked long hours for little pay. Their bosses often treated them roughly. Still, most of the immigrants stayed in their adopted land, as Asian Americans.

10. The Contributions of Asian Americans

Asian Americans form one of the most diverse groups in the United States. Today, this group includes people from many different countries in Asia, like China, Japan, the Philippines, North Korea and South Korea, Vietnam, Cambodia, Laos, Thailand, India, as well as the countries of the Pacific Islands.

Asian Americans have made many contributions to American life. When immigrants from countries in China first came to this country, some were treated very poorly. Many were forced to live in parts of a city that were unsafe. They worked together to rebuild these sections of town and turned them into places, often called Chinatowns, that people from all over the world can visit and enjoy today.

The diverse groups of immigrants that came from Asia brought new foods to the United States. They also brought new ways of cooking. As a result, today Americans enjoy many kinds of Asian foods, such as sushi and stir-fried dishes. Asian cooking has also blended with many other types of American food to create new and delicious combinations.

There are many other contributions that Asian Americans have made to American life. Today, many immigrants from Asia come to the United States to study. Once they are done with school, many choose to stay and help their fellow Americans research and create new ways to make the lives of all Americans better. What other contributions have Asian Americans made to American life?

Asian Americans come from many different countries. Each group brings new things, like different kinds of food, to the United States.

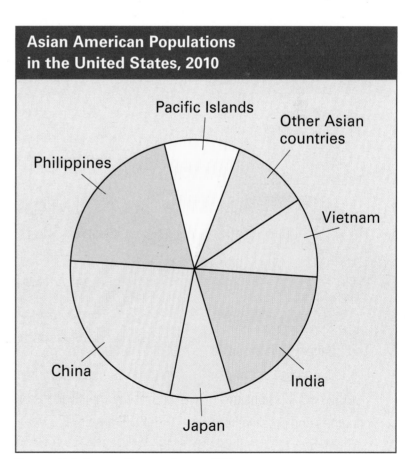

Asian American Populations in the United States, 2010

Pacific Islands

Other Asian countries

Philippines

Vietnam

China

India

Japan

Source: U.S. Census Bureau, Census 2010

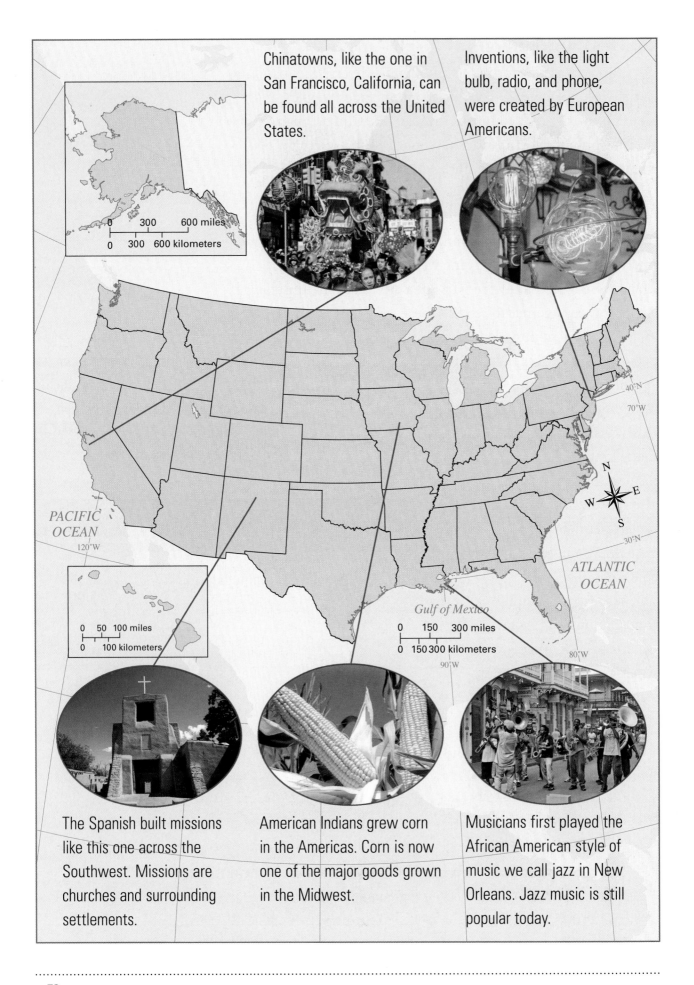

Chinatowns, like the one in San Francisco, California, can be found all across the United States.

Inventions, like the light bulb, radio, and phone, were created by European Americans.

PACIFIC OCEAN
120°W

ATLANTIC OCEAN

Gulf of Mexico

40°N
70°W

30°N

80°W

90°W

0   300   600 miles
0   300   600 kilometers

0   50   100 miles
0   100 kilometers

0   150   300 miles
0   150 300 kilometers

The Spanish built missions like this one across the Southwest. Missions are churches and surrounding settlements.

American Indians grew corn in the Americas. Corn is now one of the major goods grown in the Midwest.

Musicians first played the African American style of music we call jazz in New Orleans. Jazz music is still popular today.

These people have something in common. They are all Americans.

Lesson Summary

Sooner or later, you will hear someone describe the United States as a nation of immigrants. It's true. We all came to this land from some other place. Some made the journey thousands of years ago. Others arrived just yesterday.

Each group came for its own reasons. Ancestors of American Indians may have followed the animals they hunted to a new land. The Spanish were looking for a route to Asia. The English came seeking freedom and opportunity. Other Europeans were fleeing war and hunger. The first Africans were brought to America against their will. Asians originally crossed the ocean to find gold and work.

Immigrants are still traveling to America. Most of these new immigrants come from countries in Latin America and Asia. But people also come from many other parts of the world.

The contributions of each group of people have changed and strengthened the United States. Without any one group and its contributions, the United States would not be as richly varied as it is today.

Settling in Your State

You just read about the diverse backgrounds of the people in the United States. Your state is probably diverse. Some people may have recently arrived from other countries. Others may have lived here all their lives, but their grandparents or great-grandparents arrived from another part of the world. So, why do people live in your state?

People from other parts of the world bring their culture with them. Does your state have restaurants that serve Chinese, Indian, or Mexican food? Those recipes came from other countries. Different cultures affect other parts of your state, too. For instance, if you live in Colorado, the name of your state comes from Spain. Spanish explorers saw red rocks by a river and named the river *Colorado*, which means "the color red."

People move to states for many different reasons at different times in history. For example, in the mid-1800s, Colorado attracted thousands of gold-seekers after gold and silver were discovered. Today, people come for jobs in oil and gas production or to live by the Rocky Mountains.

Do research and find out why people have moved to your state. Start by writing questions, such as: Did people come for certain kinds of jobs? Is the scenery or climate a big attraction? Make a list of questions you want to answer.

Many people settled in Colorado during the mid-1800s once gold and silver were discovered. This is just one of many reasons people settled in this state.

GREGORY GOLD DIGGINGS, COLORADO, MAY, 1859.

Move Here!

There are many places to find answers to your questions. You can interview a neighbor or family members. Or you can go to a library and read diaries by people who moved there. Remember that these sources will give you just one person's point of view. For other viewpoints, you can look at Web sites about your state and in history books. Take notes like the ones shown here.

Now prepare a sales pitch to encourage someone to move to your state. Construct an argument that gives reasons why your state is a great place to live. Start with the question: Why should you move to my state? Write strong statements to persuade people. Do research for facts that will support your statements. For example, if people move there for jobs in a certain field, find out how many people got jobs in that field last year. If mild weather is important, list the average number of sunny days or the average temperatures each season. If your state has fun things to do, find exciting photographs to share. These are all ways to back up your argument with supporting evidence. Make posters that help you make your point. Present your sales pitch to your classmates.

Once you have found answers to your questions, prepare a sales pitch. Include information about why people moved to your state.

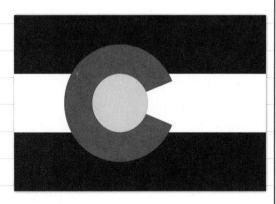

Why People Moved to Colorado

Jobs: Mining, ranching, hotels and ski resorts

Climate: Warm summers and snowy winters

Scenery: Rocky Mountains

Recreation: Skiing in winter

Geography

History

New York City: Layers of the Past

Walk down any block in New York, and you will see people from many backgrounds passing by. The same thing has been true for hundreds of years. How have different groups of people made New York City what it is today?

Corlears Hook Park is in New York City, which is in the state of New York. People of all different backgrounds live around this park.

Welcome to Corlears Hook Park located in the Lower East Side, a neighborhood in New York City. There are children laughing and running in the park today. Listen and you can hear them speak in Spanish and Chinese, as well as English, as they play.

About 100 years ago, on this very same spot, children also played. Those children spoke Dutch, English, French, German, and Yiddish.

Some 300 years before that, the children here were American Indians from the Lenape tribe. The children helped their parents to fish, grow crops, or trap animals.

Stand in Corlears Hook Park today, and you stand on layers and layers of American history. Each group of people that lived in this place has left its mark. How did they shape the New York City of today?

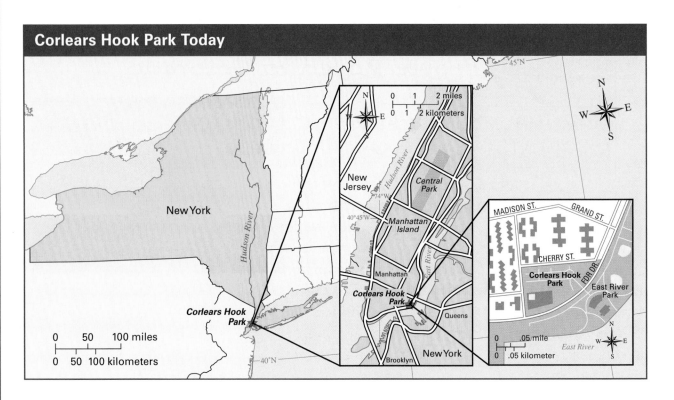

Corlears Hook Park Today

The Lenapes met Henry Hudson and his crew of twenty men. The crew of *Half Moon* wanted to trade for furs that the Lenape had.

A Meeting of Three Worlds

Manhattan Island, now a part of New York City, was first settled by American Indians more than 10,000 years ago. Thousands of Lenapes lived on the island they called Manahatta, "the hilly island." They fished, grew crops, and trapped animals such as beavers. Those beavers would eventually change life on Manahatta forever.

In 1609, the Dutch ship *Half Moon*, captained by Henry Hudson, sailed into the harbor of Manahatta. The Dutch were looking for places to settle and for people to trade with. They especially wanted furs. And the Lenapes had lots of furs.

A few years later, a free black sailor named Juan Rodriguez, who worked with the Dutch, sailed to Manahatta. It was his job to trade Dutch furs with American Indians. He was the first man who wasn't an American Indian to live on Manhattan Island.

In 1624, a Dutch fur company sent 30 families to start a colony. Their settlement at the tip of Manhattan Island was named New Amsterdam. The Dutch made changes to the island as they built their new town. They cut down trees, laid out streets, and built homes.

As more and more people arrived, three worlds came together. First were the American Indians, and then the Dutch. Later, people came from France, Ireland, Great Britain, and other European countries. Africans were part of the story, too. In 1644, a visitor to New Amsterdam said that he heard 18 different languages spoken on the streets! It was a diverse town even then.

Tenement apartments were often very crowded. Since there was very little space inside, people had to do many things outside.

Waves of Immigrants Come to New York

Since the 1600s, when the Dutch first settled there, New York City has attracted immigrants by the millions. In 1664, the English took over New Amsterdam and renamed the city New York.

In the late 1800s and early 1900s, most immigrants to the United States came from Europe by ship. They traveled past the Statue of Liberty into New York Harbor and landed at Ellis Island. In the year 1907, more than 1 million new Americans came through Ellis Island.

Many immigrants settled on the Lower East Side. The neighborhood around Corlears Hook was crowded with families that had come from Italy and Russia and other parts of Europe. Everyone—even children— worked hard to start a new life in their new country.

Many immigrant families lived in **tenements**. Sometimes, twenty families or more lived in one tenement. Each floor had several small apartments and often only one bathroom. The apartments did not have much fresh air or good light. Rats and cockroaches added to the poor living conditions.

The Confino family lived in a tenement located at 97 Orchard Street. Ten people lived in their small apartment. Like other families, the Confinos brought their traditions with them. They practiced Judaism. They ate foods like those they had eaten in Greece. They also brought their dreams to the United States. In time, they became Americans.

tenement a four- to six-story building with many small apartments

People celebrate the Feast of San Gennaro in Little Italy. For eleven days each year they honor Italian traditions.

New York City Today

The Lower East Side is still crowded. It is still a place where many new Americans first arrive. And it is still a place where you can see signs of the past. An Italian bakery or a Jewish delicatessen reminds New Yorkers of the Lower East Side that the Confinos knew.

Today, you hear different languages on the streets. In Little Italy, you once heard Italian everywhere. Now, you are more likely to hear Chinese or Spanish as you walk through the neighborhood. In fact, New York City's Chinatown is the largest Chinatown in the United States.

The Lower East Side celebrates its history all year long. It has been home to a mix of people since Juan Rodrigues first arrived. People in all groups that have come to New York City have changed the place in some way. ◆

In Chinatown, dragons dance in the street. People come from many places to welcome the Chinese New Year.

A Train Tour of the Northeast

What are different parts of the Northeast like?

Introduction

Welcome to our train tour of the historic Northeast. My name is Ms. Mariner, and I will be your guide. During this tour, we will visit many states in the Northeast. Have you been to this region of the United States before?

When I am not leading tours, I work in my town's local history center. I like to teach and learn about the early American colonies, the American Revolution, and the founding of the United States. You will learn a lot from me about the past as we go.

Our tour will take you to many different places with historical landmarks. Each place has a story to tell about the Northeast and its people. Famous events occurred in some of these places.

As we visit these places, I want you to look for answers to these three questions.

1. Why do we call the Northeast the "birthplace of our nation"?
2. Why did our nation's first factories start here?
3. What large cities are found in the Northeast?

You'll hear and see clues to the answers to these questions as we travel along.

Watch your step as you climb aboard the train. Our first stop of our journey through the Northeast will be in the beautiful state of Maine.

Social Studies Vocabulary

American Revolution

canal

Declaration of Independence

lock

mass production

peak

skyscraper

United States Constitution

◄ This train travels through a mountain range in New Hampshire, one the states in the Northeast region.

 Civics $ Economics Geography   History

The Northeast Region

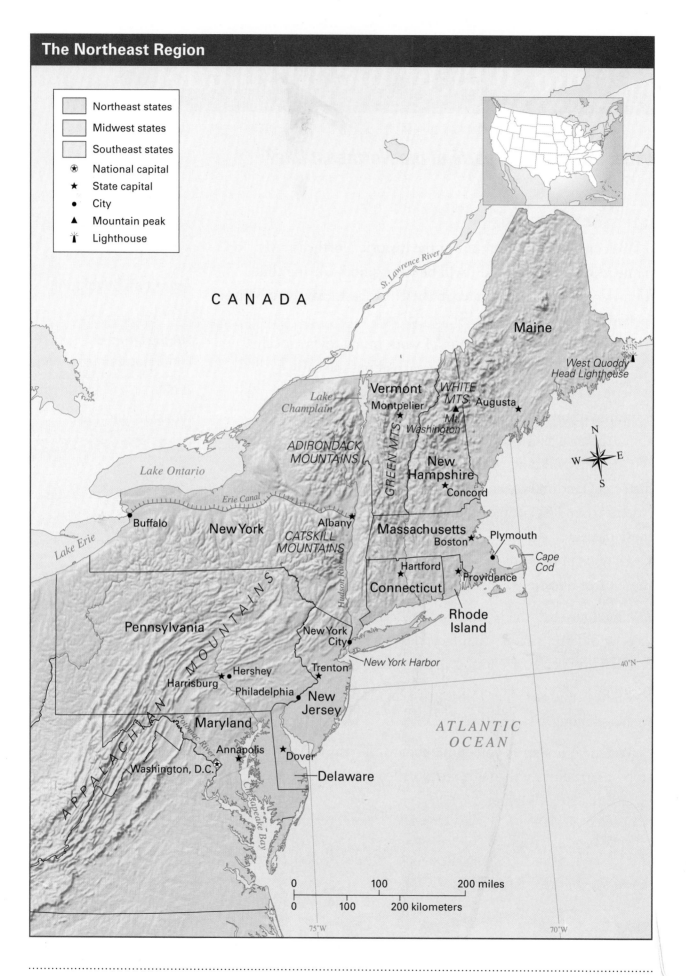

Northeast states
Midwest states
Southeast states
⊛ National capital
★ State capital
• City
▲ Mountain peak
⚲ Lighthouse

CANADA

St. Lawrence River

Maine

West Quoddy
Head Lighthouse

Lake
Champlain

Vermont
Montpelier

WHITE
MTS.

Mt.
Washington

Augusta

ADIRONDACK
MOUNTAINS

GREEN MTS.

New
Hampshire

Lake Ontario

Concord

Erie Canal

Buffalo

New York

Albany

CATSKILL
MOUNTAINS

Massachusetts
Boston

Plymouth

Cape
Cod

Lake Erie

Hartford

Providence

Connecticut

Rhode
Island

Pennsylvania

Hudson River

New York
City

New York Harbor

40°N

Trenton

Hershey

Harrisburg

Philadelphia

New
Jersey

ATLANTIC
OCEAN

Maryland

Potomac River

Annapolis

Dover

Washington, D.C.

Delaware

Chesapeake Bay

APPALACHIAN MOUNTAINS

N
W   E
S

45°N

0   100   200 miles
0   100   200 kilometers

75°W

70°W

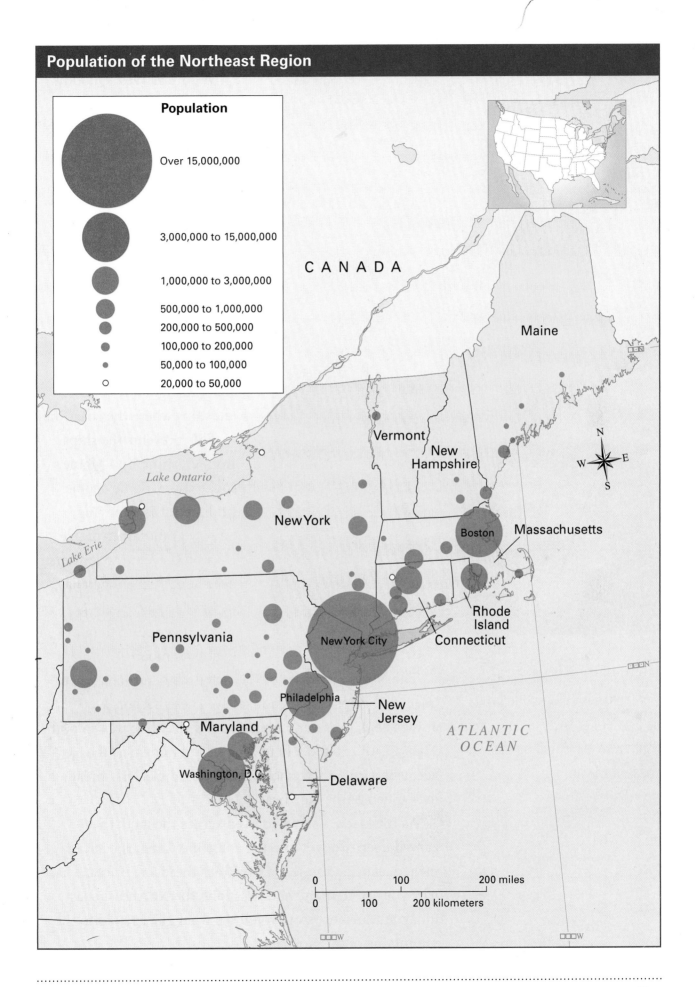

Population of the Northeast Region

Population

Over 15,000,000

3,000,000 to 15,000,000

1,000,000 to 3,000,000

500,000 to 1,000,000

200,000 to 500,000

100,000 to 200,000

50,000 to 100,000

20,000 to 50,000

CANADA

Maine

Vermont

New
Hampshire

Lake Ontario

New York

Boston

Massachusetts

Lake Erie

Rhode
Island

Connecticut

New York City

Pennsylvania

Philadelphia

New
Jersey

ATLANTIC
OCEAN

Maryland

Washington, D.C.

Delaware

N
W   E
S

0   100   200 miles

0   100   200 kilometers

1. The Northeast Coast

We are at West Quoddy Head in the eastern corner of Maine. The tribal name of the American Indians living here is Wabanoki, which means "living at the sunrise." And they are. This is the most eastern point of land in the United States, where the sun rises before anywhere else in the country.

The West Quoddy Head Lighthouse was built in 1808. Its light and foghorn tell ships where the coastline is. This prevents the ships from crashing into Maine's rocky shore. Some people find foghorns annoying, but my grandfather didn't. He would even trap lobsters near here. "On a foggy day," he liked to say, "there is no prettier sound than a foghorn's moan."

The West Quoddy Head Lighthouse is still used today as a guide for ships at sea. This lighthouse is located on the coast of Maine.

The Northeast coastline is dotted with harbors, where boats and ships can anchor safely. These harbors weren't always here, however. Long ago, this coastline was smooth. Then Earth entered a long cold period known as the ice age, when mile-thick sheets of ice called glaciers spread over much of the Northeast.

As the glaciers slowly moved across the land, they carved deep grooves into the coastline. Later, the ice melted, causing the sea to flow into these low places. That's why you see so many harbors along the Northeast coast today. At our next stop, you'll see what glaciers did to the mountains of the Northeast.

2. The Mountains of the Northeast

Welcome to Mount Washington in New Hampshire. At 6,288 feet tall, Mount Washington is the highest **peak** in the Northeast. On a clear day, visitors can see for a hundred miles from its top.

Mount Washington has some of the world's most severe weather. It can snow here all year long. The peak is also one of the windiest places on Earth.

My family visited Mount Washington when I was your age. To get to the top, we rode the Mount Washington Cog Railway, which is the second-steepest mountain-climbing railway in the world. The wind speed that day was 75 miles per hour. My mother still believes that if she hadn't held on to me, I would have blown out to sea. The highest wind speed ever recorded here was 231 miles per hour in 1934.

Mount Washington sits in the White Mountains of New Hampshire. The White Mountains are part of the Appalachian mountain range, which is one of the oldest mountain ranges in the world.

> **peak** the top of a mountain

At 6,288 feet high, Mount Washington is the highest peak in the Northeast. Many hikers climb the mountain each year.

In Plymouth Massachusetts, you can visit the *Mayflower II*. This is a copy of the Pilgrims' ship.

3. Democracy Takes Root at Plymouth

This is Plymouth, Massachusetts, where the Pilgrims landed almost 400 years ago. You can visit a reproduction, or copy, of their ship, the *Mayflower*, in Plymouth Harbor.

In 1620, the *Mayflower* left England with 102 passengers aboard. All of the passengers were headed for Virginia. Less than half of them were Pilgrims in search of religious freedom, and the rest simply wanted to make their home in America. The Pilgrims called these settlers "strangers."

Storms blew the *Mayflower* off course. Instead of Virginia, the ship reached New England. Sick of stormy seas, the Pilgrims decided to stop there instead. But they had a problem. There was no government in New England, and some of the "strangers" looked like troublemakers. What would you have done in their situation? Think about this as you leave the train to visit Plymouth.

⋆   ⋆   ⋆

Welcome back. I'll tell you now how the Pilgrims solved their problem. Before going ashore, they drew up an agreement called the Mayflower Compact. It said that they would set up a government and make laws for the good of everyone. Most of the men signed the compact, and then the passengers elected a governor to lead the government.

Today, Americans believe that people should make their own laws and elect their own leaders. We call this form of government a democracy. During the Pilgrims' time, when kings and queens ruled countries, this was a bold idea.

4. Boston Leads the Fight for Freedom

We are now visiting the Boston Common in Boston, Massachusetts. The Boston Common is America's first public park, and Boston is one of America's oldest cities. It is also where the fight for America's freedom from Great Britain began.

In 1775, many people in the 13 colonies did not want to live under British rule anymore. Fighting broke out between colonists and British troops about 20 miles outside of Boston. The conflict moved into Boston later that year.

This was the beginning of a long war called the **American Revolution**. The fighting lasted for six years. The American Revolution led to the overthrow, or end, of British rule of the colonies.

Two historic trails begin at the Boston Common. The first is the Freedom Trail. This walking tour takes you to places where the fight for freedom began. The trail ends at Bunker Hill. One of the early battles of the American Revolution was fought near this hill.

The second trail is the Black Heritage Trail. Boston was a safe place for slaves fleeing the South. In many other states, slaves were often returned to the South if they were caught. But in Boston, people worked hard to help African Americans escape slavery. On this walking tour, you will learn about the long history of African Americans in Boston. The trail ends at the African Meeting House, the oldest standing African American church building in the United States.

Which trail should you take? I recommend both. Just be sure to wear good walking shoes.

American Revolution the war in which the American colonies won independence from Great Britain

The Old State House is located in Boston. It is one of the many sights along the Freedom Trail.

5. The Erie Canal Links the Northeast and the Midwest

Have you ever sung a song called "The Erie Canal"? You are looking at the **canal** that inspired the song. A canal is a ditch dug across land, and often canals connect one waterway with another. The Erie Canal is a 340-mile-long ditch that connects the Hudson River with the Great Lakes.

Work on the Erie Canal began in 1817. At that time, there was no good way to move goods from the Northeast to the Midwest. Moving goods by horse and wagon was slow and costly. Moving goods by boat was faster and cheaper, but there was a problem. No river crossed the Appalachian Mountains, which lay between the Midwest and the Northeast.

The men who built the Erie Canal solved that problem. They dug a 40-foot-wide ditch from the Hudson River to Lake Erie. Along the way, they built 83 **locks** to help carry boats over the mountains. Locks are used to raise and lower boats in the water.

The Erie Canal opened for use in 1825, and it was an instant success. Freight prices between Lake Erie and New York City dropped from $100 a ton by road to just $10 a ton by canal. New York City was soon the nation's busiest seaport.

This is a lock on the Erie Canal. Locks are used to raise and lower boats in the water.

On clear days, visitors to the top of the Empire State Building can see parts of New Jersey, Pennsylvania, Connecticut, and Massachusetts, as well as New York.

6. New York City: Where Buildings Touch the Sky

We are in New York City, the largest city in America. More than 8 million people live here.

New York City has always been a city of immigrants. The Dutch were the first Europeans to settle here, and then people from other parts of Europe and Africa followed. Together, they made New York City a city of many cultures, or ways of life.

Today, people still come to New York City from all over the world. Just listen to people talking on the streets. You will hear English, Spanish, Chinese, Arabic, Russian, Hebrew, Italian, Korean, and many other languages.

Are you wondering how New York City finds room for all of these people? The answer is—up in the air! A hundred years ago, New Yorkers began building **skyscrapers**. People live and work in these very tall buildings.

The Empire State Building is one of New York City's most famous skyscrapers. This office building has 103 stories, or floors, and visitors can go to the very top of the building and look out at the view. You could climb the 1,860 stairs, but I suggest that you take the elevator.

skyscraper a very tall building

7. Hershey, Pennsylvania: A Town Built on Chocolate

One of my favorite movies is *Willy Wonka and the Chocolate Factory*. So I was very excited when my family visited Hershey, Pennsylvania. At last, I got a chance to see a real chocolate factory. Yum!

Later, I wondered why America's first factories were built in the Northeast. I think there were two main reasons. One reason was waterpower. The first factories were built alongside rivers that rushed down out of the mountains. This rushing water turned big waterwheels that made the machines in the factories run.

A second reason was people power. The Northeast was a good place for people who wanted to start businesses. Candy maker Milton Hershey was one of these people. And there were many people to work in these businesses.

More than 100 years ago, Hershey started a candy business here in Pennsylvania. In his factory, he used a system called **mass production,** which is a way of making very large quantities of the same product. The Hershey bar was America's first mass-produced chocolate bar. Today, Hershey's factory is the largest chocolate factory in the world.

We'll stop here to learn more about mass production. Enjoy your visit, and try not to eat too much chocolate.

mass production a way of making large quantities of products

A worker at this factory checks the quality of a large vat of chocolate. The factory is located in Hershey, Pennsylvania.

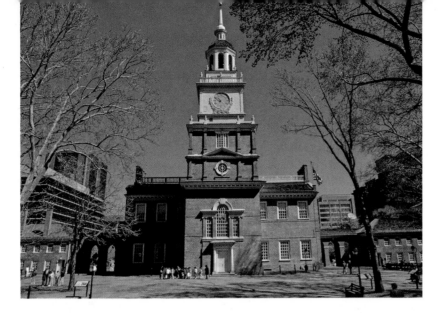

The Declaration of Independence was approved in Independence Hall in Philadelphia, Pennsylvania. Today, Independence Hall is part of a national historic park.

8. Independence Hall: The Birthplace of the United States

You are looking at Independence Hall in Philadelphia, Pennsylvania. It was here that the United States was born. We celebrate our nation's birthday each year on Independence Day.

The date of our nation's birth was July 4, 1776. On that day, leaders from the 13 colonies met in Independence Hall to approve the **Declaration of Independence**. This statement told the world that the Americans had formed their own nation. This new country was called the United States of America.

Americans fought a long war to win their independence. Great Britain finally agreed that Americans should govern themselves. But how would they do that?

In 1787, some of the best thinkers in the nation met in Independence Hall to answer that question. They talked and argued for months. Then they wrote a new constitution, or plan of government, for the country. We still live under that plan today.

The **United States Constitution** is based on the idea of democracy. Under this plan of government, we, the people, choose our leaders. The Constitution also protects our rights. You have the right to say what you think, to follow any religion you choose, and to have a fair trial. These and many others are rights that the Constitution provides and that Americans hold dear.

Declaration of Independence the document that declared the United States to be free from Great Britain

United States Constitution the plan of government for the United States

The Capitol building is in Washington, D.C., and it is the home of our national government. This is where Congress meets to make our nation's laws.

9. Washington, D.C.: Our Nation's Capital

Does this building look familiar to you? It is the Capitol building, one of the great landmarks of the city of Washington, D.C.

Washington, D.C., is our nation's capital, the home of our national government. Here, the people who have the power to make decisions for our country do their jobs. The work of our government is important because the government creates the rules we live by. Picture what life would be like without rules. Think about it as you leave the train to visit Washington, D.C.

* * *

Welcome back. Let me tell you a bit more about our government's rules, or laws.

Our government's laws help to make sure that each person's rights are protected. Our rights include the right to life, liberty, property, and the pursuit of happiness.

The government also works for the common good. This means that it tries to act in ways that serve all people, not just a few. Our government seeks to provide an equal chance for all people, and it tries to treat all people fairly.

Our government is a republic. In a republic, the power lies with the people, and they exercise their power by electing leaders. The Constitution says that Americans can choose representatives to make laws for them. People choose representatives by voting in elections. Voting is a key part of being a good citizen.

10. Our Government Buildings

The national government of the United States has three branches, or parts. Each branch has a different role. Each branch helps promote the common good and protect people's basic rights. And each has a special building it calls home.

Congress is the legislative branch. It makes laws for our country. Voters in each state elect lawmakers to represent them in Congress. Congress works in the Capitol building.

The president of the United States is the head of the executive branch. The president's main job is to make sure that laws passed by Congress are carried out. The president is also elected. The president lives and works in the White House.

The president of the United States lives and works in the White House. The president is the head of the executive branch.

The judicial branch is the third branch of government, which is made up of the nation's courts. This branch guarantees that the laws passed by Congress are obeyed. The courts also seek truth and justice, and they decide questions and disagreements about our laws. For example, courts decide whether someone has broken a law.

The top court in the United States meets in the Supreme Court Building. The Court is located next to the Capitol building.

The highest court is the Supreme Court. Its home is also in Washington, D.C.—in the Supreme Court Building. One of the Supreme Court's jobs is to make sure that laws passed by Congress follow the United States Constitution. The Constitution explains what the U.S. government and its leaders can and cannot do. The Supreme Court also helps make sure that government treats all people fairly.

11. Our National Monuments

Washington, D.C., is more than a home to government. It also has many famous landmarks. You have visited the Capitol building and have seen the White House and the Supreme Court Building. Other buildings honor the ideas and the people that have helped make our country great while others hold some of our national treasures.

Washington, D.C., has many monuments. These are buildings that help us remember important people or events. The Washington Monument celebrates George Washington, the first president of the United States. The Jefferson Memorial honors Thomas Jefferson, our third president. Jefferson also wrote the Declaration of Independence. This document says, "All men are created equal," and it gives some of the main ideas that have shaped our government. In Washington, D.C., you can see the signed copy of the Declaration of Independence. It is at one of the city's great museums—the National Archives.

The Lincoln Memorial (left), Washington Monument (middle), and the Capitol (at right) are all located in Washington, D.C. These are three of the most famous American landmarks in the country.

The United States National Archives is located in Washington, D.C. This museum holds important records such as copies to the Constitution, the Bill of Rights, and the Declaration of Independence.

The National Archives also holds the U.S. Constitution and the Bill of Rights. The Bill of Rights, which lists our most cherished freedoms, was added to the Constitution in 1791. Thanks to the Bill of Rights, we have the freedom of speech. We can speak out if we are unhappy with our government and the Bill of Rights also promises us freedom of religion.

As you have learned, there is much to see and do in Washington, D.C. You can find out about our nation's history. You can learn about the ideas that are important to our country and celebrate our past. I hope you have enjoyed your visit!

Lesson Summary

Do you remember the questions I asked you when we began our journey? The first question was why we call the Northeast the "birthplace of our nation." Boston is where the American Revolution began. And Philadelphia is where Americans first declared their independence from Great Britain.

I asked you why the nation's first factories were built in the Northeast. This region had a lot of waterpower for running factories. And it had people who enjoyed the challenge of starting new businesses and people who wanted to work in them.

My last question was what large cities are found here. You visited some of the largest cities in the Northeast: Boston, New York City, Philadelphia, and Washington, D.C. You also stopped at two smaller towns, Plymouth and Hershey.

Our tour of the Northeast is ending now. I hope you enjoyed your trip as much as I enjoyed being your guide.

The Most Important Cities in Your State

Every state has a variety of cities. Each city has features that make it special. These might be buildings, colleges, sports teams, historical places, or outdoor activities.

Illinois, for example, has the third largest city in the United States—Chicago. It sits on Lake Michigan and has many skyscrapers. The city of Springfield is the state capital and was home to Abraham Lincoln before he became president. Then there is Champaign, a city where more than 40,000 students attend the big, exciting University of Illinois.

Which city do you think is the most important in your state? Can you persuade someone else to agree with you? First, you should research some strong facts about three cities. Then you must develop and present a convincing argument about the best city in your opinion.

Before you start your research, draw a blank research table similar to this example. Pick three well-known cities in your state, and write the city names in the top row. Then find out the size, job opportunities, and points of interest of each. Do your research in several reliable sources. For example, do an Internet search for a city name and choose Web sites that have current information. They could be on government Web sites or the state tourism office. You can also look in encyclopedias and reference books.

A student made this table about three Illinois cities. She can use the information to argue why she thinks that one city is the most important city in the state.

Illinois Cities	Chicago	Springfield	Champaign
Population	2,718,782	117,006	83,424
Popular Jobs	• Telecommunications and publishing • Manufacturing	• Government jobs • Transportation and warehousing	• Jobs at university • Health care
Points of Interest	• Millennium Park • Wrigley Field • Lake Michigan	• Lincoln Home National Historic Site • State Capitol Building	• University of Illinois • Orpheum Children's Museum

Build Your Case!

Which is the most important city in your state? There is not one right answer. People have different opinions, and there are many reasons to be a fan of a city. Some people think the state capital is most important, while others like the city with the most people. And others may choose a small city with lots of parks and activities.

You and your classmates should each pick what you think is the most important city in your state. Prepare a presentation to try to convince others to agree with you.

First, state your opinion using "opinion words" like *I think, I believe,* and *most important.* Next, support your opinion with three reasons. They may include the city's size, activities, historical places, sports teams, work opportunities, or natural features. Support each reason with facts from your research. Facts are true statements that tell *who, what, when, where,* and *how much.* You can check that a fact is true by looking in other sources that you trust.

Present your argument to a classmate, and then listen to your classmate make his or her argument. Evaluate your classmate's presentation. Did it begin with an opinion? Was it supported with reasons? Were the reasons supported with strong facts? Did the presentation change your opinion? Tell your classmate what you thought of his or her presentation and why.

There are many reasons why a city is important. Illinois government leaders work in the Capitol building in Springfield (top). Chicago has tall buildings, a large lake, and manufacturing jobs (bottom).

Civics   Economics   Geography   History

Lowell, Massachusetts: Factory Life

In the early 1800s, the Northeast was filled with factories. Many of them made just one item—cotton cloth. People around the world wanted cotton goods. In Lowell, Massachusetts, thousands of women took jobs to make these goods. What was it like to work in Lowell's cotton mills?

mill a factory in which people make products out of raw materials

Many girls spent their childhoods working in massive mill buildings.

In the still dark just before dawn, loud bells awoke the New England town. Sleepy young women and girls, some only 10 years old, dressed quickly. The sun wasn't up, but their day had begun.

It was 4:30 A.M. They had to arrive for work at the factory in 30 minutes and if they got there even one minute late, they might lose their jobs. At the very least, they would surely receive an unpleasant scolding. The girls walked hurriedly to their jobs at the textile **mills,** where they would make thread and cloth, in the growing town of Lowell, Massachusetts.

Gate

Canal

Water Pipe

Gear

Turbine Gear

Loom

Power House   Mill

Cotton, Cotton, Cotton!

Lowell was established in 1822. Mill owners in the Northeast had wanted to expand to make more cotton thread and cloth—and more money. So they looked carefully in the region for a place to build a brand new mill town.

They chose the area where the Merrimack and Concord rivers meet. The two rivers made this area the perfect location to create factories. Rivers meant water, and water powered factories. The mill owners built miles of canals to move water from the rivers through the town. This water brought the factories to life, as it turned the mill's turbines, or wheels with blades. These turbines used the power of flowing water to turn gears, which powered the machines inside the mill. With waterpower, the Lowell mills produced millions of yards of cloth in a year.

More than five miles of canals carried river water through Lowell. This water turned large wheels that powered the machines inside the mills.

The Lowell mills grew quickly. Factory buildings lined a mile of the Merrimack River.

Workers Needed

The mill owners needed many workers to produce so much cotton thread and cloth. And because owners continued to build new mills, they needed new workers to fill them. Clever business owners knew that there were not enough men for them to hire for all of those jobs. They choose to hire women— thousands of them—to work in the factories.

In the early 1800s, many Americans felt that women should not work, and the thought of women doing factory work shocked them. But the hum of the mill cities attracted young women and girls from all over the Northeast. Most came from farms. Workers also arrived from Canada and parts of Europe. And men eagerly took jobs in the mills, too. Still, most of the workers were women. They soon became known as "mill girls." Lowell quickly became one of the most important factory towns in the United States. By 1850, 40 large mill buildings stood side-by-side for a mile along the Merrimack River. And the mills had hired 10,000 women, girls, and men to work in them.

Women came from all over to work in Lowell. These women are from Portugal.

Women could earn more money at the mills than they might have otherwise. This gave them some independence.

Why Did They Come?

In the early 1800s, women could hold only a few types of jobs outside of the home. For example, they could be servants, or they could sew clothes, but these jobs did not pay much. Harriet Robinson, who worked in one of the Lowell mills from age 10 to 23, described the other options:

> If she [a woman] worked out as servant, or 'help,' her wages were from 50 cents to $1.00 a week; or if she went from house to house by the day to spin and weave, or do tailoress [sewing] work, she could get but 75 cents a week and her meals.

At $2.00 a week, the factories offered good, steady pay. That was hard for many mill girls to ignore as they saw a mill job as a way to a better life.

At the mills, women could earn their own living. They could be independent. Some used their earnings to help pay for a brother's education or a family debt. The girls had more options than they might have had otherwise.

One young mill girl, named Ann Swett Appleton, explained, "The thought that I am living on no one is a happy one, indeed."

Some women ran the spinning machines. Others worked the weaving looms.

Long, Hard Days

But life in the factories was tiring and boring. Women often ran the spinning machines or weaving looms. Spinning machines turned strands of cotton into thread and looms turned thread into cloth. Workers repeated the same tasks for 13 or 14 hours a day.

Today, there are laws that prevent children from working, but in the 1800s, there were not. Even young teens worked from 5 A.M. until the bell announced the end of the workday at 7 P.M. And the mill girls were allowed only two half-hour breaks each day— for breakfast and dinner. Inside the mills, the noise was deafening as hundreds of machines screamed and squealed all day long.

And many factory owners kept all windows shut, even in summer. They wanted the air inside to stay warm and moist. That kept the thread from breaking easily and sometimes workers fainted from the heat.

At times, the stomach-turning smell of burning whale oil filled the air. The oil burned in lamps that lit the dim factories in the dark days of winter.

Often, workers left their jobs because they were unhappy with the working conditions. Others left to return to their families or get married. But many stayed, day after day, for several years and some even stayed as long as 15 years.

Women Speak Out

Mill owners ran crowded boarding houses where mill girls had to live. In 1836, the owners decided to charge women more for their rooms. The owners also lowered **wages,** saying that they had to because the country was facing hard times. As a result, mills were losing money.

Many mill girls could not afford to lose that much pay. About 1,500 women went on strike, or left their jobs in protest. Harriet Robinson described the day:

> One of the girls stood on a pump and [stated] the feelings of her companions in a neat speech. . . . This was the first time a woman had spoken in public in Lowell.

There was community support for the striking workers. But, unfortunately, the factory owners did not change their minds and soon the girls went back to work.

The strike did some good, though. It showed that female workers would join together to fight for better treatment and they did that again and again during the next 75 years. Eventually, mill workers won better pay and working conditions.

The Lowell mills buzzed with activity into the 1900s. But in the 1920s, many of the factories began moving south. By 1955, Lowell's noisy mills had fallen silent. Yet the strong voices of Lowell's mill girls have not been forgotten. ◆

wage a payment of money for work

The *Lowell Offering* published the writings and thoughts of the mill girls.

LOWELL OFFERING

December, 1845.

"It is said also among the prophets."

A REPOSITORY
OF ORIGINAL ARTICLES, WRITTEN BY
"FACTORY GIRLS."

LOWELL: MISSES CURTIS & FARLEY.
Boston: JORDAN & WILEY, 121
Washington street.
1845.

Population Density and Life in the Northeast

How do people live in the Northeast?

Introduction

Have you ever seen a photograph of the United States taken from space? During the day, you might be able to see physical features like mountains or lakes. But at night, you will not be able to see features at all. Instead, you may see many bright dots of light and you might see nothing at all.

The bright areas are where lots of people live. You see the lights of homes, businesses, street lights, and other lit objects. People live close together in towns and cities there. We can say that these areas are heavily populated. The dark areas are where fewer people live. These are less populated areas, and people live far apart there.

What do you see when you look at the photograph of the Northeast region from space? Do you notice the long, bright area near the coast? This bright area is filled with hundreds of towns and cities where millions of people live. Starting north of Boston and ending south of Washington, D.C., this series of cities stretches more than 400 miles. People sometimes call this area "Boswash."

In this lesson, you will read about the people who live in the Northeast. You will also learn how the large population affects people's daily lives.

> **Social Studies Vocabulary**
>
> megalopolis
>
> population density
>
> pollution

◀ Some areas have many lights while others do not. Bright areas on the map have more people than the dark areas.

Geography

New York City has more than 27,000 people per square mile. Small towns in the Northeast are much less crowded.

population density a measure of the average number of people living in one unit of area

1. Living in the Northeast

Where do you live? Do you live in a big city? Maybe you live in a medium-sized suburb. Maybe you even live in a small town or rural area. Each of these places has a different **population density**. Population density is a measure of how many people live in a given amount of land. It is often shown as the number of people per square mile of land. The word *per* means "for each." A square mile is a square piece of land measuring one mile on each side.

Population density affects how people live. Many rural areas often have fewer than 1,000 people per square mile. This means that there are, on average, fewer than 1,000 people living on each square mile of land. Larger areas have more than 1,000 people per square mile. Some urban areas can have over 25,000 people per square mile.

There are good things about living in both rural and urban areas. In small towns, people can get to know each other more easily, and neighbors often help each other. Life can be quiet and peaceful there.

Cities may not seem as friendly as small towns, but cities offer people more choices. There are many places to shop, and restaurants serve food from many places around the world. There are many exciting things to do in a city.

2. Reading a Population Density Map

Some maps show the population density of places in the United States. They often show how many people per square mile live in different parts of the nation. Population maps have map keys. Some population maps use colors to represent different numbers of people per square mile.

In the Northeast, population density is very high along the coast. This area is a **megalopolis**. The word megalopolis means "great city." The megalopolis of Boswash stretches from Massachusetts south through parts of Rhode Island, Connecticut, New York, New Jersey, Pennsylvania, Delaware, and Maryland.

Look at this population density map of the Northeast. What do you notice about the population density of Boswash? Now look at the states of Vermont, New Hampshire, and Maine on the map. How is the population density of these states different from that of Boswash?

megalopolis a "great city" consisting of a string of towns and cities where many people live

This map shows the population density of the Northeast. The map key shows what areas have more people per square mile.

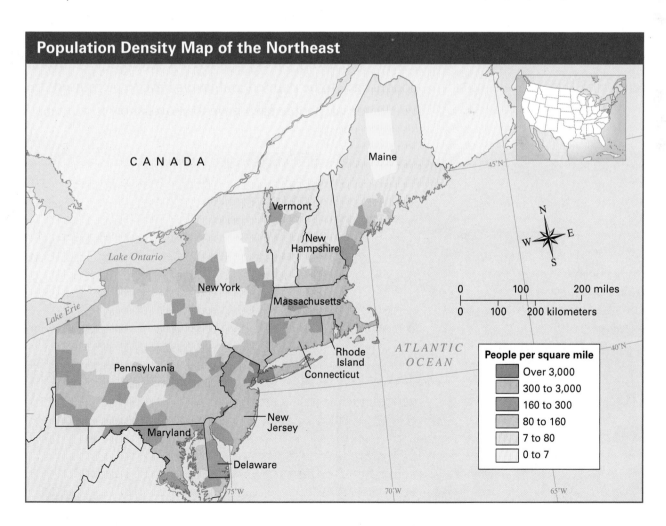

Population Density Map of the Northeast

People per square mile
- Over 3,000
- 300 to 3,000
- 160 to 300
- 80 to 160
- 7 to 80
- 0 to 7

3. Places to Live

Population density affects people's daily lives in many ways. One way it affects people is in the kinds of homes available to them.

In densely populated cities, many people live in apartment buildings. Apartments are usually stacked on top of each other and side by side. Some apartment buildings are towering skyscrapers while others are just a few stories high.

Many people like living in apartment buildings. They may like having lots of neighbors. They may also like living near shops and restaurants.

On the other hand, people live close to each other in apartment buildings. At times neighbors can be noisy. If people play loud music or make a lot of noise in an apartment, their neighbors may not like it!

In small towns and rural areas, many people live in houses. Many houses have yards where children can play. People can make more noise in a house without bothering their neighbors.

However, taking care of a house and yard is a lot of work. Houses have to be painted and lawns have to be mowed. In the Northeast, people even have to shovel snow in winter.

Thousands of people may live on one city block. Just one family may live on several acres in the country.

4. Making a Living

Population density also affects the kind of work people do. There are many more jobs in cities than in rural areas.

Small towns and rural areas have fewer businesses. Some people may work on a farm. Others may work in stores or provide services that people need. Often, there are only a few kinds of jobs in a small town. That is one reason why some people move to cities.

There are lots of different kinds of jobs in cities. Many people who live in a city work in offices. Other people work in restaurants and stores.

Newspapers and television stations have offices in cities as well. These businesses create jobs for writers, photographers, and designers.

Cities are also centers for the arts. They attract people who want to work as actors, musicians, or artists.

Large hospitals and health care centers are located in cities. These businesses create jobs for doctors, nurses, and other health care workers.

Many people like to visit cities. Tourism is the business of taking care of people visiting a place. Tourism creates jobs for tour guides, hotel workers, taxicab drivers, and others.

Small towns often have only a few businesses, like this country store. Big cities may build new buildings for businesses every day.

In New York City, cars and taxis fill the streets. You may not see many cars in a small town.

5. Getting Around

Population density affects what types of transportation people use. Getting from place to place in a densely populated area can be difficult. Driving a car is usually the worst way to get around in big northeastern cities. Many of these cities' streets are narrow. Others are wide but crowded. Think of all the cars, buses, trucks, and taxis that fill city streets today. They cause traffic to move slowly.

It is not easy to find a place to park a car in a large city. Parking garages help solve this problem, but they can be expensive. Bicycles fit well on narrow city streets, but riding a bike in city traffic can be dangerous.

Because city streets are often crowded, many people walk wherever they want to go. For longer trips within cities, people often need to use public buses, taxis, or subway trains.

Driving is much easier in small towns. There is much less traffic, and parking is usually free. Country roads are usually safe for both cars and bikes.

However, it can be hard to get around in rural areas without a car. Many small towns in less populated areas have no public bus or taxi service. The places that people want to go may also be very far apart. This can be a problem for people who do not drive or own a car.

6. People and Pollution

Population density also affects the level of **pollution** in an area. Pollution is anything that makes our air, water, or soil dirty or unsafe to use. Many things people do cause pollution. When we toss trash on the ground, we pollute the land. When we drive cars, we pollute the air. When we dump waste into rivers, we pollute the water.

In urban areas, pollution can be a big problem. People living in cities throw away mountains of trash each day. Some of the trash can be recycled. The rest must be carried off to landfills. If left on the streets, trash attracts insects and rats. These pests often carry harmful diseases.

Air pollution is a problem as well. Smoke from cars, factories, and homes can hover over cities. This dirty air can cause our eyes to burn, and it can also damage our health.

Dirty water from city streets and sewers may run into rivers and lakes. The result is water pollution. Polluted water is not safe to drink or swim in.

In rural areas, there are fewer people to cause big pollution problems. Air and water are generally cleaner there than in cities. Without as many cars or homes, there is less smoke, so people in rural areas can look up at night and see thousands of stars.

> **pollution** any substance that makes air, water, or soil dirty or unsafe to use

Air pollution is a big issue in cities. Rural areas tend to have much cleaner air.

7. Finding Fun Things to Do

What do you do for fun on weekends? Your answer may depend partly on where you live.

People living in rural areas often enjoy outdoor activities year-round. Many people in rural areas may live close to mountains or forests. These areas are great places for people to hike and explore. Other people in small towns live near lakes or rivers. They can choose to spend their weekend fishing or swimming. They can also spend summer evenings at the movies or meeting friends for dinner.

People who live in cities can also go to the movies or eat dinner with friends, but they have different options for what they can do as well. In cities, there are many things to do close to home. Suppose that it is a sunny summer Saturday in New York City. What could you do? You might choose to

- go to a Yankees or Mets baseball game.
- tour an aircraft carrier or an old submarine.
- walk through a rainforest at the Bronx Zoo.
- explore the New York Botanical Garden.
- ride a roller coaster at Coney Island.

In the summer, people from towns of the Northeast can go hiking in mountains. People in New York City can ride this roller coaster at Coney Island.

In the winter, many people in rural communities can sled in the snow. In the city, people can go ice skating.

In winter, people have other options for what they can do. During the winter, people in rural areas might enjoy the snow outside. In cities, people have many different options to choose from. Suppose that you are looking for something to do on a cold and snowy day in New York City. You might choose to

- ice skate at Rockefeller Center.
- climb the Statue of Liberty.
- create a puppet at the Children's Museum of the Arts.
- try indoor soccer or rock climbing at Chelsea Piers.
- make a movie at the American Museum of the Moving Arts.
- see a circus or a play just for kids.

There are so many options in a city that people who live in small towns might choose to go to a city for a day of fun. People that live in a city can also go to a rural area for the day.

Lesson Summary

In this lesson, you learned how population density shapes people's daily lives. In the Northeast, many people live in very densely populated areas. But other people live in less densely populated areas. For the people of the Northeast, life in a city is very different from life in a small town.

You saw how population density of an area affects the kinds of homes people choose and the work that they do. You also saw how population density affects the types of transportation that people use, and how pollution affects different places and people in the Northeast.

Finally, you saw how population density affects what people do for fun in both rural and urban areas. Population density affects many different parts of people's lives.

Population Density in Your State

What is the population density in the area you live in? How does it compare to other areas in your state? Creating your own population density map can help you answer questions like these.

The first step in making a population density map is choosing the places you want the map to represent. For example, you might choose San Francisco, Santa Barbara, and Redding, which are all places in California.

Next, you will find the population density of each area. You need to research each place's population data. You can look at the U.S. Census Bureau Web site to get this information. Then record it on a table, like the one shown here. Divide the population by area to get the population density for each place. As you can see, population is very different from place to place.

Once you have the population information, you can make your map. First, make a map of the places you chose. In this example, you might make a map of California. You might also show physical features, landmarks, or natural resources on the map. Make sure to make a key that shows how you represent these other features. Triangles could represent mountains, and blue circles could represent lakes.

You can make a table to compare the population density of different cities.

City	Area in Square Miles	Population	People Per Square Mile
San Francisco	46.87 sq mi	837,442	17,867/sq mi
Santa Barbara	19.47 sq mi	90,412	4,644/sq mi
Redding	59.65 sq mi	91,119	1,528/sq mi
Los Angeles	468.67 sq mi	3,884,307	8,288/sq mi
Eureka	9.38 sq mi	26,913	2,869/sq mi
Merced	23.32 sq mi	81,102	3,478/sq mi
San Bernardino	59.2 sq mi	213,708	3,610/sq mi

You will also have to make a key for your map that shows population. For instance, you could use different colors to represent different numbers. Here, red is used to show population density of 15,000/sq mi and up. Look at the key. What does yellow represent? Orange?

When you make your map, use your key to mark up your map. Look at your table and read the population density for each city. Pick the appropriate color that represents it. Then mark the area of the city in this color. Look at this map of California. Which place has the lowest population density? Which has the highest?

Analyzing your map can help you understand why populations are different from place to place. San Francisco and Los Angeles are close to water. People might move there because they can easily ship goods and use natural resources from the ocean. Redding is in the mountains. Less people might move there because it is harder to get to, and they are far from water. How else does population density affect people's daily lives?

This map of California shows the population density of three cities.

California Population Density Map

Population Density
- 15,000+/sq mi
- 5,000–10,000/sq mi
- 0–5,000/sq mi

Redding

Sierra

San Francisco

Nevada

California

PACIFIC OCEAN

Los Angeles

| 0 | 100 | 200 miles |
| 0 | 100 | 200 kilometers |

Inventing New Ways of Living

The Northeast is known for its big cities with bright lights, towering buildings, and crowded streets. Whom do we have to thank for the inventions that helped make modern cities possible?

It was just one little light bulb that glowed for about 13 hours before it burned out. Yet, the people in 1879 who saw the experiment were amazed. The famous inventor had his own laboratory in Menlo Park, New Jersey. There, he and his team worked to create new inventions. Making a safe, usable light bulb was just one example.

In 1882, Thomas Edison helped create the nation's first electric power plant in New York City. The plant was powerful enough to produce electricity to light all the houses for several city blocks.

The late 1800s were an exciting time to live in a city for everybody. People were constructing taller and taller buildings, and more people began using streetcars to get around the city. Daily life was changing very rapidly. What were some of the new inventions that helped make life feel modern? Who invented them? How have those inventions helped create the cities of today?

Advertisements are a way to introduce new inventions to people. Today, old ads are a way to learn about the past.

Building Higher and Stronger

When you think of cities, you may picture tall buildings called skyscrapers. The first skyscraper was built in the late 1800s, but before that time, most buildings had only a few floors.

Two important inventions helped make skyscrapers possible. One was the use of steel. Steel is a strong but lightweight metal that can support a tall, thin building. In the 1850s, Henry Bessemer found a cheaper way to make the metal, which made it easier for builders to use. By using steel, builders could now build structures with ten floors or more.

This skyscraper was built in 1902. Look at the steel beams at the very top. Without steel, these skyscrapers would have never been possible.

Another new invention that helped people build skyscrapers was the passenger elevator. Before elevators, few people wanted to live or work more than a few stories above the ground. Think of all the stairs they had to climb! Building owners had trouble renting out spaces on high floors, and therefore no one wanted to build tall buildings.

The first elevators were unsafe, so they were mostly used to move boxes or supplies instead of people. Elisha Otis, of Vermont, helped solve this problem. In 1853, he invented a special kind of brake that kept elevator cars from falling if their ropes broke. People felt much safer in elevators.

People began putting elevators in their buildings. People now wanted to live and work high above the city streets. It was quieter and cleaner there. Soon, skyscrapers began to appear on city streets.

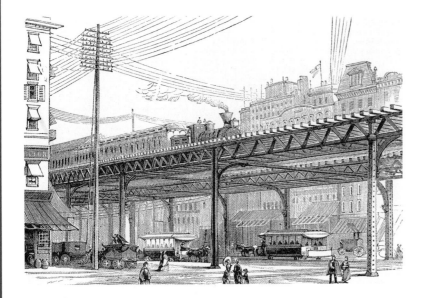

Before New York City had subways, people often rode trains that ran on elevated tracks through the city.

Moving People Here to There

In the late 1800s, cities grew quickly. Thousands of Americans moved from farms to cities and even more people came from Europe. They crossed the ocean in boats, and many of them settled in the big cities of the Northeast. New York City's population grew more than five times bigger between 1870 and 1920.

As the cities grew larger, transportation became an immense challenge. People had to get to work. Each day, thousands of workers traveled over large areas, and more and more people crowded the streets. Many of them rode in streetcars, which were horse-drawn carriages that ran on rails. The rails helped the streetcars roll easily through town. It took fewer horses to pull more people, and fewer horses meant less crowding. It also meant less of a smelly mess on the streets.

In the late 1880s, streetcars began to run on electricity in the United States. These electric streetcars were called trolleys. A man named Granville Woods invented a system that used overhead wires to power the trolleys.

Later, some cities built subways. Unlike many other forms of transportation, subways ran underground. In 1897, Boston opened the first subway in the United States. Within 10 years, New York City and Philadelphia had subways, too.

Trolleys, like this one, carried people around cities. They often had no walls or windows.

Early Road Travel

Other improvements were made to transportation in big cities as well. For example, in 1870, people in Newark, New Jersey, used asphalt to pave a road. Asphalt is a tar-like material, and it can be pressed down to make smooth, hard surfaces. It makes an excellent road surface.

In the early 1900s, a new invention appeared on the road—the automobile, or car. Few people had cars in 1900, but the new machines quickly became popular. By 1920, cars filled the streets.

Trolleys and cars changed people's lives. They also changed city life forever because they made it possible for people to live far away but still work in the city. Many city people moved to homes outside the city center. These new settlements were called suburbs. Over time, suburbs grew and began to fill with more people. New suburbs formed, even farther out from the cities. The area of dense population spread outward.

Today, we can see the effects of this spread that started hundreds of years ago on the East Coast. New technology and inventions have led to dense settlement of towns and cities throughout all the regions of the United States. ◆

Before cars, people used horse-drawn carriages. The first cars were built more like these carriages than like cars made today. They were much slower and simpler than modern cars.

A Boat and Bus Tour of the Southeast

What factors have shaped the culture of the Southeast?

Introduction

Hello, I'm Mr. Davis. You can probably tell from my uniform that I'm a park ranger. As part of my job, I get to take groups like yours on tours.

During the next few days, we will use a bus and four different kinds of boats to tour the Southeast. We will start on an airboat through the Everglades. We will sail on a fishing trawler, from Florida to Virginia. From there, we'll take a big bus and cross the Appalachian Mountains. Then we'll board an old-time riverboat and sail down the Mississippi River to the port of New Orleans. A port is a place where ships load and unload their goods. We'll take a short motorboat ride to an oil rig in the middle of the Gulf of Mexico. Then it's back on board the bus for our final two stops in Mississippi and Alabama.

As we travel, keep your eyes, ears, and minds wide open. Notice the land and how each place is used in different ways. Listen for the sounds and music of this region. Think about how the Southeast has changed over time.

The captain says he's ready. So put on your life jackets, and let's go.

Social Studies Vocabulary

bayou

delta

hurricane

mineral

petroleum

plantation

savanna

segregation

strip mine

swamp

◀ Airboats are a common type of boat in the Southeast. They allow people to easily travel through swamps.

 Civics   Economics   Geography   History

The Southeast Region

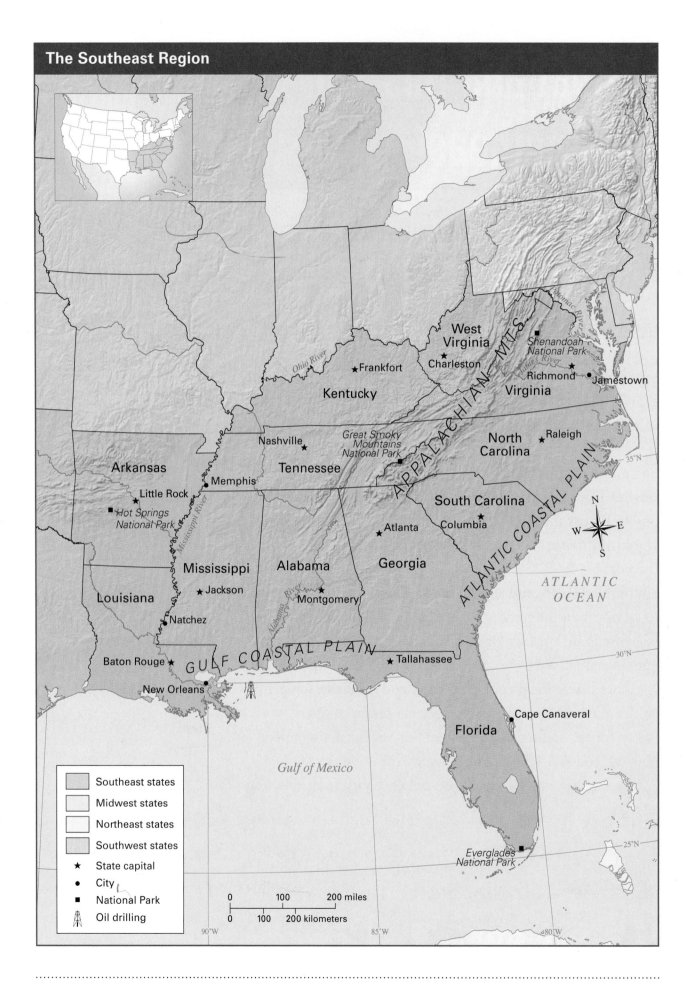

West Virginia

Shenandoah National Park

Charleston

Frankfort

Kentucky

Ohio River

Richmond

Jamestown

Virginia

APPALACHIAN MTS.

Nashville

Great Smoky Mountains National Park

North Carolina

Raleigh

Arkansas

Memphis

Tennessee

35°N

Little Rock

South Carolina

Hot Springs National Park

Mississippi River

Columbia

ATLANTIC COASTAL PLAIN

Atlanta

Mississippi

Alabama

Georgia

N

W E

S

ATLANTIC OCEAN

Louisiana

Jackson

Alabama River

Montgomery

Natchez

GULF COASTAL PLAIN

Baton Rouge

Tallahassee

30°N

New Orleans

Gulf of Mexico

Cape Canaveral

Florida

Southeast states

Midwest states

Northeast states

Southwest states

★ State capital

● City

■ National Park

Oil drilling

Everglades National Park

25°N

0   100   200 miles

0   100   200 kilometers

90°W   85°W   80°W

Important Ports in the Southeast Region

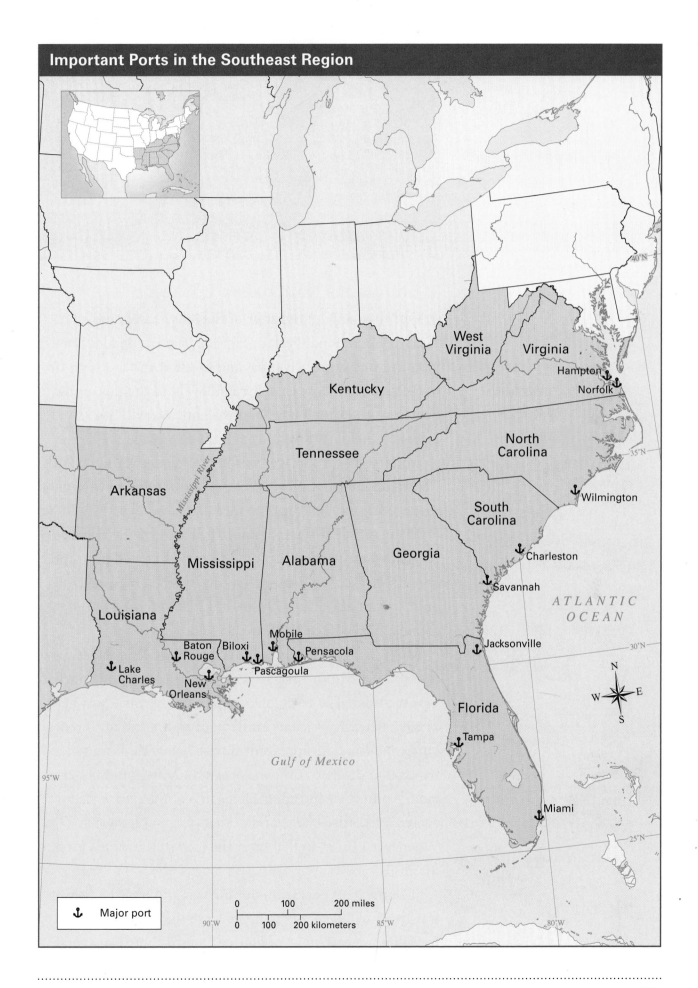

West Virginia

Virginia

Hampton

Norfolk

Kentucky

North Carolina

Tennessee

Arkansas

Mississippi River

Wilmington

South Carolina

Charleston

Mississippi

Alabama

Georgia

Savannah

ATLANTIC OCEAN

Louisiana

Jacksonville

Baton Rouge

Biloxi

Mobile

Pensacola

N

W   E

S

Lake Charles

Pascagoula

New Orleans

Florida

Tampa

Gulf of Mexico

Miami

⚓ Major port

| 0 | 100 | 200 miles |

| 0 | 100 | 200 kilometers |

95°W

90°W

85°W

80°W

40°N

35°N

30°N

25°N

Many waterways flow through the flat land of the Everglades. These waterways are home to many different types of plants and animals.

swamp a low area of land that is covered by water at least part of the year

savanna a flat grassland

hurricane a storm, with heavy rains and high winds, that develops over the ocean and often moves toward land

1. Everglades National Park, Florida

Our first stop on our tour of the Southeast is the Everglades National Park in Florida. The Everglades is a vast area of swamp, savanna, and forest at the southern tip of Florida. A **swamp** is an area of low land that is covered by water. A **savanna** is a flat grassland. We will use an airboat to help us travel through the Everglades.

My first job as a ranger was in Everglades National Park. I had studied geography in college and wanted to work in a real live swamp. But I had no idea just how alive it would be!

Many different types of animals live in the Everglades. Alligators, crocodiles, turtles, and snakes can all be found here. Deer, bears, panthers, bobcats, otters, and other animals can also live in the park. I like to record the sounds that these animals make.

More than 300 kinds of birds live in the Everglades. I get up early many mornings to record their calls on my pocket tape recorder. The park looks peaceful now, but I was here in 1992 when Hurricane Andrew hit southern Florida. A **hurricane** is a dangerous storm with heavy rains and high winds that develops over the ocean and often moves toward land. Andrew's winds damaged some of the park's visitor center. I recorded the sound of that storm at its worst. Whenever I listen to that tape, the roar of the winds gives me chills.

It's time to depart from our airboat and board a fishing trawler. It will head north as we leave the Everglades and travel up the east coast of Florida toward Cape Canaveral.

2. The John F. Kennedy Space Center at Cape Canaveral, Florida

Florida is in a part of the United States called the Sunbelt. The Sunbelt stretches across the country from Florida to California, and states in the Sunbelt have a mild climate all year long. A mild climate means that it is usually warm and sunny there.

Florida's sunny climate makes it a popular place to visit. People from all over the world travel to Florida for vacation. People who travel for fun are called tourists.

Many tourists visit Florida every year. Some come to enjoy the sunshine and the beaches. Disney World's Magic Kingdom alone sees more than 17 million visitors every year.

I like to visit the John F. Kennedy Space Center at Cape Canaveral. In 1961, the people at the space center launched Alan Shepard into space in a rocket-propelled ship. He was the first American to travel in space. Today, Cape Canaveral is home to our nation's space shuttles.

Visitors of the Kennedy Space Center learn all about space exploration. They may even see a shuttle launch. I saw a launch last year and recorded the sound. The blast from the rockets was so loud that the ground shook under my feet.

The Kennedy Space Center is home to our nation's space program. A space shuttle, like this one, uses rockets to blast off its launch pad.

Today, you can visit Jamestown. People demonstrate what life was like in the 1600s.

3. Jamestown, Virginia: England's First American Colony

We have traveled quite a distance along the east coast of the United States and have reached the state of Virginia. You are looking at the site of Jamestown, Virginia. Jamestown was the first permanent English settlement in America.

In the spring of 1607, settlers from England chose this spot on the James River to build a colony. John Smith, one of their leaders, called it "a very fit place." He was wrong! The land was swampy. Mosquitoes also made life miserable, and they carried a dangerous disease called malaria.

By summer, many people in Jamestown were hungry. The forests around Jamestown were full of food, but the colonists didn't know how to find it. By fall, many of the colonists were dead. For many years, the pattern continued—new colonists arrived during the spring, but by winter, most had died.

However, in 1612, things started to get better. The colonists found a crop that grew well in this area. It was tobacco. Virginia tobacco sold well in England, and the colony began to make money.

In 1619, an English ship arrived in the Virginia colony. Its cargo included 20 Africans. They had been taken from Africa by force and were sold as workers. By the mid-1600s, Africans were being sold as slaves in the American colonies.

My ancestors were Africans. They were brought to the Americas in the late 1600s, and they were forced to work as slaves on large farms.

It is time to leave the trawler now. We have a bus waiting for us that will take us on the next part of our journey.

4. A Coal Mine in Appalachia

Welcome to Appalachia. This mountain area is located in the southern part of the Appalachian mountain range. Appalachia has no exact borders. It covers most of West Virginia and parts of several other states, including North Carolina, South Carolina, and Georgia. A bus is a good way to travel through these mountains.

Appalachia is too hilly for large-scale farming, but it is rich in **minerals**. Minerals are natural substances found in rocks. One important mineral is coal. Coal is used to heat homes and produce electricity.

There are underground coal mines in Appalachia. Miners have dug tunnels into the mountains to get at the coal hidden inside. Some coal also comes from **strip mines** like the one you see here. Strip mines are mines that are found on the surface. Miners use heavy machinery to strip away the dirt and rocks covering the coal. Then they use giant shovels to dig the coal out of the mountain.

Last fall, I went to a bluegrass music festival near this mine. Bluegrass is the traditional music of Appalachia. It is played on banjos, guitars, and fiddles. I recorded a lot of old songs. The fast beat of this music always makes me feel good. Let's get back on the bus to learn more about the music of the Southeast.

mineral a natural material found in rock

strip mine a place where minerals are scraped from the ground

Miners dig coal out of strip mines such as this one. Coal is often used to produce electricity for homes and businesses around the United States.

Riverboats have been used to move goods and people down the Mississippi River. Today, they are still used to tour the river.

delta a triangle-shaped area of land at the end of a river

Memphis is famous for its blues music. Many places play blues for locals and tourists alike.

5. Musical Memphis, Tennessee

We've reached Memphis, Tennessee. From here, we'll be traveling on a riverboat like the one you see here.

Memphis is at the northern end of the Mississippi Delta region. Now, a true **delta** is a triangle-shaped area at the end of a river. Soil carried downstream by the river slowly builds up, creating a delta. The Mississippi River's delta is in Louisiana, and it juts out into the Gulf of Mexico.

Where we stand today is not a true delta, though. What geographers call the "Mississippi Delta" is really a basin of land mostly in Mississippi that lies between the Mississippi and the Yazoo rivers. The area is laced with rivers, and the land here is fertile and good for farming.

In the early 1800s, the Delta's rich soil attracted cotton planters to this region. At that time, cotton was a valuable crop. Many planters brought slaves with them. Slaves did most of the work of planting and picking cotton.

Slaves led hard lives. They worked from sunrise until sundown most days of the year, and they were given no right to choose what they wanted to do. Since these planters thought of slaves as property, slaves could be bought and sold.

Slaves would sometimes sing about their sorrows. These sad songs contributed to a musical style that became known as the blues. In 1912, W.C. Handy, an African American songwriter in Memphis, wrote the first popular blues song, which he called "Memphis Blues." Today, Memphis is famous around the world as one of the birthplaces of the blues.

6. The French Quarter in New Orleans, Louisiana

Welcome to New Orleans, the largest city in Louisiana. French colonists built the city near the mouth of the Mississippi River. Here, in the French Quarter, you can still see homes similar to those the original colonists built.

In 2005, Hurricane Katrina did serious damage to many parts of New Orleans when it caused the Mississippi River to overflow. Today, the people of New Orleans continue to work hard to restore the city.

Ships from all over the world come to New Orleans. It is an important port in the United States.

New Orleans is also the birthplace of jazz. African American musicians living in the area created this new style of music. One of the most famous jazz musicians of all time was Louis Armstrong, known for his great trumpet playing. There are many kinds of jazz. One of the oldest is called Dixieland. You can hear great Dixieland jazz right here in the French Quarter.

Louisiana's nickname is the Bayou State. A **bayou** is a stream flowing through swampy land. In the 1700s, French colonists from Canada settled along Louisiana's bayous. They called themselves Acadians. Over time, the name was shortened to Cajuns.

Cajuns and their way of life used to be hidden away in the bayous. Not anymore! Cajun food is all the rage in New Orleans. It has a lot of seasonings, and it is delicious. Cajun music is even more popular. It's as great as Cajun food—and it makes your toes tap!

We will now leave our riverboat. It is time for us to board a motorboat for the short journey to an oil rig in the Gulf of Mexico.

bayou a stream that flows through a swamp

The French Quarter is the oldest neighborhood in New Orleans. It is the part of the city that most tourists visit.

7. An Oil Rig in the Gulf of Mexico

Many people who live near the Gulf Coast are oil workers. Another name for oil is **petroleum**. The state of Louisiana has more than 58,000 wells that pump petroleum out of the ground.

Petroleum is a thick, black liquid that is found deep in the soil and under the ocean floor. Drilling for oil under the ocean is not easy, and oil workers build huge platforms, called rigs, to hold their machinery. Then they drill down under the sea until they find oil.

Once the oil is pumped out of the earth, it is sent to a factory. This factory is called a refinery, and it turns petroleum into useful products. The product you probably know best is gasoline for cars.

Oil is also used to make petrochemicals, a big word that means "chemicals made from oil." Petrochemicals are used in all kinds of products, from medicines to plastics. I'll bet you're wearing a petrochemical product right now. It might be a button, a zipper, or the soles of your running shoes.

Let's take the motorboat back to New Orleans. We still have two more places to visit by bus on our journey through the Southeast.

petroleum a thick, black liquid found underground

From shore, you may see oil rigs like this one all along the Gulf of Mexico. They drill for oil that can be used around the United States.

This plantation home is in Natchez, Mississippi. Plantation homes are often very large.

8. A Cotton Plantation in Natchez, Mississippi

Our bus has brought us back to Natchez, Mississippi. You are looking at a cotton **plantation** home. A plantation is a large farm.

In the early 1800s, cotton planters settled this area. Many of them became very rich growing cotton, and they spent their wealth building big homes like this one. Then they filled their homes with the best things money could buy.

In the mid-1800s, many planters wanted to start new plantations on western lands that belonged to the United States. They wanted to use slave labor, but other people felt that slavery should not spread into new areas. Who had the right to decide—the federal government or the Southern slave owners?

It took a war to settle this argument. Divided into North and South, Americans fought the American Civil War for four long years. Much of the Southeast was damaged in the fighting, and more than 600,000 people died.

One good thing came out of this terrible war. Slavery was ended forever in the United States. I wonder how my slave ancestors felt when they heard they were free. It must have been an amazing feeling.

Natchez escaped most of the fighting, so many of its beautiful homes were not damaged in the war. Today, they are one of the city's main tourist attractions. Let's get on our bus for one last trip.

plantation a large farm, usually worked by many laborers

The Civil Rights Memorial shows the names of 40 men and women who were killed during the civil rights movement.

9. Montgomery, Alabama: Birthplace of the Civil Rights Movement

You are looking at the Civil Rights Memorial in Montgomery, Alabama. This memorial honors 40 Americans who were killed during the civil rights movement.

After the American Civil War, blacks in the South were free. But many still did not treat them as equal. They were denied many of the rights other white citizens had. At the same time, **segregation** became a way of life. Segregation is the separation of people because of race, religion, or gender. African Americans were often segregated from white people. They could not go to school with whites. They could not eat at white lunch counters. They couldn't even sit beside white people on a bus.

African Americans were unhappy that they were not being treated equally. For several years, African Americans fought against this unfair treatment. Montgomery was home to one of the important milestones in the struggle to achieve racial equality.

In 1955, a minister named Martin Luther King Jr. led a protest against segregation on buses. Before 1955, African Americans could not sit at the front of the bus and had to stand if a white person wanted their seat. African Americans in Montgomery refused to ride the buses until they were treated the same as whites.

segregation the separation of people because of race, religion, or gender

Most African Americans back then did not have cars. They needed the bus to get to their jobs. But the people of Montgomery, like my grandma, chose to walk to work every day for a year rather than ride on a segregated bus. Thanks to all the people who protested using the buses of Montgomery, bus segregation was finally ended here.

When I was little, I asked my grandma how her feet held up during the protest. She told me something a woman named Mother Pollard had once said: "My feet were tired, but my soul was rested."

Throughout our travels, we have seen many different places and have learned about our nation's history. I hope you have enjoyed this adventure!

In the 1950s, African Americans could not sit with white people on buses. The civil rights movement ended segregation.

Lesson Summary

I asked you to keep your eyes, ears, and minds wide open on this journey. Now I'll tell you why.

I wanted you to use your eyes to see the different ways in which the land is used in the Southeast. In Everglades National Park you saw land that people are trying to protect. But, in Appalachia, you saw a mountain being mined for coal.

I wanted you to use your ears to hear some of the sounds of the Southeast. You heard the sounds of nature—even the roar of a hurricane. You also listened to the music of this region, like bluegrass and jazz.

Finally, I wanted you to learn how the Southeast has changed over time. Slavery and segregation are part of this region's past—but not its future. As my grandma likes to say, "Times have changed, and they've changed for the better."

Landmarks of Your State

You just read about different points of interest in the Southeast. Many of these places are called *landmarks* or places that stand out because they are very important in some way.

Your state probably has several landmarks. If you live in Pennsylvania, you may know about the Liberty Bell in Philadelphia. It is a symbol of American freedom, and it has a mysterious crack. Another landmark in Pennsylvania is the Leap the Dips in Altoona, which is the world's oldest roller coaster.

What do you think is the most important landmark in your state? Pick a landmark. At the end of this activity, you will make a presentation to convince your school to send your class on a trip to this landmark.

You will need to support your argument with facts that you find in research. Facts are different from opinions.

An opinion tells what someone thinks or believes. You may read opinions on someone's blog. ("The Battle at Gettysburg should never have been fought.") You may read them in advertisements ("Philadelphia has the best pizza in the state.") You can't prove that an opinion is correct. Facts, on the other hand, can be proven or checked with reliable sources. Look for Web sites that end with ".gov." These may be government Web sites that give facts about national or state monuments. Other reliable sources include an encyclopedia or the official Web site for the landmark.

Make a table like this one. In the left column, write strong facts about your favorite landmark in the state. For each fact, list your source. In the next column, tell why that source is one that you trust.

Facts about the Liberty Bell	Why I trust this source
The Liberty Bell cracked on the first test ring. Source: http://www.nps.gov	This is a government Web site.
In the late 1800s, the bell traveled across the country so people could see it. Source: http://www.nps.gov	This is a government Web site.
The Liberty Bell weighs 2,080 pounds. Source: *World Book Encyclopedia*, Vol. 12, page 232	This is an encyclopedia in our school library.

Students in Philadelphia may choose the Liberty Bell as a favorite landmark in their state. Visitors like to look at and learn about the mysterious crack.

Let's Visit a Landmark!

Pretend that your school can send your class to visit one of your state's landmarks. Try to convince the teachers to choose the landmark that you think is most important.

Write a persuasive letter. At the beginning of the letter, state which landmark you want to visit. Then support your argument with opinions. If you live in Pennsylvania, you might say, "The Liberty Bell is one of the most important historical symbols." Also support your argument with facts from reliable sources. For example, you might say, "The 2,080-pound Liberty Bell traveled across the country before it returned to Philadelphia." Be sure your facts tell why the landmark is important and a good place to visit. At the end of the letter tell what you want the reader to do. It might say, "Please decide to send our class to this landmark."

Exchange letters with a classmate. Read each other's letters, and write a reply. Tell you classmate if his or her letter was persuasive. Ask questions about the facts or sources and revise your letter, if needed. Then give copies of your letter to some teachers and hope you can persuade them!

The Quilters of Gee's Bend

Gee's Bend is a small, out-of-the-way town in Alabama. There, its people have created a great tradition of art. For many years, the women of Gee's Bend have made quilts of great beauty. How has the isolated location of the town helped shape this art?

To many people, the quilts of Gee's Bend are great treasures. In 2006, the U.S. Postal Service created a set of stamps that show their quilts.

Not too long ago, most women in Gee's Bend hardly ever left their area. After all, Gee's Bend is a rural community. It took about an hour to travel by road to the nearest town.

But times have changed. Since the 1960s, women such as Arlonzia Pettway have done a lot of traveling. They have visited big cities, like New York City and Houston, Texas. In those cities, they have gone to fine art museums. Arlonzia Pettway and the women of Gee's Bend have made these trips to see their own art, for they are now famous artists. The quilts they have made are considered great treasures.

"I felt so good," said Pettway, after she saw her quilt in a museum exhibit. "I had the happiest time I had in my life to see our quilts hanging on the wall, and peoples just praising our quilts, and everybody's eyes full of water."

The quilts of Gee's Bend certainly are beautiful. They also help tell the story of an amazing place.

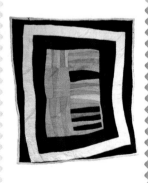

This old photograph shows the ferry that people used to take to get to Gee's Bend. In recent years, the ferry has been re-opened.

An Out-of-the-Way Place to Live

Gee's Bend is located on a small piece of land five miles wide and eight miles long. It is almost an island. The muddy Alabama River bends around—and nearly surrounds—the community. To get to Gee's Bend, you must take a ferry or travel the one road into town.

That makes Gee's Bend an isolated place to live. An isolated place is a long way from large towns and might be difficult to reach.

The community is named for its first white owner. His name was Joseph Gee. The land later passed to another white man, named Mark Pettway. Around 1845, Pettway brought his family and 100 slaves to Gee's Bend. After the American Civil War ended, the slaves in Gee's Bend were free men and women.

Over time, all the white people in Gee's Bend left. The African Americans, however, stayed and continued to farm the land.

For most of the people of Gee's Bend, life was hard in the late 1800s and early 1900s. Even though they were free, they struggled to make a living. Most of them were very poor.

The women of Gee's Bend learned to make use of every little thing they had. They learned not to throw out pieces of old fabric. For example, scraps of worn-out work pants and dresses or bits of burlap sack could all be used again. They could be used to make quilts, which would help keep a person warm at night.

Gee's Bend is located on a small piece of land that is hard to reach.

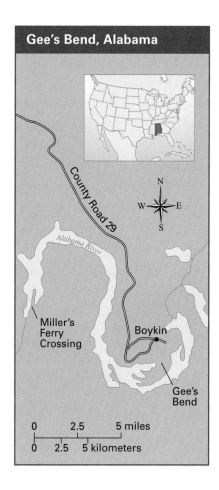

Gee's Bend, Alabama

Arlonzia Pettway (far right) is not the only woman in her family who makes quilts. All the quilters shown here with their quilts are her relatives.

From Parent to Child

While quilting was a way of making something useful out of worn-out fabric, it was also a way of making something beautiful. The quilters of Gee's Bend never thought that they were making art, but they did work hard to make something that would please the eye.

The making of quilts is an old tradition in Gee's Bend. For as long as anyone there can remember, the women of Gee's Bend have been gathering in groups to piece together bits of fabric. They have been sharing ideas about new designs, and they have been telling each other stories about their lives.

They have also been teaching their children. In this way, the craft of quilting has been passed down from parent to child, on and on over the decades. Stories and memories have also been kept alive.

For a long time, the only people who enjoyed these quilts were the people of Gee's Bend. Few people from outside the community ever visited there. And few of Gee's Bend's residents ever left the community.

That changed in the 1960s. Civil rights workers came to visit Gee's Bend. They noticed the fantastic quilts drying on the clotheslines. They saw the vibrant colors and the exciting designs. The quilters of Gee's Bend had been discovered.

Sharing Their Talent with the World

What makes the quilts of Gee's Bend so special? Of course, the bright colors are beautiful, and the skill of the quilters is outstanding, each quilt being sewn with great care. But it is the startling designs of the quilts that make them so remarkable.

Usually, quilts follow a rigid pattern. Lines are straight, and the shapes repeat in an orderly way. But the Gee's Bend quilts are different. The patterns shift and change, and the lines are not straight. Each quilt is unique. Yet, certain styles keep coming up in quilt after quilt. You can see how ideas were shared by the quilters, changed a bit, and then passed on to others.

Some experts think that the Gee's Bend quilts look like modern art. Although the quilts seem to have simple designs, they are actually very complex. In fact, they have **abstract** designs. Something is considered abstract if it makes use of shapes and patterns, rather than showing people or things as they actually are.

When people outside the community of Gee's Bend saw the quilts, they wanted to buy them. Museums wanted to put them on display. The quilters of Gee's Bend began their own business to make and sell their quilts, which helped improve their lives.

This style of quilting is found only in Gee's Bend. But now, the quilters are also happy to share their work with the rest of the world. ◆

abstract making use of shapes and patterns, rather than showing people or things as they actually are

Gee's Bend quilts have traveled the country. They have stopped at museums in New York City, Boston, Washington, D.C., Houston, Atlanta, and other large cities.

The Effects of Geography on Life in the Southeast

How has geography helped shape daily life in the Southeast?

Introduction

If you brought your lunch to school today, what did you bring? For some of you, the answer may be "a bit of the Southeast."

Start with the paper lunch bag itself. It may be made of paper that came from a southern pine tree. These trees are used to make paper. Papermaking is important throughout the Southeast, and the paper products that are made here are sold around the United States.

What's in your lunch bag? Maybe you brought a peanut butter and jelly sandwich to school today. You may have also packed some orange juice or a piece of fruit. Much of the contents of a typical lunch could have come from the Southeast. Georgia grows more peanuts than any other state. Florida grows more than half of our nation's oranges. Even the plastic wrap around the sandwich may have been made from oil found in the Southeast.

In this lesson, you will find out why so many of the things we use or eat every day are from the Southeast. At the same time, you will see how geography has shaped life in the Southeast long ago and today.

◀ Geography affects where cities are in the Southeast. Many cities in the Southeast are near rivers.

Social Studies Vocabulary
agriculture
fall line
floodplain
foothills
industry
natural resource
navigable
tornado

 Economics

 Geography

Lowlands are common in the Southeast. During high tide, seawater flows onto these lowlands.

1. Elevation: Lowlands and Highlands

The Southeast is a region of lowlands and highlands. The low Coastal Plain stretches along the southeastern coast from Virginia to Louisiana. The water level of the rivers and swamps in this region rise and fall with the ocean tides each day. When the ocean rises at high tide, seawater flows onto this lowland area. When the tide pulls back, water levels drop.

The Coastal Plain ends at the **foothills** of the Appalachian Mountains. This area of low, rolling hills is called the *Piedmont*. Piedmont, in French, means "foot of the mountains." Beyond the Piedmont rise the Appalachian Mountains. Some of the peaks in this mountain chain are more than 6,000 feet high.

Elevation affects life here in many ways. For example, elevation affects climate. The higher the elevation of a place, the colder it is. Plants that grow well in the warm lowland freeze in the cool highland. Elevation also affects soil. Lowland soil is rich and good for farming. Highland soil is rocky and not easy to farm.

Elevation also affects travel. Travel in the lowlands is faster and easier, while travel in the highlands is slower and more difficult. People from the mountains sometimes joke that the only way to get to some of the tiny Appalachian towns is to be born there!

foothills a hilly region at the base of a mountain range

The Appalachian mountain range stretches through many states. These mountains are in North Carolina.

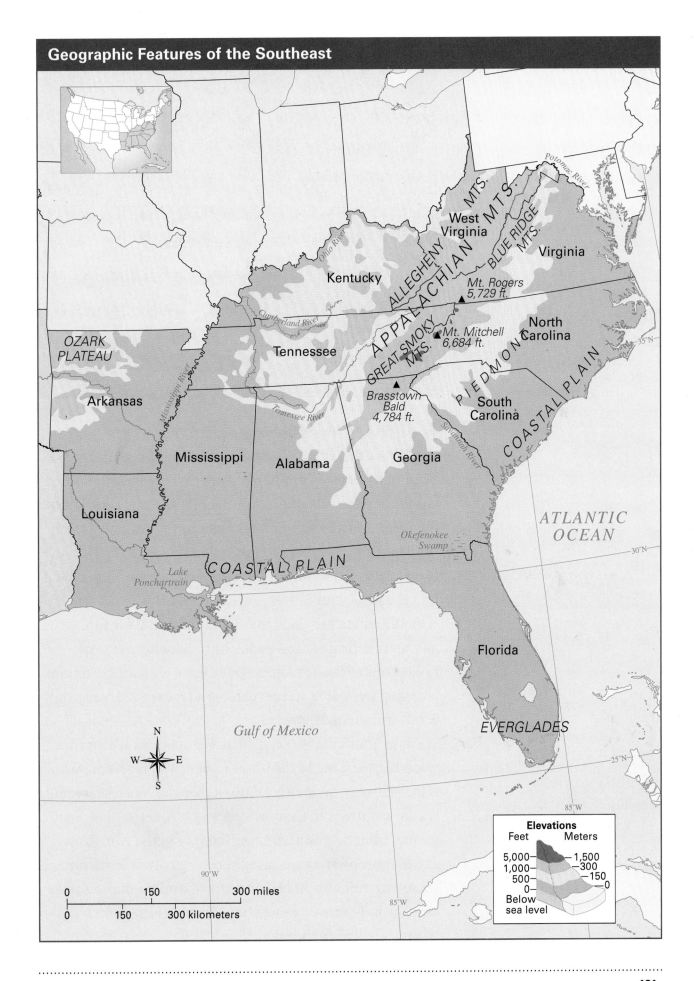

Geographic Features of the Southeast

OZARK PLATEAU

Arkansas

Louisiana

Mississippi

Mississippi River

Lake Ponchartrain

COASTAL PLAIN

Alabama

Tennessee

Tennessee River

Cumberland River

Ohio River

Kentucky

West Virginia

ALLEGHENY MTS.

APPALACHIAN MTS.

BLUE RIDGE MTS.

Virginia

Potomac River

Mt. Rogers 5,729 ft.

GREAT SMOKY MTS.

Mt. Mitchell 6,684 ft.

North Carolina

Brasstown Bald 4,784 ft.

PIEDMONT

South Carolina

Georgia

Savannah River

COASTAL PLAIN

Okefenokee Swamp

ATLANTIC OCEAN

35°N

30°N

Florida

EVERGLADES

25°N

Gulf of Mexico

N
W E
S

90°W

85°W

85°W

0   150   300 miles
0   150   300 kilometers

Elevations

Feet   Meters

5,000 — 1,500
1,000 — 300
500 — 150
0 — 0
Below sea level

Shipping by boat is important for cities in the Southeast. These cargo ships are carrying goods along the Mississippi River.

2. Rivers and Ocean

The Southeast has a long coastline and many rivers. Most of its rivers begin in the Appalachian Mountains. On the eastern side of the Appalachians, rivers flow across the Piedmont and the Coastal Plain to the Atlantic Ocean. In the southern Appalachians, rivers flow into the Gulf of Mexico. On the western side of the mountains, they flow into the Mississippi River.

Southerners use their rivers and the ocean for fun. Swimming, fishing, and boating are popular water sports.

People here also use their waterways for transportation. Shipping by boat is an inexpensive way to move crops and goods over long distances.

Many port cities developed along the coast where rivers reach the sea. One of the busiest port cities is Miami, which is located near the southern tip of Florida. Much of its trade is with countries in Central and South America. For this reason, Miami calls itself the "Gateway of the Americas."

The port of Miami is also home to many cruise ships. Each year, millions of people leave Miami on cruise ships for vacations at sea. No wonder Miami is also known as the "Cruise Capital of the World."

3. The Fall Line

Many of the rivers that cross the Coastal Plain are **navigable**. A navigable river is one that is both deep and wide enough for ships to use. But when ships reach the Piedmont, they stop. The place where they stop is called the **fall line**. A fall line is an imaginary line at the point where rivers drop from higher land to lower land.

In this case, the fall line is where the Piedmont meets the Coastal Plain. The edge of the Piedmont drops sharply at this point. As rivers flow over this drop, they form waterfalls. Ships cannot continue to sail upstream beyond these falls.

For early settlers in the Southeast, the fall line was a problem. Settlers on the Coastal Plain depended on rivers to send their crops to market. But when settlers moved up to the Piedmont, they had no good way to ship their crops to the coast.

Some people saw this problem as an opportunity. Traders set up trading posts right on the fall line, where goods that arrived by boat from the coast could be traded for meat and crops raised in the highlands.

Other people settled on the fall line because they knew how to use falling water to run machines. They built sawmills, flour mills, and workshops that ran on waterpower. Many fall-line towns—like Richmond, Virginia; Raleigh, North Carolina; and Macon, Georgia—grew into large cities.

navigable deep enough and wide enough for ships to use

fall line an imaginary line, marked by rapids and waterfalls, where rivers start to drop from higher land to lower land

This powerful rapids area of the Potomac River shows the presence of a fall line. Ships cannot travel past the fall line to trade goods.

4. Natural Resources

While many people choose to live in the Southeast for its many rivers, others live in the area because it is rich in **natural resources**. Natural resources include land, oceans, forests, minerals, and fuels.

Land was the first natural resource that attracted people to the Southeast. Growing crops and raising animals were two of the largest **industries** for many years. An industry is all the businesses that produce one kind of good or provide one kind of service.

Today, many industries are important to the economy of the region. On your tour of the Southeast, you learned about two industries that developed from resources hidden under the ground. One is the coal-mining industry. Another is the oil industry.

The Southeast's steel industry is built on another hidden resource. In the 1800s, people discovered iron at Red Mountain in Alabama. Iron ore is used to make steel. Built at the foot of Red Mountain, Birmingham, Alabama, became a steelmaking center.

Some industries are based on the Southeast's large forests. Sawmills cut trees into lumber. Paper mills grind wood into gooey wood pulp. This pulp is then used to make paper. Furniture makers turn trees into tables and chairs. Right now, you may be sitting on a chair that was made in the Southeast.

natural resource a material found in nature that is useful to people

industry an organized economic activity connected with the production, manufacture, or construction of a particular product or range of products

A forest is an important natural resource in the Southeast. Industries, such as the paper industry, use this resource to make goods we want.

5. A Long Growing Season

The business of growing crops and raising animals is called **agriculture**. Agriculture is an important part of the economy of the Southeast. Most farmers need three things from nature: good soil, plenty of rain, and a long growing season. The Southeast has all three.

Many crops grow well in the Southeast, cotton being a good example. Cotton plants need plenty of water and six months of warm weather, and the Southeast meets these needs perfectly.

In the 1800s, cotton was the main crop grown in the Southeast. Then disaster struck when a little bug called the boll weevil invaded cotton fields. The boll weevil destroyed the cotton before it was ready for harvest, leaving many farmers ruined. Those who survived learned a hard lesson. No longer could they depend on just one crop.

Today, the Southeast is a region of mixed agriculture. Farmers on the Coastal Plain grow rice, cotton, peanuts, and other warm-weather crops. Orange groves cover large parts of Florida. Piedmont farmers raise dairy cattle, peaches, and tobacco. Farmers in Appalachia grow corn and apples in mountain valleys.

Citrus fruits and cotton are important crops in the Southeast. People around the United States use these crops every day.

agriculture the business of growing crops and raising animals

6. Dangerous Weather

Not every day is sunny in the Southeast. The Southeast has many different types of weather. Some weather is dangerous and can hurt people or destroy property.

Rain falls all year long in Southeast. Sometimes, storms bring too much rain, which sometimes results in a flood. During a flood, a river fills with more water than it can hold. The extra water flows over the river's banks onto its **floodplain,** or a low, flat land along a river.

Most rivers flood from time to time, but floods become dangerous when people live and work on floodplains. Floods do much more than cover the floodplain with muddy water. The water can destroy homes, crops, and people's lives.

Though floods can cause a lot of damage, the most dangerous storms are hurricanes. Hurricanes are powerful storms with winds of 74 miles per hour or more. Hurricanes form over warm water, but they can move onto land. As a hurricane grows, it produces heavy rain and high waves. Almost every year, at least one hurricane strikes the Southeast.

floodplain the low, flat land along a river that may be underwater during a flood

Floods can cause lots of damage to buildings in towns and cities. In Miami, store owners put sand bags in front of doors to prevent water from getting inside.

Tornadoes are another threat to the Southeast. A tornado is a violent and powerful windstorm shaped like a funnel. Tornadoes form over land and can have wind speeds of 300 miles per hour. The winds of powerful tornadoes are strong enough to lift cars and destroy houses. The people of the Southeast have to prepare for several tornadoes each year.

It is hard for scientists to predict the paths of hurricanes and tornadoes. Many cities in the Southeast have tornado and hurricane warning systems so that people can do their best to prepare for them.

Tornadoes are very dangerous. They can cause a lot of damage to property and nature.

tornado a violent and powerful windstorm that is shaped like a funnel

Lesson Summary

No matter where you go in the Southeast, you will find that geography helps shape how people live in the region. You will also find that geography will affect people differently because of where they live.

If you were in Miami, Florida, people might talk about the importance of the ocean. But in New Iberia, Louisiana, people might talk about dangerous weather. You might hear some scary stories about floods and hurricanes.

People in Dawson, Georgia might tell you about the importance of a long growing season. In High Point, North Carolina, people might mention the importance of forests. Though geography affects everyone in the Southeast, different types of geography affect people differently.

Your State's Natural Resources and Natural Hazards

We all depend on natural resources. People need clean water for drinking, fishing, boating, and shipping. We need healthy soil for growing food. And we need minerals and fuels from under the ground. Your state has natural resources. What are they?

Look in books, encyclopedia articles, and Web sites about your state. Make a list of some of the important natural resources there. For example, if you lived in Wisconsin, you might discover that almost half the state is covered in forests. These trees are an important natural resource. They are important for building homes, making paper products, and providing shelter for animals. Lakes are another important natural resource in Wisconsin. There are thousands of lakes in that state. People use them for fishing, boating, and swimming.

Unfortunately, natural resources can be destroyed. Many things threaten the health of resources such as clean water, clean air, and healthy soil. People cannot always protect our resources from the threats like tornados, hurricanes, and wildfires. We can, however, control such threats as air pollution, water pollution, and destructive animals.

There are 15,000 lakes in Wisconsin. Thousands of volunteers work to protect the lakes from pollution and fast-spreading weeds.

Groups that want to save the trees put signs like this one up in forests and parks.

Threats to Your Natural Resources

Many natural resources face serious threats. However, people and groups often work to solve these problems. For instance, trees in Wisconsin have been invaded by beetles called emerald ash borers. They came to the United States accidentally, in wooden shipping crates from China. The insects eat through ash trees, killing them by the thousands.

Wisconsin's Department of Natural Resources works hard to keep these beetles from killing more trees. With signs and events, it is telling people in their state not to move affected trees, leaves, or firewood from one place to another. The beetles can hitch a ride in any of these things and spread out to kill more trees.

Pick one of your state's natural resources that you especially care about. What are the biggest threats to this resource? It may be wildfires, insects, pollution, or something else. You can find out more about a particular place or a topic, like forests, in trustworthy sources, such as books or Web sites.

Research Web sites for groups that are trying to protect this or a similar natural resource. Help this group by educating people in your community. Start by talking to your teacher, parents, and classmates. Explain why it is important to work together on this problem and how you think your actions will help. With your classmates, choose some ways to communicate your message. You might write a letter to a mayor or governor. You could write an article for your town newspaper or perform a play at your school. Also you could make signs and post them in your community.

Hurricane Andrew

Hurricanes are a fact of life in the Southeast. But Hurricane Andrew was different. It was one of the worst disasters in the history of the United States. How did Hurricane Andrew affect daily life in Florida?

On August 24, 1992, Hurricane Andrew hit south Florida. The howling winds sounded almost hungry to some people.

David Fisher turned on his television to find out what was happening. The news reporter said that the instruments measuring the wind had just blown off the roof of the National Hurricane Center. Then the lights—and the television—went out in the Fisher house.

Dan Sanabria also remembers the noise. He thought that it sounded like a jet plane taking off. He will also never forget what the storm did to his house. "When the eye of [the storm] passed over, I went out for a look, and we had no roof."

After Hurricane Andrew, the Shropshire family had only one thing left. It was the bed that Pearlie Shropshire and her son, Travis, were hiding under. Everything else was gone.

This picture was taken about one day before Hurricane Andrew hit Florida. The dot on this satellite photograph shows the eye, or center, of the storm.

A Storm Is Coming

One week before Hurricane Andrew hit Florida, the National Weather Service announced that a storm was on the way. It said that the first tropical storm of 1992 was moving slowly toward the United States. It had winds of about 50 miles per hour, which meant that it was already a stronger storm than most. However, not many people paid attention because many storms and hurricanes occur in Florida every year.

The warm, sunny climate is one of the main reasons why so many people go to Florida—to visit and to live. In fact, Florida is one of the fastest-growing states in the country. More than 5,000 people move to Florida every week. However, the warm climate there also leads to the formation of hurricanes.

The number of hurricanes that threaten Florida each year varies. An average year might have about three big hurricanes. But not all of them hit land. In 2004, four hurricanes hit Florida. That was more than in any other year on record. In 2006, not one hurricane hit the state.

Hurricanes like Andrew are rare. But three-fourths of all people in Florida live on or near the coasts. So, when a storm like Andrew hits, it creates problems for most people in the state.

More than 13 million people live along Florida's coasts. They live in small towns and in big cities like Miami.

Hurricane Andrew brought violent winds and flooding rains to Florida and other states. This person is walking through the powerful winds of the hurricane.

The Storm Hits

As Hurricane Andrew came closer to the United States, its winds grew stronger and stronger. Now people began to pay attention.

Television and radio announcers urged people to leave the area. More than a million people did leave. As they did, highways going north became jammed solid with cars. But millions of other people chose to stay.

According to scientist David Fisher, "the scariest place on Earth is directly in the path of an onrushing hurricane." Others have compared the energy of a hurricane to that of a very powerful bomb exploding.

Andrew was 60 miles wide before it touched land. Compared to other hurricanes, it wasn't large, but it was very strong. Its winds reached 175 miles an hour. That is strong enough to tear buildings apart, blow big trees down, and pick up cars and people as if they were toys.

Scientists choose a number from 1 to 5 to describe the force of a hurricane. Category 1 is the mildest. Hurricane Andrew was named a Category 5 hurricane.

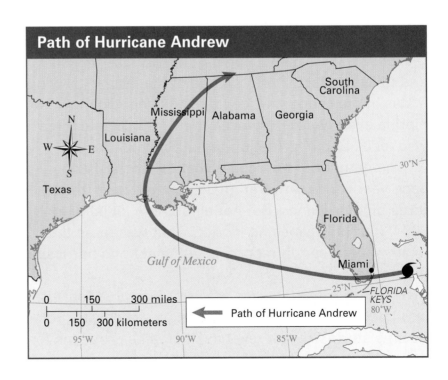

Path of Hurricane Andrew

South Carolina
Mississippi Alabama Georgia
Louisiana
N
W E
S
Texas
30°N
Florida
Gulf of Mexico
Miami
25°N
FLORIDA KEYS
80°W
0 150 300 miles
0 150 300 kilometers
← Path of Hurricane Andrew
95°W 90°W 85°W

Hurricane Andrew's winds caused a lot of destruction around Miami. This car was overturned by the hurricane.

After the Storm

Eventually, Andrew moved on into the Gulf of Mexico toward Louisiana. But it left behind a huge disaster in Florida.

More than forty people were dead. More than 250,000 people were homeless, and thousands of houses were completely destroyed. Many businesses were gone. The damage to homes, businesses, and land eventually cost about 30 *billion* dollars.

People's lives were changed forever. "I went to bed with two jobs and a home," Charles Wilson said. "I woke up with no jobs and a piece of a home."

Many people went back to Florida to rebuild their homes and communities. But about 30,000 people left the heavily populated south Florida county, Dade County, for good.

For a long time after the storm, whenever Dan Sanabria walked outside, he would look around for places he could take shelter in a storm. For Dan and for all those people who lived through Hurricane Andrew, the memory of that fierce storm is hard to forget. ◆

Hurricane Andrew devastated Florida's communities. But the people of Florida worked together to help others find food, clothing, and shelter.

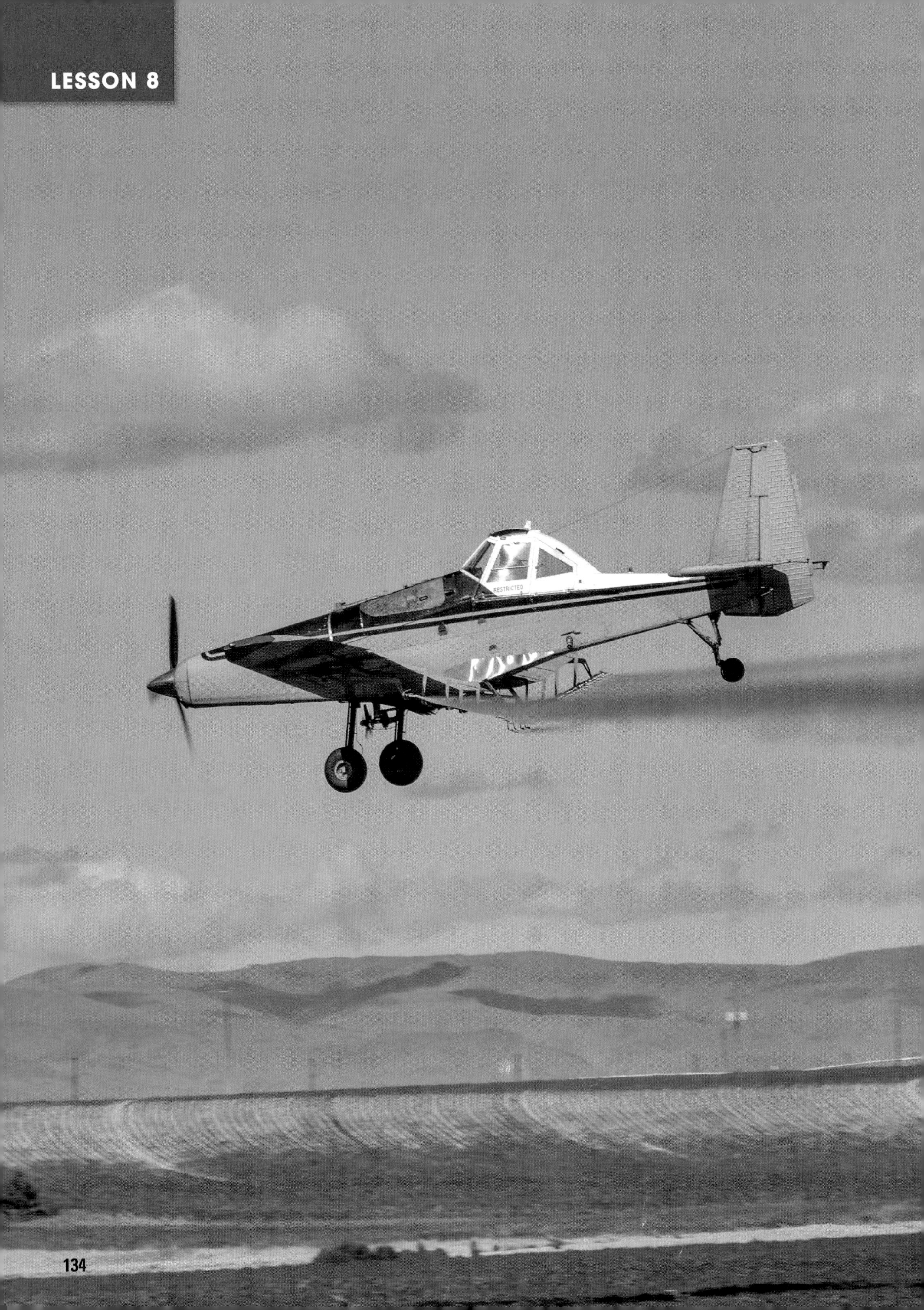
RESTRICTED

A Crop Duster Tour of the Midwest

Why do we call the Midwest "America's Heartland"?

Introduction

Hi. My name is Mr. Ortiz, and I'll be your guide as we explore the Midwest. I'm not normally a tour guide. I work as an economist at a bank in Chicago. My job is to study how people make, use, and manage goods and services. I wanted to lead your tour for several reasons. I want you to learn about the economy of the Midwest. I also want to show you the geography of this region and tell you about its colorful history. And most of all, I love to travel.

Over the course of this tour, we will visit nine of my favorite places in the Midwest. You'll see great monuments, open spaces, an engineering solution to a problem, factories and towns, airports, and even a shopping mall. Along the way, look for answers to this question: How did this one region earn these two very different nicknames— "America's Breadbasket" and "America's Heartland"?

We will be touring in little planes called crop dusters. Most of the time, farmers use these planes to spray chemicals on crops. Because of their small size, crop dusters can fly close to the ground, so we should get some great views.

Fasten your seat belts for takeoff. Our first stop will be in Missouri, nicknamed the "Show Me State."

> **Social Studies Vocabulary**
>
> assembly line
>
> feedlot
>
> fertile
>
> frontier
>
> livestock
>
> meatpacking
>
> prairie
>
> reservation
>
> transportation hub

◀ A crop duster, like this one, flies close to the ground. Crop dusters often fly over fields in the Midwest.

 Civics   Economics   Geography   History

The Midwest Region

0   150   300 miles
0   150   300 kilometers

CANADA

Lake of the Woods

Lake Superior

Soo Locks

North Dakota
★ Bismarck

Minnesota

Lake Huron

South Dakota
★ Pierre

■ Mt. Rushmore Monument

Mall of America ■ ★ St. Paul

Wisconsin

Mississippi River

Lake Michigan

Michigan
Lansing ★

Detroit ●

Lake Erie

Madison ★

O'Hare Airport ■

Wrigley Field

Cleveland ●

Iowa
● Des Moines

Chicago ●

Nebraska

Missouri River

Ohio
Columbus ★

Lincoln ★

Illinois
★ Springfield

Indiana
★ Indianapolis

Kansas
Topeka ★

Kansas City ●

Jefferson City ★

St. Louis ●

Ohio River

Dodge City ●

Missouri

★ State capital
● City
■ Point of interest

MEXICO

Gulf of Mexico

100°W   90°W   80°W

Corn, Wheat, Milk, and Milk Products in the Midwest

CANADA

Lake of the Woods

Lake Superior

Lake Michigan

Lake Huron

Lake Erie

North Dakota

Minnesota

South Dakota

Wisconsin

Michigan

BLACK HILLS

Iowa

Nebraska

Illinois

Indiana

Ohio

Kansas

Missouri

MEXICO

Gulf of Mexico

0 150 300 miles

0 150 300 kilometers

N
W   E
S

100°W   90°W   80°W

Corn

Milk and milk products

Wheat

Other land use

This is the Gateway Arch in St. Louis. It is a memorial to the pioneers who helped settle the West.

frontier the beginning of unexplored land

1. St. Louis, Missouri: Gateway to the West

Welcome to St. Louis, Missouri, and its Gateway Arch. I chose St. Louis as our first stop because of its history. This was also the first stop for many people who were traveling west to settle.

St. Louis began as a **frontier** town. The frontier was a region of wild country, unexplored by Europeans. French traders were the first people to settle in St. Louis. They chose this spot because it is near two mighty rivers, the Mississippi and Missouri. These rivers come together just north of St. Louis.

Pioneers were the first Americans to settle the West. Many of these pioneers started their journey by heading west from St. Louis. This is why St. Louis is called the "Gateway to the West." The Gateway Arch was built to honor those pioneers. It is a proud reminder of St. Louis's history.

The Gateway Arch is one of the most famous arches in the world. Made of gleaming stainless steel, it rises about 630 feet above the Mississippi River. Visitors can ride a tram inside it to the top. I did this a few years ago with my family. The cars are small and the ride is bumpy, but the view from the top is great.

2. The Farm State of Iowa

One of my best friends from college said, "If you wanted to invent a farming state, you couldn't do much better than Iowa." He grew up on an Iowa farm that looks a lot like the one you see here.

"First," he said, "you would want your farm state to be mostly flat." Iowa began as **prairie** land. A prairie is an area of flat or rolling land covered mostly with tall grasses. Later on, farmers planted crops on the prairie.

Next, you would want **fertile** soil. The word *fertile* means "able to produce good crops." Iowa has so much fertile soil that farms cover almost all of the state.

Finally, you would want good transportation. Iowa lies between the Mississippi and Missouri rivers. Before there were trains, Iowa farmers used these rivers to send their crops to market.

Today, Iowa farms produce huge crops of corn, soybeans, and oats. Much of this harvest is fed to **livestock**. Livestock are animals raised on farms, such as cattle, hogs, and chickens. Iowa farm products are used in all kinds of foods. In fact, the chances are good that the next bag of popcorn you pop was grown on an Iowa farm just like this one.

> **prairie** flat or gently rolling land that is covered with tall grasses and wildflowers
>
> **fertile** able to produce good crops
>
> **livestock** animals that are raised on farms, such as cattle, hogs, and chickens

The state of Iowa has fertile soil for its many farms. The Midwest grows many different types of food that we use every day.

3. Dodge City, Kansas: Where the Cattle Once Roamed

Welcome to Dodge City, Kansas. Kansas—a land made up of mostly flat plains—has long been famous for wheat and cowboys.

The plains of Kansas make it a wonderful place to grow wheat. In fact, Kansas produces more wheat than any other state. If you travel through Kansas in the early summer, you will see mile after mile of golden wheat.

Back in the 1870s, cowboys from Texas used to herd cattle across the Great Plains to Dodge City. Herding cattle is hot, dusty, smelly work, and cattle drives took weeks or months. When the cattle finally reached Dodge City, they were loaded onto trains and shipped east for sale.

Today, fewer cattle graze on the plains. Cattle are mostly raised on a **feedlot**. Feedlots are areas or buildings where livestock are kept while being fattened for slaughter. Dodge City is home to some of the biggest **meatpacking** plants in the country. Meatpacking is the preparing of meat for sale. It's an important industry in the Midwest.

When I was your age, I wanted to be a cowboy—or, as my dad would say in Spanish, a *vaquero*. Some people still work as cowboys today, but they likely go home at the end of the day. We'll stop here to learn more about cowboys from long ago.

feedlot an area or a building where livestock are kept while being fattened for slaughter

meatpacking the preparing of meat for sale

Dodge City's streets were once filled with horses, wagons, and cattle. Today the streets look much different.

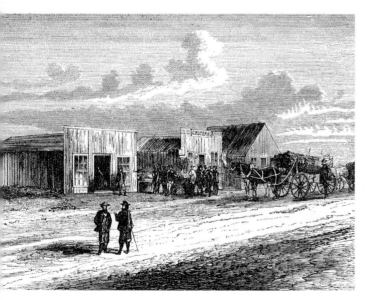

4. South Dakota's Heroes

Two huge monuments are carved into the Black Hills of South Dakota. The first is Mount Rushmore National Memorial. It shows the faces of four American presidents: George Washington, Thomas Jefferson, Theodore Roosevelt, and Abraham Lincoln. Each head is six stories tall.

The second monument honors an American Indian named Crazy Horse, who was chief of the Oglala tribe. It is still being carved into the Black Hills. When it is finished, Crazy Horse Memorial will be the world's largest statue.

The Black Hills are sacred to the American Indians who lived in this region. When white settlers moved into this area, they began pushing American Indian tribes off this land. American Indians fought back to keep their homeland. This struggle led to war with the United States.

During that war, an American leader named George Custer attacked a group of American Indians who were camping by Little Bighorn River in Montana. Crazy Horse led his warriors into battle. Soon, Custer and his men were dead.

Despite this victory, the American Indians lost most of their land over time. Many American Indian tribes, like the Oglala, were pushed by white settlers onto **reservations,** or special areas set aside for American Indian tribes to live.

Mount Rushmore National Memorial honors four American presidents.

The Crazy Horse Memorial honors the Oglala chief Crazy Horse. It is still being built today.

reservation public land set aside by the government for use by American Indians

The back gates open and the ship enters the lock. Then the gates close.

Water is taken out of or released into the lock to lower or raise the ship.

The front gates open and the ship leaves the lock.

In Lake Superior, a ship approaches the Soo Locks. The water in Lake Superior is higher than the water in Lake Huron. The Soo Locks will lower the ship to Lake Huron. The diagram shows how the lock raises and lowers ships between the two lakes.

5. Michigan's Soo Locks: Linking the Great Lakes

You are looking down on one of my favorite sights: the Soo Locks. Locks are used to raise and lower ships between different bodies of water. The Soo Locks are two of the longest locks in the world, and they can raise and lower ships that are about 1,000 feet in length. Many people say that these locks are one of the greatest wonders of the world.

The Great Lakes are part of a water highway that stretches from the Midwest to the Atlantic Ocean. Ships move from lake to lake along canals. Because the lakes are at different water levels, locks are used to lift and lower ships from one lake to the next. The Soo Locks raise or lower ships the 21 feet between Lake Huron and Lake Superior.

Many ships pass through the Soo Locks each day. Some are small passenger boats. Others are oceangoing ships filled with iron ore, coal, grain, or other cargo. People call these ships "salties" because they have journeyed from the Atlantic Ocean.

6. Detroit, Michigan: America's Motor City

In 1896, a Michigan farm boy named Henry Ford built his first car. At that time, automobiles were very expensive to buy. People saw cars as toys for the rich.

But Ford had different ideas. He dreamed of building cars that most people could afford. Ford's dream gave birth to the American automobile industry.

In 1903, Ford started an automobile factory in Detroit, Michigan. He needed a way to keep his costs down. In the past, workers could build only one car at a time. So Ford installed a moving **assembly line**. A moving belt carried unfinished cars past workers. Each worker did one task. One worker might install a windshield. Another might screw on a door handle. The time needed to assemble a car dropped from 12 hours to just 93 minutes. The assembly line lowered the cost of each car by reducing the time it took to make it.

Ford's success brought other carmakers to Detroit. Detroit became known as "Motor City," or "Motown" for short. The automobile industry attracted many other businesses to the Midwest, too.

Today, Midwest industries continue to look for better ways to manufacture goods. One example is the invention and use of robots, or computer-controlled mechanical devices, to speed up assembly lines.

We'll stop here and learn more about Ford's original assembly line.

assembly line a process in which each worker assembles one part of a product before passing it to the next worker down the line

Ford began using assembly lines to build his cars. Assembly lines sped up how fast each car could be created.

7. O'Hare International Airport: The Midwest's Transportation Hub

You are looking at O'Hare International Airport in Chicago, Illinois. It is one of the busiest airports in the United States. Hundreds of thousands of people pass through O'Hare each day. That adds up to millions of airplane passengers a year.

Chicago has been a **transportation hub,** or a center for moving goods and people, for almost 200 years. In the 1800s, railroad tracks fanned out from Chicago across the Midwest. Trains left Chicago every day, carrying goods from factories to small farming towns. The trains returned loaded with corn, wheat, and livestock for the big cities.

Today, railroads, highways, airports, rivers, and lakes move more people and goods into and out of Chicago than they do in any other American city. Moving all these people and goods is a big business. O'Hare International Airport, by itself, employs about 40 thousand workers.

As an economist, I know how important transportation is to the economy of the Midwest. Last year, for example, my college friend from Iowa sold his entire soybean crop to a buyer in Japan. Without a good transportation system, how could my farmer friend move his crop halfway around the world?

transportation hub a city that serves as a center for moving goods and people

People from the Midwest can travel all over the world. Many of them leave from O'Hare International Airport.

8. Chicago's Wrigley Field

For me, this is one of the best views in the world. You are looking down at Wrigley Field, home of the Chicago Cubs.

Sports are popular in the Midwest. The first professional baseball team played in the city of Cincinnati, Ohio. But soon sports teams began to appear in other cities around the Midwest.

As a kid, I listened to the Cubs play baseball on the radio. I became a big fan even though the Cubs had not won a championship called the World Series in a long time. After 108 years, the Cubs won the World Series again in 2016.

Wrigley Field is a special place for people who like baseball. It is the second-oldest baseball park in America, built in 1914. A lot of historic events have happened here. The most famous one may be Babe Ruth's "called shot," during Game 3 of the 1932 World Series. As the story goes, when Ruth came up to bat, he pointed to the bleachers. Then, on the next pitch, he hit a home run to that very spot. I wish I'd been there to see it.

Baseball is a popular sport in the Midwest. Many famous games have been played at Chicago's Wrigley Field.

9. Minnesota's Mall of America

Our last stop is the Mall of America, in Bloomington, Minnesota. This is the largest indoor shopping mall in the United States. The Mall of America was built in 1992.

The nation's first mall covered by a roof was built in 1956. Its purpose was to make shopping a more pleasant experience by protecting shoppers from bad weather.

People in the Midwest have to pay a lot of attention to the weather. In winter, storms called blizzards bring heavy snow and freezing winds. Spring brings hailstorms that drop hailstones, or lumps of ice, instead of rain. Spring is also when tornado season begins. When the weather gets bad, indoor malls are a good way to protect shoppers. These malls also offer customers lots of choices about what to buy.

The Mall of America has more than 500 stores. If you spent just ten minutes in each one, it would take you four days and three nights to visit the entire mall. And that time doesn't include eating in any of the 50 restaurants, visiting any of the 14 movie theaters, or playing in the amusement park.

The Mall of America has over 500 stores and an amusement park. It is one of the largest malls in the world.

The Mall of America is more important than just its size, though. As an economist, I have studied how big of an impact the Mall of America has had on the economy of the area. Each year, over 40 million people visit the Mall of America. That is more than the entire population of Canada! Many of these visitors come from different countries. Because of all these visitors, the Mall of America brings a lot of money to the area. This money is used by the state to improve people's lives in many ways. The Mall of America also provides jobs for thousands of people.

Many people visit the Mall of America each year. These visitors have a large impact on the economy of the state.

Lesson Summary

When we began, I asked you why the Midwest is called "America's Breadbasket." The answer is that Midwestern farmers grow a lot of the wheat we use to make bread.

I also asked you why we call the Midwest "America's Heartland." There are many answers to this question. One answer looks at geography. The Midwest lies at the heart, or center, of the United States. But it is also the point where pioneers began their westward journeys. The Midwest is also the heart of farming and industry. From corn to cars, many products you use every day come from America's economic heartland.

Our crop dusters are about to land. Thank you very much for coming on my tour.

The Industries of Your State

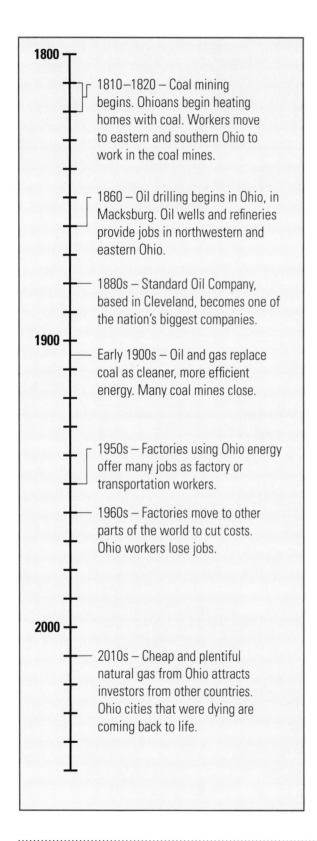

1800

1810–1820 – Coal mining begins. Ohioans begin heating homes with coal. Workers move to eastern and southern Ohio to work in the coal mines.

1860 – Oil drilling begins in Ohio, in Macksburg. Oil wells and refineries provide jobs in northwestern and eastern Ohio.

1880s – Standard Oil Company, based in Cleveland, becomes one of the nation's biggest companies.

1900

Early 1900s – Oil and gas replace coal as cleaner, more efficient energy. Many coal mines close.

1950s – Factories using Ohio energy offer many jobs as factory or transportation workers.

1960s – Factories move to other parts of the world to cut costs. Ohio workers lose jobs.

2000

2010s – Cheap and plentiful natural gas from Ohio attracts investors from other countries. Ohio cities that were dying are coming back to life.

You just read how industries help cities grow. Industries are groups of businesses, such as the automobile industry or entertainment industry. Do you know the biggest industries in your state? One place to find out is in an encyclopedia. Look up your state and then find a section called "Economy." One of the major industries in Ohio is energy. These are companies that produce power to run machines and create light and heat.

Pick one of the important industries in your state. Write the name of the industry at the top of a piece of paper. Then write this question: How has this industry affected our state? You will need to do research to answer this big question. Find books, encyclopedias, and reliable Web sites that write specifically about this one industry in your particular state.

Research the history of the industry in your state and write your facts on a timeline like this one. Include a year or time period, what happened, and how it affected the state. Keep in mind that the growth of industry can make a city grow, but when an industry changes or leaves a state, this can cause problems such as unemployment.

This timeline shows how the industries in Ohio have grown and changed. You can write a timeline for industries in your own state.

What Happened in Your State?

Through the years, companies in Ohio have mined coal, drilled oil, and produced natural gas. Coal mining, oil drilling, and other activities changed some of Ohio's physical land. People have been affected, too. When mines and oil and gas companies started, they created new jobs. When they closed, people lost jobs. When people lose jobs, they cannot buy goods in local stores. This affects the income of store owners.

Write a three-paragraph explanation that tells how one industry affected your state. Your first sentence should ask the question: How has the _____ industry affected our state? Use your timeline and research notes to construct an explanation to that question. Write your answer in a logical sequence, perhaps from its beginning to the present. Give examples of the different kinds of businesses and jobs in the industry. Add details about how industry affected the land, homes, jobs, daily life, or health in their communities. Add data, or number details, from charts, graphs, and articles that you find. For example, in 2013, 69 percent of Ohio's electricity came from coal, 15 percent from natural gas, and 12 percent from nuclear energy.

Exchange your explanation with a classmate. Read what your classmate wrote and tell him or her if you feel the reasoning, sequence, examples, and details are strong. Use your classmate's comments to revise your explanation.

Cleveland, Ohio, is a large city. There, in the late 1800s, Standard Oil Company was one of the first and largest oil companies in the nation.

Economics   History

Detroit During World War II

Detroit was already an important center of industry in 1941. That year, when the United States entered World War II, the city became even more important. People looked to Detroit to build the tanks and planes needed for the war. How did wartime change one Midwestern city?

Louise Thompson, an African American woman, already had a job. But in 1941 she heard that one of Detroit's factories was looking for workers. The factory made planes for the United States to use in World War II. It was paying high wages, and Louise was interested.

In the early 1940s, there were few good jobs open to African American women. But wartime was changing many things since many men were away fighting the war. This meant that thousands of workers were needed in factories and many of these jobs were open to women. Thompson decided to train for one of the factory jobs. It was a great opportunity, and she could help her country.

These women learned a new job—assembling planes. During World War II, many women were hired to work in factories.

Mr. and Mrs. Castle also saw an opportunity. Before the war, they had run a small business in their home, about 150 miles outside Detroit. When the war started, they closed their business and moved to Detroit. Both of them found jobs at the airplane factory near the city. But they had to live in a tiny trailer near the factory. It was a difficult change for the Castles, but they, too, wanted to help their country and themselves.

Willow Run workers built thousands of planes during World War II. The use of the assembly line allowed the workers of Willow Run to make a new bomber every hour.

Changes in Industry

Before World War II, Detroit had been home to the nation's auto industry. Many people worked to make cars in Detroit, and most of these workers were men.

In 1939, several countries went to war in Europe. Before long, countries in many parts of the world became involved. The United States entered World War II in December 1941.

The war brought many changes to the auto industry in Detroit. The country no longer needed new cars. People could make do with old cars during wartime. So the auto factories stopped making cars, and instead, some auto companies made tanks. Others made ship engines or airplanes.

Henry Ford built a new factory called Willow Run. This factory made a special kind of airplane called the B-24 bomber. The new factory was huge. The people who ran it wanted to use many of the same ideas that Ford had introduced to make cars, so they decided to use an assembly line to make planes.

It was a new idea for building planes, and the results were amazing. Before the war, building an airplane could take many workers several days to complete. By the summer of 1944, however, the workers at Willow Run were able to complete a new bomber every hour.

At Willow Run, many workers lived in dirty and unsafe conditions. They lived in these houses so they could have good jobs.

Changes in Everyday Life

It took many workers to keep Willow Run's assembly lines moving. By June 1943, more than 42,000 people worked at the factory. The large number of new workers created some changes for Detroit.

Workers needed to live near the factories, but at Willow Run and other factories, there were not enough houses for all the new workers. Many people, like the Castles, lived in small trailers, and some families even moved into old chicken coops. A lot of people were willing to accept such hardships to have a good job.

There were also shortages of many things. Goods such as gasoline and rubber were needed for the war, so the government put a limit on how much of these products people could use at home.

The Castles had trouble finding bottled gas for cooking. Once, they had to drive 150 miles to fill their bottles. They also had to pay high prices for things like restaurant meals. With so many new customers coming in, restaurants could charge more money for their food.

African Americans like Louise Thompson had to face similar problems, and more. Even though Thompson had been trained to work in a war factory, she had trouble finding a job. Even during wartime, some factories would not hire African Americans.

Conflict and Opportunity

With factories like Willow Run growing quickly, Detroit suddenly had thousands of new residents. Some longtime residents were unhappy to see their communities changing. Tension grew between the residents and newcomers as some of these newcomers were made to feel unwelcome.

Occasionally, these stresses and challenges led some people to become violent. In 1943, conflict between white and black Americans led to fighting in the streets of Detroit. Thirty-four people died before the fight was over. Hundreds were hurt.

But there were also many times when the people of Detroit worked together to meet the challenges of war. Workers at Willow Run made 8,685 airplanes. The Chrysler Company made 25,000 tanks. General Motors also made tanks. Other auto factories made engines for planes and ships. The people and the factories of Detroit played a key role in helping the United States win the war.

The war created many opportunities for individuals and families. Many people entered the workforce for the first time. Women had a wider range of jobs open to them. Different groups of people met and worked together for an important cause. ◆

People in Detroit worked together in new ways to support the war effort. This factory built tanks during the war.

Agricultural Changes in the Midwest

How has farming changed in the Midwest over time?

Introduction

"Tickle the land with a hoe," boasted a Midwestern farmer, "and the crop will laugh to the harvest."

In the 1800s, boasts like this one were common in the Midwest. Many Midwesterners liked to brag about their farms. They bragged about the farm boy who got stuck on top of a cornstalk because the corn grew faster than he could climb down it. They boasted about pumpkins so large that cows could live inside them. They even told stories about giant watermelons that were so big that they had to be pulled out of fields on sleds.

Many of these boasts were false. However, this much is true: the Midwest has some of the richest soil anywhere. And many crops grow well in the climate there.

Still, farming in the Midwest has never been as easy as tickling the land with a hoe. The first farmers who settled there struggled to overcome hardships. Farming has changed a lot since then. New technology and machines have replaced most hand tools and animal-driven plows. Large farming businesses have replaced many small farms. But Midwestern farmers still have to work hard to make a living from the land.

> ### Social Studies Vocabulary
> agribusiness
> canning
> combine
> dairy
> fertilizer
> pesticide
> reaper
> self-sufficient
> sod

◄ The Midwest prairie has some of the richest farmland in the United States.

 Economics Geography History

At first, farmers avoided the grassy plains of the Midwest. But they soon learned that the prairie soil was deep and rich and good for farming.

1. Farming in the Midwest in 1800

In 1800, almost all Americans lived on farms. In fact, about 90 out of every 100 people in America lived on a farm. Most farms had only as much land as needed to feed one family, which was often about 10 acres.

Most of these farms were east of the Appalachian Mountains. However, farmland was scarce there. Settlers had begun to cross the mountains looking for new land to farm. By 1810, more than a million Americans lived west of the Appalachians.

People settled in Ohio, Michigan, and Indiana. These areas were mostly covered with forests. Before farmers could plant anything, they had to chop down the trees to clear the land.

As people moved further west into Illinois and Wisconsin, they found land where the forests grew thinner. Instead of forests, there were patches of prairie covered with grasses and wildflowers. At first, farmers avoided these prairies because prairie grass has deep, tangled roots. Farmers did not think that they could clear the land to get anything else to grow there. But they soon learned that prairie soil was deep and rich and good for growing crops.

It was hard work to clear forests and prairies for planting. Most farmers felt that they were doing well just to raise enough food to feed their families.

2. Farm Tools in 1800

The tools farmers used in 1800 were simple ones. Farmers used axes to cut down trees. Saws were then used to cut the trees into logs to build log cabins. Wood from trees was also used to make fences and furniture.

A plow with an iron blade was used to prepare soil for planting. As this blade was dragged across a field, it dug a long groove called a furrow.

If farmers were lucky, they would have had a team of oxen to pull these plows. Even then, plowing was slow work. The thick prairie soil stuck to the iron blades. Farmers had to stop every few steps to scrape dirt from their plows.

Farmers planted their crops by hand. They walked up and down their fields, dropping seeds into the fresh furrows. They hoped the seeds would take root in this loose soil.

Farmers used a scythe, a curved knife on a long handle, to harvest their grain crops. Later on, they threshed the grain by beating it with a tool called a flail. Threshing separates the seeds of the grain from the rest of the plant.

With these tools, a farmer had to work about 300 hours to raise 100 bushels of wheat. For this amount of wheat, he had to plow, plant, and harvest five acres of land.

Farmers used simple tools during the 1800s. A plow with an iron blade tilled the thick prairie soil.

3. The Family Farm in 1800

The first farmhouse most families built was a log cabin. The typical cabin had one main room furnished with a table and a few stools. There was a stone fireplace for cooking and heating.

Cabins could be gloomy inside. Glass was expensive to buy, so people used greased paper to cover their small windows. At night, the only light in the cabin came from the fire and lamps. Farm families went to bed early. Family members slept under quilts made from scraps of cloth and on mattresses stuffed with oak or beech leaves.

Farm families raised almost all of their own food. They planted vegetable gardens and fruit orchards. They kept cows for milk, butter, and cheese. They raised chickens for eggs and hogs for meat. They raised sheep for wool that was used to make clothes. What they couldn't produce themselves, they bartered, or traded for, with neighbors.

Farm families faced many hardships, some of which prevented families from getting enough to eat. Wolves attacked farm animals such as chickens and hogs. Rabbits and deer raided their gardens. Squirrels and raccoons stole corn from the cornfields.

Disease could strike family members at any time. Injuries were also common. Women could hurt themselves cooking over open fires. Men could hurt themselves working in the fields. With no doctors nearby, families did their best to care for themselves.

A farmhouse in 1800 was a one room cabin. Farm families raised almost all their own food.

By 1900, farmers began to sell crops and livestock for cash. With money in hand, farmers could buy just about everything they might need at the country store.

4. Farming in the Midwest in 1900

In the year 1900, less than half of all Americans lived on farms. About 40 out of every 100 people in America lived on a farm. Most farms were much larger than the farms 100 years earlier. The average farm was about 150 acres.

The first farmers on the prairie had worked hard to be **self-sufficient**. Being self-sufficient means doing everything necessary to take care of yourself on your own. Like the farmers in the 1800s, these farmers raised their own food and made their own clothes. They did not make much money. But they did not have much need for money, either.

By 1900, farms covered the Midwest. Farmers on the Central Plains raised corn, pigs, and cows. Farmers on the Great Plains raised wheat, cattle, and sheep.

No longer did farmers plant crops on just enough land to feed their families. Instead, farmers raised large crops of grain and great herds of animals. These crops and livestock were sold for cash. Some farmers had **dairies**. A dairy is a farm that produces milk and milk products that can also be sold for cash.

With more money in their pockets, farmers could buy more land. They could purchase machines to help them work that land. And they could buy the useful new goods coming out of American factories—such as iron stoves, sewing machines, and telephones.

self-sufficient doing everything necessary to take care of yourself on your own

dairy a farm that produces milk and milk products

By 1900, many new farm tools helped farmers plant and harvest their crops. A reaper helps these farmers harvest piles of hay.

reaper a machine for cutting grain

combine a machine for cutting and threshing grain

5. Farm Tools in 1900

By 1900, Americans had invented many new farm tools. Many of these tools had to be pulled through fields by teams of horses.

The most important new tool for prairie farmers was the steel plow. A man named John Deere invented it in 1837. Deere's plows were made with steel blades rather than iron. Steel blades were sharper and smoother than iron blades. As a result, steel plows could cut through the thick prairie soil far more easily than the earlier iron plows.

Another new tool was a grain-cutting machine called a reaper. A man named Cyrus McCormick invented it in 1834. A farmer could cut much more grain with McCormick's reaper than with a scythe.

Other machines became common on farms in the Midwest in the 1900s. One machine was the horse-drawn seed drill. It planted seeds much faster than a farmer could by hand. Another machine was the horse-drawn combine. A combine could cut and thresh a field of grain at the same time.

These inventions helped Midwestern farmers grow more food with less effort. In the early 1800s, a farmer needed to work 300 hours to raise 100 bushels of wheat. By the 1900s, a farmer needed to work only 50 hours to raise the same number of bushels.

6. The Family Farm in 1900

For most families on the prairie, their first home was a tent, a log cabin, or a soddie. Soddies were houses made of blocks of **sod,** or dirt mixed with grass roots. When it rained, soddies dripped mud. "Life is too short," wrote one farm woman, "to be spent under a sod roof."

As soon as farm families had money saved, they built houses made of wood boards. By 1900, the typical farmhouse had lots of windows and a big porch. The largest room was often the kitchen. Few farmhouses had bathrooms. Instead, families used an outhouse that stood outside the main house.

Only the richest farmers could afford such wonders as electricity and running water. Most farm families used candles or oil lamps for lighting. They cooked on wood-burning iron stoves. They used hand pumps to draw water from wells.

Everybody worked. Men plowed, planted, and harvested crops. Women cooked, cleaned, and cared for the children. In summer, farm women spent hours **canning** food from their gardens.

Every child had farm chores, as well. Children helped out by chopping wood, drawing water, and weeding the garden. They also gathered eggs, milked cows, and fed the animals.

> **sod** a mixture of dirt and roots of grass
>
> **canning** preserving food by cooking and sealing it in cans or jars

Farmhouses built during the 1900s had wood boards, a front porch, and many windows. This Nebraskan family poses proudly in front of their new home.

7. Farming in the Midwest Today

Today, very few Americans live and work on farms. Only 2 out of every 100 people in America live on a farm. Some farms are almost ten times the size of farms 200 years earlier. The average farm today is just under 450 acres in size.

Farming in the 21st century is a big business. If you look at the total number of farms, most are still owned and run by families. But if you look at the total amount of farm acres, most are owned by big companies. We call these companies **agribusinesses**.

Farming in the Midwest has changed in many ways over the past 100 years. Today, most farm work is done by machines. Most farmers add **fertilizers** to the soil to make plants grow better. Some fertilizers are natural products. Other fertilizers are made from chemicals. Farmers also use chemicals to kill insects and other pests that attack their crops. These products are called **pesticides**.

These changes have helped farmers grow more food than ever before. But they have also created new problems. Chemicals used on crops can be harmful to other living things. For example, fertilizers and pesticides wash into rivers. There, they can kill fish and other wildlife.

agribusiness farming on a large scale by big companies

fertilizer a substance added to the soil to improve plant growth

pesticide a substance used on crops to kill insects and other pests

Crop sprayers can apply pesticides over large areas of a field at once. Today much of the work on farms is done by machines.

8. Farm Tools Today

By the year 2000, most of the work of plowing, planting, and picking crops was done by machines. Gasoline engines supply the power for these machines.

The most important new farm machine of the last 100 years has been the tractor. Farmers can use tractors in two ways. One way is to pull heavy loads. A modern tractor can pull more weight than 100 horses can. The other way is to power other farm equipment. Farmers use tractors to pull plows, seed drills, and machines that harvest their crops.

For dairy farmers, nothing has been more useful than the milking machine. Before the invention of the milking machines, dairy farmers had to milk each cow by hand. This was slow work. Milking machines allow a farmer to milk many cows at the same time. As a result, dairy farms are much larger today than they were in 1900.

New tools have also helped Midwestern farmers grow more food on less land. In 1800, a farmer needed five acres to grow 100 bushels of wheat. By 2013, the same amount of wheat could be grown on about two acres.

New machines have also reduced the time it takes to raise 100 bushels of wheat. In 1800, it took farm workers 300 hours of labor to raise that much wheat. Today, it takes less than 3 hours to raise 100 bushels of wheat. That's a big difference.

Today, machines help farmers produce more with less. Combines and milking machines reduce the amount of time it takes one farmer to harvest wheat or milk a cow.

9. The Family Farm Today

Throughout U.S. history, as the nation expanded westward, the number of farms increased. By the 1920s, there were more than 6 million farms in the United States. Today, there are only 2.2 million farms left in the United States. Of these, more than 95 percent are owned by families and individuals. The rest are agribusinesses.

Why has the number of farms decreased? In the 1930s, hard times hit the family farm. Crop prices fell so low that farmers could not make any money. Then a long drought struck the Midwest. With no rain, fields turned to dust. Many families gave up farming. Since then, farmers have seen some good times and some bad times. But the number of family farms has decreased year by year.

Farm families live like most other American families. They buy their clothes in department stores. They send their children to school. They participate in service and sports organizations. Families have computers and use the Internet. But being rural has its challenges. Internet and television broadband service doesn't always extend far away from a town. So, rural farms may use a satellite to connect.

Events from the past have shaped the lives today's farmers. What changes will the future bring?

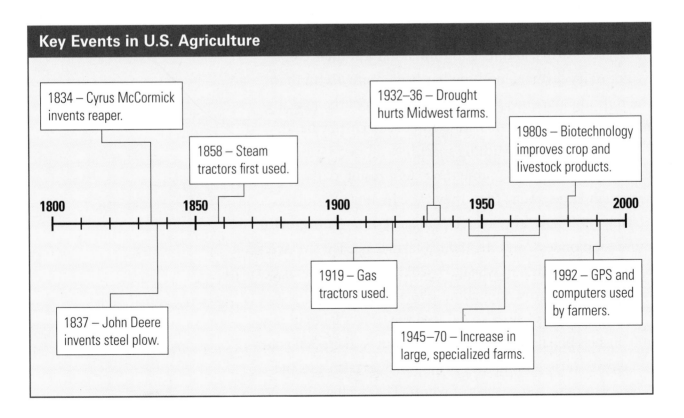

Key Events in U.S. Agriculture

- 1834 – Cyrus McCormick invents reaper.
- 1858 – Steam tractors first used.
- 1932–36 – Drought hurts Midwest farms.
- 1980s – Biotechnology improves crop and livestock products.
- 1837 – John Deere invents steel plow.
- 1919 – Gas tractors used.
- 1945–70 – Increase in large, specialized farms.
- 1992 – GPS and computers used by farmers.

1800　1850　1900　1950　2000

Every year, however, more families are leaving the farm way of life. Some get tired of the hard work. Others do not like the loneliness of farm life. But the most common reason why some people are choosing to leave farming today is simply the day-to-day struggle to make enough money to pay their bills.

Today, large agribusinesses compete with family farms. Farmers who cannot make profits have moved on.

Lesson Summary

As you have seen, farming in the Midwest has changed greatly in 200 years. In 1800, farmers used only hand tools and muscle power to work the land. Most farmers were able to raise just enough food to feed their families.

Today, large agribusinesses employ workers with gasoline-fueled tractors and machines to farm the land. Farmers may also use fertilizers that allow more food to be grown on fewer acres of land. As a result, one farm can raise enough food to feed many families.

In 1800, farm families grew or made almost everything they needed to live. They bought very little. Today, farmers grow large amounts of crops for sale. With the money they earn from selling these crops, farm families can buy goods they need in stores.

Some things have not changed much in 200 years. Farming was hard work in 1800. It is still hard and risky work today.

Agriculture in Your State

You just read about how farming has changed the lives of people in the Midwest. What kind of agriculture happens in your state? Are there small farms where families raise their own food? Are there large farms that ship their crops and animals around the world?

There are many books and Web sites with information about your state's agriculture. Do an Internet search for the name of your state with the words *farming* and *agriculture*. If you live in Virginia, you could find all kinds of information on the Web site http://vafarmbureau.org. Be careful when you choose sources of information since not all are trustworthy. You can usually trust sources that come from governments (ending in .gov) or large organizations (.org). Be careful with sources that were created for class projects or are by individuals.

Make a list of your state's farm products. Research and write down facts about each, such as where is it grown or raised. You might also ask questions like: How much is produced each year? Where is it sold? Do factories in the state put the food in packages?

For example in Virginia, chickens are one of the top agriculture products. The Shenandoah Valley has many poultry farms and packaging factories. About 250 million chickens are raised in the state each year. They are sent to China, Canada, and other countries.

Virginia has more than 46,000 farms. Some of its top products are apples, peanuts, turkeys, and chickens. Agriculture provides more than 357,000 jobs in the state.

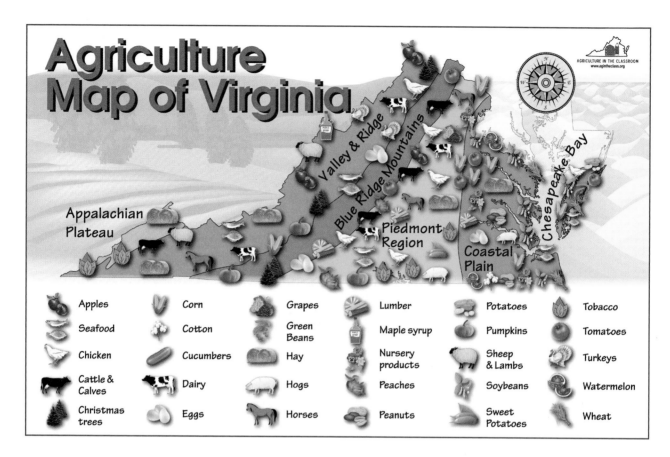

Agriculture Map of Virginia

Valley & Ridge

Blue Ridge Mountains

Appalachian Plateau

Piedmont Region

Coastal Plain

Chesapeake Bay

AGRICULTURE IN THE CLASSROOM
www.agintheclass.org

Apples	Corn	Grapes	Lumber	Potatoes	Tobacco
Seafood	Cotton	Green Beans	Maple syrup	Pumpkins	Tomatoes
Chicken	Cucumbers	Hay	Nursery products	Sheep & Lambs	Turkeys
Cattle & Calves	Dairy	Hogs	Peaches	Soybeans	Watermelon
Christmas trees	Eggs	Horses	Peanuts	Sweet Potatoes	Wheat

Farms Make a Difference

Next, make a large map of your state that you can use to show how agriculture affects the land and the people. Start with a blank state map. Label your state's regions or large cities. Label bodies of water, highways, and railroads that may be used to transport farm products. Add pictures of the crops that are grown and the animals that are raised.

Now, use your map and researched facts to explain to your classmates why farms may be located in certain regions and how the farms affect the people who live in your state. This will include the food people eat, the jobs they have, and what their environment looks like.

Tell your classmates how farms also affect the people in your state's cities. For example, there has been an apple-processing factory in Winchester, Virginia, since 1908. Many people who work there have grandparents who worked there years ago. The factory makes applesauce from apples grown in local Virginia orchards.

Summarize your explanation. Ask your classmates to tell you what they learned about agriculture in your state.

This is a map of the agriculture products in Virginia. The map of your state may show similar crops and animals.

 Economics Geography

Corn: Key Crop of the Midwest

In the United States today, farmers grow more corn than any other crop. Midwest farmers produce more than 650 billion pounds of corn every year. Why is corn such an important crop in the Midwest?

For most people, the word *corn* brings to mind either fresh corn on the cob like people eat at summer barbecues or a crunchy snack eaten while watching television. But in Mitchell, South Dakota, people celebrate corn in every way possible. Their high school sports teams are called the Kernels (for corn kernels). The school mascot is a giant ear of corn named "Cornelius." The name of the radio station is KORN. And on the main street of Mitchell, you can visit the world's only corn palace. The outside of this large building has murals made with all parts of a corn plant: corn cobs, husks, tassels, and stalks. A new mural is created every year.

Why would anyone care enough about something as simple as corn to build this huge structure? Why does the United States grow so much corn? And how do people use the corn we grow? Keep reading to find out.

Mitchell's first corn palace opened in 1892. It was built for citizens to celebrate the corn harvest.

Corn Long Ago

Corn has a long history in the Americas. About 7,000 years ago, the people of central Mexico developed a plant, called maize, from wild grass. Maize is a tall plant that produces large cobs of sweet corn.

Corn proved to be a very useful plant. The kernels were good to eat. The leaves were good to chew. Corn could even be popped. People used corn husks to make things like baskets, shoes, masks, and bed frames. They burned dried cobs for fuel.

As American Indians moved north, over thousands of years, they took corn with them. When European settlers arrived, American Indians were growing corn throughout North America.

When European settlers began to grow and harvest corn, they quickly realized what a valuable crop it was. They sent word of what they had learned—along with seeds—back home. Before long, people in other parts of the world were growing corn and other crops from the Americas.

These crops grew so well and fed so many people that they contributed to population increases around the world. For example, in southern Europe, from 1500 to 1900, the population grew from about 15 million people to about 70 million people. Today, people grow corn on every continent, except Antarctica.

The corn plant has many uses. Parts of it can be used for food, baskets, toys, and furniture.

Corn Today

Today, many Americans depend on corn just as the early settlers once did. The Midwestern states of Iowa, Illinois, Nebraska, and Minnesota raise more than half of the country's corn. These states are part of what we call "the Corn Belt."

The number of ways in which people use corn today might surprise you. Corn is used in thousands of products. Take a look at the chart below. It shows what happens to some of the corn grown in the United States.

Corn is used in many products today. Many of these are from corn grown in the Midwest.

How Corn Is Used Today

Animal Feed

More than half of all U.S. corn goes to feed animals such as cows, pigs, and chickens, and even our dogs and cats.

Food

Corn is found in many foods, from breakfast cereals to tortilla chips. Corn adds "crunch" to foods.

Fuel

Ethanol is a fuel that can be made from corn. It can power cars. Its use helps reduce air pollution.

Cornstarch

Made from corn, cornstarch is a powder that is used in food and many paper and plastic products. Your picnic utensils might be made from corn.

Corn Sweeteners

Corn sweeteners are found in many foods, from lunch meats to salad dressing. Corn sweeteners keep frozen yogurt from turning into ice.

Dried Corn Products

Dried corn is an ingredient in many household products. The pillow you sleep on and the comforter keeping you warm could have corn in them.

Day 0   **Day 12**   **Day 33**   **Day 45**

Corn is also being used to run cars. That may sound strange, but a fuel called ethanol lets us do just that. Ethanol is made from corn and can be used to power automobiles. Henry Ford's first cars could run on ethanol or gasoline or a combination of both. Burning ethanol creates less pollution than burning other types of fuel. Most gas stations today offer a blend of gasoline and ethanol for their customers that is friendlier to the environment.

And think about this the next time you use plastic plates at a picnic. When you throw the plates away, they may sit in the trash dump forever. Could we make plates out of a new material that would fall apart over time and become part of the soil? Scientists are working on ways to make just such a form of plastic out of cornstarch.

Did you brush your teeth this morning? If so, your toothpaste may get its flavor and smoothness from corn. Corn is used in many different personal care products from toothpaste to makeup, and from soap to shampoo. As you fall asleep tonight, think about all the different ways you may have used corn. And thank our Midwest farmers! ◆

This fork is made from a corn-based plastic. It decomposes safely and quickly—in just 45 days.

LESSON 10

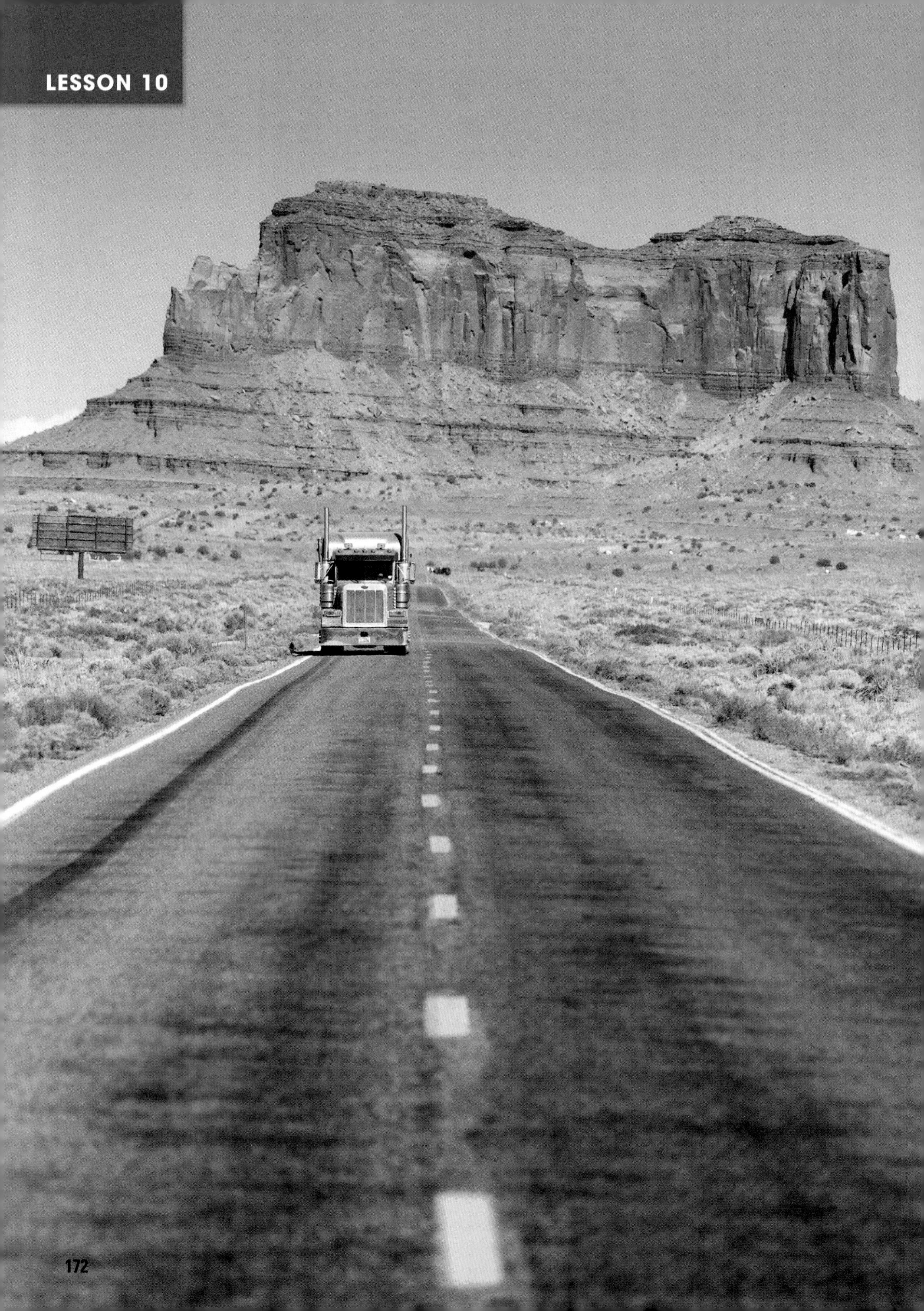

A Big Rig Tour of the Southwest

How have geography and history shaped life in the Southwest?

Introduction

Welcome to the Southwest. My name is Mr. Nakai, and I will be your guide for this region.

Let me tell you a little about myself. I am an American Indian, from the Navajo tribe. Until I retired last year, I was a truck driver. I drove my big rig—that's what truckers call their trucks—all over the Southwest. I know this region like the back of my hand.

When I was asked to lead this tour, I thought about how I could make it really special. Then, it hit me! I'm a trucker. Why not take you on a truck tour? My big rig holds only three people, but some of my trucking buddies have been nice enough to offer to help out. Together, we rounded up enough trucks to take your whole class.

During the tour, you'll see where I grew up as part of the Navajo. You'll visit big cities and small towns. This region has some incredible sights, both natural and manufactured. And, the region is full of history. You'll visit some places that are important to our past.

The view from high up in a big rig can't be beat. So pick a truck, buckle your seat belt, and let's go. We'll begin our trip in Arizona.

◀ A truck travels through the hot, dry U.S. Southwest.

 Civics   Economics   Geography   History

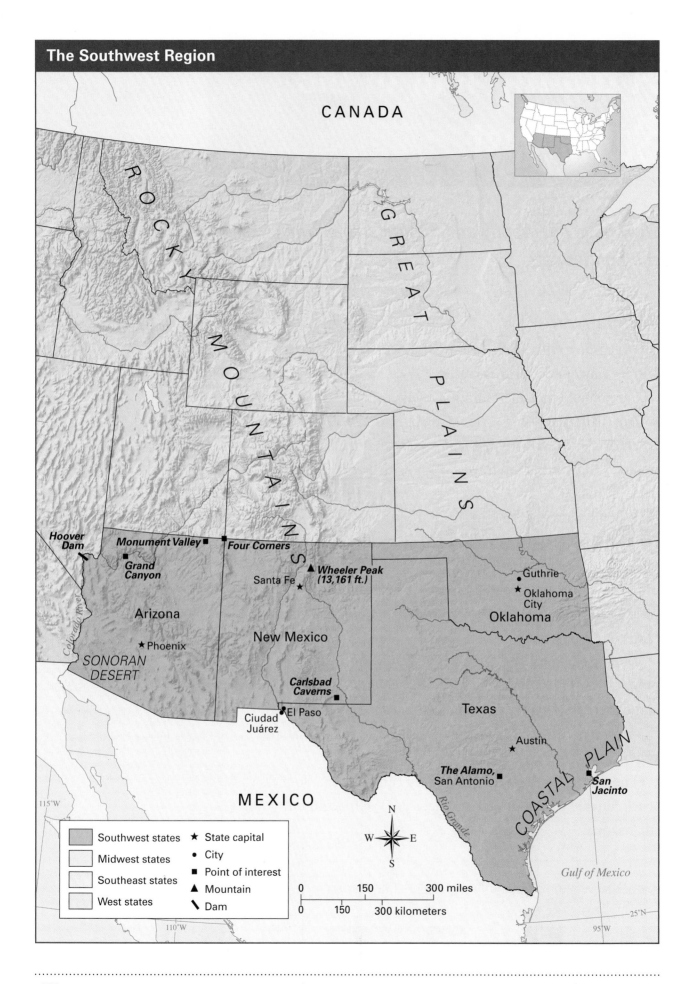

The Southwest Region

CANADA

ROCKY MOUNTAINS

GREAT PLAINS

Hoover Dam

Monument Valley ■

■ Four Corners

Grand Canyon ■

▲ Wheeler Peak (13,161 ft.)

Santa Fe ★

Guthrie ●

Oklahoma City ★

Arizona

Colorado River

New Mexico

Oklahoma

★ Phoenix

SONORAN DESERT

Carlsbad Caverns ■

Texas

Ciudad Juárez

●El Paso

Austin ★

The Alamo, San Antonio ■

MEXICO

Rio Grande

COASTAL PLAIN

■San Jacinto

115°W

110°W

95°W

25°N

Gulf of Mexico

	Legend
▦ Southwest states	★ State capital
☐ Midwest states	● City
☐ Southeast states	■ Point of interest
☐ West states	▲ Mountain
	＼ Dam

N
W E
S

0   150   300 miles
0   150   300 kilometers

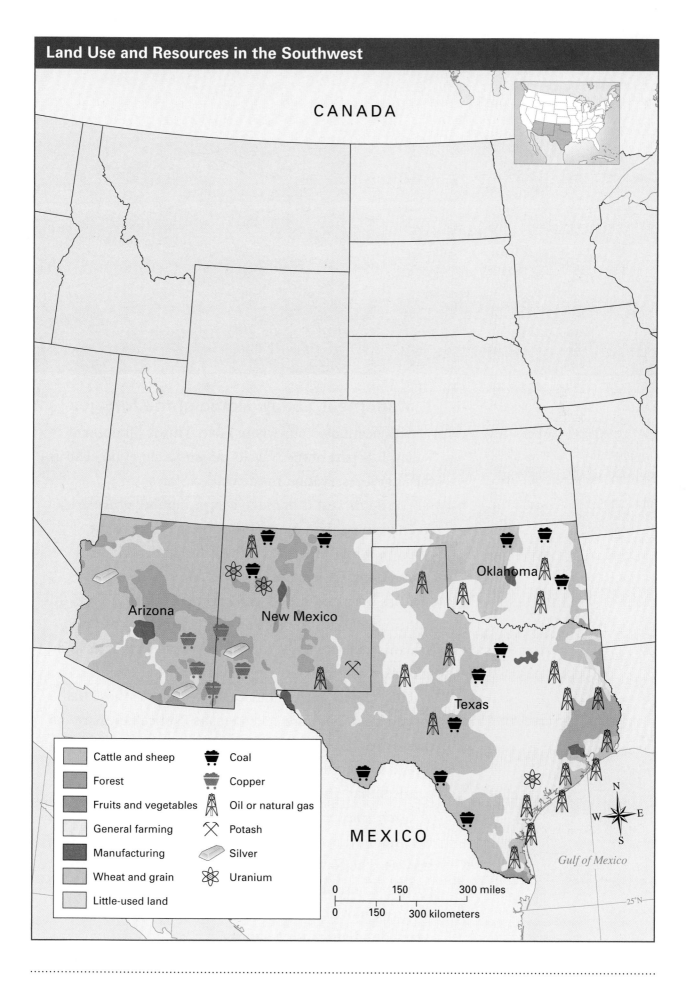

Land Use and Resources in the Southwest

CANADA

Arizona

New Mexico

Oklahoma

Texas

MEXICO

Gulf of Mexico

Cattle and sheep		Coal	
Forest		Copper	
Fruits and vegetables		Oil or natural gas	
General farming		Potash	
Manufacturing		Silver	
Wheat and grain		Uranium	
Little-used land			

0   150   300 miles

0   150   300 kilometers

25°N

People, plants, and animals have adapted to living in the dry land of Monument Valley. Flat-topped mesas dot the landscape.

mesa a flat-topped hill

desert an area of land that receives very little rain

adapt to change in order to survive

1. Monument Valley: Home of the Navajos

Let's begin our tour where I live. This is Monument Valley. It is part of the Navajo Indian Reservation. This is the largest reservation in the United States.

The Southwest is home to a large number of American Indians, more than most of the other regions of the country. Many American Indians live and work on reservations. Others live in towns and cities.

I was born and raised in Monument Valley. To me, this is the most beautiful place on Earth. Moviemakers also love this valley for its setting. Many western movies and television commercials are filmed here.

Look closely at this landscape. Do you see those flat-topped hills? They are called **mesas**. Notice how bare the mesas are. Not enough rain falls in Monument Valley for forests to grow. Much of the Southwest is **desert**. A desert gets less than 10 inches of rain a year.

Over time, plants, animals, and people have all **adapted** to living in this dry land. To adapt means to change to survive. The Navajos, for example, learned how to grow corn and raise sheep, even with little rainfall.

As we move on, look for other ways that people have adapted to living in the desert.

2. Phoenix, Arizona: America's Hottest City

This is Phoenix, Arizona, America's hottest large city. During July, temperatures here can soar to over 110 degrees Fahrenheit.

A hundred years ago, Phoenix was a small town. Not many people wanted to move to Arizona in those days. Some folks said that it was too hot, dry, and lonely here. What I call the three "A's" changed their minds.

The first "A" was air conditioners, which use electricity to cool the air in a room. Air-conditioning allows people to live in comfort no matter how hot the day is outside.

The second "A" was **aqueducts**. An aqueduct is a large pipe or canal that moves water over a long distance. Aqueducts are used in the Southwest to move water from lakes and rivers to farms and cities. Aqueducts make it possible for people to have regular showers and green lawns in Phoenix.

aqueduct a pipe or canal for carrying water over a long distance

The third "A" was automobiles. Travel in the Southwest used to be hard, and even dangerous. A traveler stuck in the desert could die of thirst.

Cars, along with good roads, made travel safer and easier. People began to come to the Phoenix area as tourists. Some liked the hot, dry weather so much that they came back here to live. Since 1940, Phoenix has grown at an amazing rate.

Air conditioners, a water supply, and automobiles helped make Phoenix a place where people want to live. Phoenix is now the sixth largest city in the United States with an ever-growing population.

3. Hoover Dam: A Concrete Marvel

You are looking at one of America's greatest manufactured structures, Hoover Dam. A **dam** is a wall built across a river to stop the water from flowing.

Hoover Dam was built for two main reasons. The first reason was to control flooding on the Colorado River. The dam slows the rush of water down the river during flood times. The second reason was to store water. Water stored behind Hoover Dam flows through aqueducts to farms and cities.

Hoover Dam was built more than 70 years ago. At that time, nobody had ever built such a huge dam. Many people said it couldn't be done. Some said the Colorado River could never be stopped long enough to build a dam. Other people did not think a dam could be made strong enough to hold back so much water. My dad helped prove these people wrong by helping to build Hoover Dam.

My dad knew a great many facts about Hoover Dam. He told me that there is enough concrete in the dam to pave a road from California to New York. He said that the lake behind the dam holds enough water to flood the entire state of Pennsylvania with one foot of water. That's a lot of concrete holding back a lot of water!

Hoover Dam helps control flooding of the Colorado River. The dam also stores water and creates electricity for use by cities and farms.

4. The Grand Canyon: Arizona's World-Famous Wonder

Wow—what a view! You are looking into the Grand Canyon, the most famous natural feature in the United States.

A **canyon** is a deep, narrow valley with steep sides. There are many canyons in the Southwest, but this one is the grandest of them all.

The Grand Canyon is about 277 miles long and one mile deep. It is so deep that the canyon's top and bottom have different weather. It can be cold here on top and hot down below. It is so deep that when I stand here on the rim, I sometimes see eagles flying below me.

canyon a deep, narrow valley with steep sides

The American Indian tribe known as the Havasupais lives at the bottom of the Grand Canyon. According to Havasupai legend, the canyon was formed when a flood covered the world. To end the flood, a god dug a hole in the Earth. The floodwater rushed down the hole, carving out the Grand Canyon as it went.

Scientists tell a different story. They say the Grand Canyon began to form anywhere from 6 to 17 million years ago. It has been carved slowly out of the Earth by water and wind. The Grand Canyon is still growing today, even while we are here looking at it.

Water and wind formed the Grand Canyon. Its walls are so high that the weather is different at the top and bottom.

Visitors look small in the Big Room of Carlsbad Caverns. This national park is entirely underground.

cavern a large cave

5. Carlsbad Caverns: Big Rooms and Bats in New Mexico

At most national parks, the big attractions are found above the ground. Not here! At Carlsbad Caverns National Park in New Mexico, the show takes place underground. About 100 caves and **caverns** lie beneath this park. A cave is a natural hole found in the Earth, and a cavern is a large cave.

According to local legend, some cowboys, including one named Jim White, found Carlsbad Caverns. One evening, they saw what looked like a plume of smoke rising into the sky. That plume of smoke turned out to be a big cloud of bats flying out of a cave entrance.

A bat looks like a mouse with wings. Hundreds of thousands of bats sleep in the caverns during the day. At night, the bats leave in a great, whirring cloud to hunt for food. If you come to the entrance at sunset, you may see them take flight. It's a very pretty sight.

More than a half million visitors tour Carlsbad Caverns each year. One of the most popular stops is a huge chamber known as the Big Room. The Big Room is about 25 stories high and a third of a mile wide. It could hold six football fields and still have space left over. Can you see the tourist in this Big Room photo?

6. El Paso and Ciudad Juárez: Two Cities, Two Countries, One Border

We are at the **border** between the United States and Mexico. A border is a line that people agree on as a boundary to separate two places. The border between the United States and Mexico is a river called the Rio Grande.

The Rio Grande separates two countries and divides two busy cities. El Paso, Texas, an American city, lies north of the border. Ciudad Juárez, a Mexican city, lies south of the border.

Forty years ago, El Paso and Juárez were sleepy little border towns with few people or trucks. Today, a total of about 2 million people live in the two cities. And the area is crawling with trucks.

The reason for this change is simple. American businesses have built hundreds of factories in Juárez. Americans build factories across the border because Mexican workers will work for much lower pay than American workers. This reduces the cost of doing business. These factories, called *maquiladoras* (mah-kee-luh-DOHR-uhs), assemble all kinds of goods. The goods are then trucked across the border for sale in the United States.

Many Mexicans move close to the border to take *maquiladora* jobs.

border a boundary line that separates two places

The Rio Grande forms part of the border between the United States (left) and Mexico (right). The river begins in Colorado.

7. San Antonio, Texas: Home of the Alamo

Welcome to San Antonio, Texas. San Antonio is a city famous for its Spanish **missions**. A mission is a Spanish settlement where priests once taught American Indians the Christian religion.

San Antonio's missions were built in the early 1700s. At that time, Texas was a colony of Spain. Later on, Texas became part of Mexico.

The Alamo is San Antonio's most famous mission. More than 2.5 million people visit the Alamo every year. They come to see where a small band of men fought and died so that Texas might be free.

In 1836, Americans living in Texas declared their independence from Mexican rule. A Mexican general named Antonio López de Santa Anna led 2,000 troops to Texas to crush this **rebellion**. A rebellion is an armed fight against one's government.

A band of 183 Texas freedom fighters gathered at the Alamo. Their goal was to stop the Mexican army there. Instead, the Mexican forces captured the mission and killed every one of its defenders.

News of the killings at the Alamo outraged Americans. Hundreds picked up their guns and headed to Texas to join the rebellion. Their battle cry was "Remember the Alamo!"

Texas won its independence from Mexico in 1836. For nine years, Texas was a free nation. Then, in 1845, Texas joined the United States as the 28th state.

mission a Spanish settlement built to teach Christianity in North America

rebellion an armed fight against a government

The Alamo is one of many missions built in San Antonio. It is a symbol of Texas independence.

8. Austin: The Capital of Texas

The government of Texas is in Austin, the **capital** of the state. A capital is a city where the government of a country or state is located.

Like our national government, state governments have three branches—legislative, executive, and judicial. The legislative branch is the state legislature. The Texas legislature meets in the building you see here with the large dome on top.

State legislatures make laws for all the people in a state. Most of the traffic laws in each state are passed by the state legislature. As a truck driver, I have to know and obey all these laws.

State legislatures decide how much people must pay in taxes to the state. They also decide how that money will be spent. Truckers always want state legislatures to spend more money on improving the roads.

The executive branch is headed by the state governor. It's the governor's job to make sure that all the laws passed by the state legislature are carried out.

State courts make up the judicial branch. State courts judge people who are accused of breaking state laws. If a person is found guilty of breaking a law, the courts decide how that person should be punished.

Austin is the seat of the Texas government. The capitol building is where the state legislature meets to make laws for the people.

capital a city where the government of a country or state is located

9. Guthrie, Oklahoma: Center of the Land Rush

Most of the Southwest was settled slowly, over time. Guthrie, Oklahoma, was settled in one day.

For many years, the U.S. government kept Oklahoma closed to everyone but American Indians. Then, in 1889, the government decided to open 2 million acres of land to new settlement. This area was to be given away in a one-day land rush. The first person to reach and claim a piece of land on that day could keep it.

On April 22, 1889, between 50,000 and 100,000 people gathered at the starting line for the land rush. Most were European Americans. Some were African Americans. Black or white, everyone wanted the same thing—free land.

At noon, a bugler blew some notes on his horn. The rush was on! People raced off in wagons, on horses, and on foot. In a few hours, every inch of land was taken.

Not everyone waited for the land rush to begin. Some settlers cheated and entered the area sooner than the government allowed. One of these "sooners" was found tending a garden full of vegetables. Oklahoma's soil was so rich, he claimed, that the plants had all sprouted up that day.

Guthrie, Oklahoma, was born during the land rush. At noon, Guthrie wasn't much more than a patch of grass. Six hours later, the town had a population of 10,000 people.

Most of the Southwest was settled slowly. However, settlers raced to grab land in Oklahoma during a one-day land rush in 1889.

Today, the town of Guthrie still has about 10,000 people living there. Most of the downtown buildings in Guthrie still look like they did in the late 1800s.

Like Guthrie, Oklahoma City got its start during the land rush of 1889. But today, it is the largest city in the state. Oklahoma City and nearby towns form a community of more than 1 million people. The city is the capital of Oklahoma, which is nicknamed the Sooner State.

Guthrie, Oklahoma, was settled in a hurry. It sprang up during the land rush of 1889. Today, many beautiful buildings that went up soon after the land rush can still be seen.

Lesson Summary

I hope you enjoyed this big rig tour of the Southwest. We passed through the states of Arizona, New Mexico, Texas, and Oklahoma.

On the way back, I asked the children in my truck what words they would use to describe the Southwest. The first word they came up with was *big*. This region has big caverns, a big canyon, a big capitol building, and a big dam. Their next two words were *hot* and *dry*. Much of the Southwest is desert. Plants, animals, and people all have to adapt to its hot, dry climate to survive.

The last word the children chose was *beautiful*. I asked them which places seemed beautiful. "Monument Valley," they answered "along with the Grand Canyon and Carlsbad Caverns." After thinking about this some more, one child added, "I think Hoover Dam is beautiful, too." My dad would have liked that answer. He would have liked it a lot.

Researching a City in Your State

You just read about different cities in the Southwest and the landforms in these areas. How do landforms and resources affect where cities are located? To answer questions like this one, you can learn more about the settlers who established a city. This can help you understand why cities are located in some places but not others.

Researching Landforms in a City

Most states have several large cities. To learn why a city in your state is located where it is, you can research that city. First you need to choose a city to research. For example, if you live in Minnesota, you might choose to learn more about the city Minneapolis.

Landforms can affect where people establish cities. A valley might attract more settlers than a place with lots of mountains. A desert that is hot and dry might attract less settlers than a plain with healthy soil.

To find what landforms are near a city, first make a map of that state, like this one of Minnesota.

Place the city on it. Use the Internet or an atlas to research what landforms are near the city. Make a key for these landforms. For instance, in this map, triangles represent mountains, and wavy blue lines represent rivers. Mark the landforms on the map. Which landforms are near the city you chose?

To learn why an area attracted settlers, you can research a city's landforms and resources. This map of Minnesota shows the features near the city Minneapolis.

A Physical Map of Minnesota

CANADA

0 50 100 miles
0 50 100 kilometers

Lake of the Woods

Upper Red Lake
Lower Red Lake

Lake Winnibigoshish

RED RIVER VALLEY

Leech Lake

Lake Superior

Mille Lacs Lake

Minnesota

Mississippi River

N
W E
S

Minnesota River

★ St. Paul

Forest
Plain
Valley

Writing an Explanation About a City

Now it's time to observe the map you made. Based on your observations, write an explanation about why you think the city is located where it is. For instance, based on the Minnesota map, an explanation might be that people settled in Minneapolis because there is the Mississippi River running through it and people could use the water. There are also no mountains there, which makes it easy to access.

When you have written down your explanation, you can research the city's history. Use sources from the Internet or library to learn about why settlers lived there. You can also research the resources in that area that the settlers used. How did landforms and resources influence settlement?

The settlement of Minneapolis began in 1849, and it became a city in 1867. There is a waterfall there that helped the city flourish by providing power. With this resource, Minneapolis had a thriving flour and lumber industry that attracted people.

Revise your explanation based on your research, and then share it with a partner. Have your partner answer these questions: Does your evidence support your explanation? How could your explanation be improved?

Minneapolis is on flat land located near the Mississippi River and waterfalls. These features attracted settlers.

Civics   Economics   Geography   History

Freedom—or Death

Before Texas was a state, it was the home of American Indians. It was a colony of Spain and then Mexico. And then it was an independent nation. How did one battle help shape the history of Texas?

BOOM! BOOM! The walls of the Alamo shook as the cannons fired. The sound of rifles was heard nearby. The shouts of the men outside grew more desperate as the Mexican army advanced. No one expected to make it out of the room alive. Would this be the end of their dreams for Texas?

The date was March 6, 1836. For days, a small army of Texan soldiers had been defending the mission. It was their small army against thousands of Mexican soldiers. They had hoped that other Texans would join them, but no help arrived.

General Santa Anna's army was outside the walls. Mexican soldiers had circled the Alamo cutting off escape routes. His men flew a red flag that meant the general would show no mercy to the Texan rebels. No prisoners would be taken. This small group of Texans was determined to try to win their freedom. For Texas, they were willing to fight until death.

Texan soldiers fought the Mexican army at the Battle of the Alamo. They would fight until death for Texas.

Between Two Countries

For thousands of years, American Indians lived in Texas, hunting and farming in the hot, dry climate. In the 1500s, Spanish settlers arrived, and built missions and towns. Spain claimed Texas as part of its Mexican colony.

In the summer of 1821, an American named Stephen F. Austin rode his horse through Spanish Texas. The United States was not yet 50 years old, but already Americans were pushing west. Austin's father had permission from Spain to settle 300 families in Texas, and Stephen was looking for good land.

Stephen decided to build a settlement between the Colorado and Brazos rivers. Each family would receive a large amount of land for a very low cost.

In 1821, Mexico won its independence from Spain. At first, Mexico was happy about the new settlers in Texas. To the Mexicans, U.S. settlers would be good citizens who would help protect Mexican land. To the new settlers, the colony was a chance for cheap land—and new lives.

Stephen F. Austin brought new settlers to Texas. Each family got more than 4,400 acres of land.

The Texas Revolution Begins

Within ten years, thousands of Americans had settled in Texas. They were used to living in the United States. They wanted more independence than they had in Mexico. So they demanded that Texas become a separate Mexican state.

Mexican leaders were worried. Too many Americans were moving to Texas and making demands. Mexican officials said that no more Americans could move to Texas. And Mexico refused to let Texas become a state.

Stephen F. Austin visited Mexico to smooth things between the Texans and the Mexican government. But officials threw him in jail. Some officials thought Austin wanted independence for Texas. Austin spent more than a year in jail. When he got out, he understood that Texans needed to fight Mexico for their freedom.

In October 1835, tensions between Texas and Mexico erupted into war. Austin led 400 soldiers to San Antonio to fight. The Texans won that small battle.

In February 1836, General Santa Anna brought his army to San Antonio. The Texans were ready for him. Brave fighters, including Davy Crockett, Jim Bowie, and William Travis, stood up against Santa Anna's troops. For 13 days, the Texans and the Mexicans had a standoff at the Alamo.

During fighting, Texan soldiers dared Santa Anna to "come and take" their prized cannon. At the Alamo, this cannon remains as a reminder.

Freedom for Texas

Texans declared their independence on March 2. Texas became the Republic of Texas, a free nation. But Mexico would not let Texas go.

On March 6, the Mexican army attacked the Alamo again. The Texans put up a fierce fight, but the mission fell under Santa Anna's control. Only the women and children, and a few enslaved African Americans, survived the bloody fight. Stories from those who witnessed the battle enraged Americans. Many people now joined the Texan army to fight the Mexicans.

A few weeks later, a Texan general named Sam Houston defeated Santa Anna's army at the Battle of San Jacinto. Texas then declared victory. The rebels had won their independence from Mexico.

Today, the Alamo sits in downtown San Antonio, Texas. Much of the old mission is gone, but a small chapel still stands. Its walls show scars from the fighting. People from all over the world visit the Alamo. They listen to guides describe the fighting, and they learn how the Texans fought for their freedom.

For Texans, the battle at the Alamo was an important step in their battle for freedom. It led the way for Texas to become an independent nation, if only for a short time. ◆

Many flags have flown over Texas during its history. Above, you can see six of them, including the U.S., Mexican (green, white, and red) and Spanish (red, yellow, red) flags.

A Case Study in Water Use: The Colorado River

How do people depend on the Colorado River and share its water?

Introduction

Many rivers flow through the United States, but few of them are as important as the Colorado River. The people who live in the West and in the Southwest depend on the Colorado River for many things. The river provides drinking water for more than 36 million people. It supplies water for more than 3 million acres of farmland. Dams on the river help produce much of the electricity used in the Southwest.

The Colorado River begins high in the Rocky Mountains. The beginning of a river is called its source. The Colorado wanders south and west through some of the driest parts of the country. Then it crosses into Mexico, where it ends in the Gulf of California. The river's total journey is 1,450 miles long.

Many smaller rivers flow into the Colorado. Rivers that join other, larger rivers are called tributaries. Each tributary adds water and soil, called silt, to the Colorado. This silt gives parts of the river a reddish brown color.

The history of the Colorado River Basin shapes how people use and share this river. Current challenges will affect its future. How can we use this resource wisely?

> **Social Studies Vocabulary**
>
> conservation
>
> drought
>
> habitat
>
> irrigation
>
> municipality
>
> reservoir
>
> river basin
>
> wastewater

◀ The Colorado River flows through the Grand Canyon on its way to the Gulf of California in Mexico.

 Civics   Geography   History

A spring continuously fills this natural well in central Arizona. The well was a valuable water source used by early settlers of the region.

river basin the area around a river and its tributaries

drought a long period of time when little or no rain falls

1. The First Settlers in the Colorado River Basin

Today, millions of people live in the Colorado River Basin. A **river basin** is the area around a river and its tributaries. In the past, the Colorado River Basin was mostly an empty desert.

Two of the American Indian groups that once made their homes in this dry region were the Anasazis and the Hohokams. The Anasazis lived in the Four Corners area. This is where the states of Arizona, New Mexico, Utah, and Colorado meet today. The Hohokams lived in central Arizona.

The Anasazis and the Hohokams were farmers. They raised corn, beans, and squash in desert fields. Not enough rain fell to water their crops, so they built canals to carry water from rivers to their fields. Some Hohokam canals were so well built that they are still used today.

Around 1350, the Anasazis left their villages. Around the same time, the Hohokams also left. The name Hohokam means "those who have vanished."

Why did these people leave their homelands? No one is sure, but the most likely answer is **drought**. A drought is a time when little or no rain falls. When no rain came and their rivers ran dry, the Anasazis and the Hohokams probably had two choices. They could leave and live, or stay and most likely die. They chose to leave their villages to live in other parts of the Southwest.

2. Explorers Arrive

Spanish explorers were the first Europeans to visit the Southwest. In 1540, a Spanish soldier named Francisco Vásquez de Coronado led an army north from Mexico. Coronado hoped to find cities made of gold. Instead, he found American Indian villages built from mud and stone.

In their search for gold, some of Coronado's men came upon the Grand Canyon. From high up on the canyon rim, the river at the bottom looked like a trickling creek. The men didn't bother to give it a name.

Spanish settlers eventually followed Coronado into the Southwest and lived off the land by farming and ranching. These settlers eventually named the muddy river flowing through the Grand Canyon. They called it the Colorado, which means "reddish color" in Spanish.

In 1869, an explorer named John Wesley Powell and a crew of nine men navigated down the Colorado in small boats. These men were the first Americans to see the Grand Canyon from the bottom. The trip took three months.

In 1871, Powell made a second trip down the Colorado. He wrote a report on the Colorado River Basin. He said that the region was too dry for much settlement. He believed that there wasn't enough water to support a large number of people.

John Wesley Powell explored the Colorado River in the 1800s. During his second journey, Powell made a map of the Colorado River.

3. A Wave of Settlement

Powell's warning did not stop settlers from coming to the Colorado River Basin. Some of them were farmers. Like the Anasazis and the Hohokams, they found that they could grow crops in the desert. They just had to bring a lot of water to their fields.

To do this, farmers used **irrigation**. Irrigation is a way to bring water to a dry area. Some irrigation systems use canals, pipes, and ditches to carry water from one place to another. This is how farmers irrigated the Colorado River Basin.

Other settlers became cattle and sheep ranchers. Sheep and cattle could live off plants that grew wild in the Southwest. But ranchers had to find drinking water for their animals. Some ranchers also needed water to raise crops of hay for their animals.

As the number of settlers grew, towns appeared in the basin. A few—such as Las Vegas, Nevada, and Phoenix, Arizona—grew into cities. People living in these towns and cities needed water for drinking, washing, and watering their gardens. All of these people looked to the Colorado and its tributaries for their water needs.

irrigation a way to bring water to dry land, using water from another location

Canals in the river basin irrigate fields and provide drinking water for animals. Farming and ranching is only possible by bringing in lots of water.

Representatives from the seven basin states signed the Colorado River Compact on November 24, 1922. Mexico was not included in this agreement.

4. Sharing the Water: The Colorado River Compact

At first, the Colorado River had enough water for everyone. Water was divided up following the rule of "first in time, first in right." This meant that people who settled first were first in line to draw water from the river. Those who came last were last in line.

This way of dividing water created a problem because those settlers first in line lived mostly in California. This meant that California had the right to use almost all of the river's water. This didn't seem fair to other states in the river basin.

In 1922, the seven states in the river basin reached an agreement known as the Colorado River Compact. The compact divided the basin into two parts. The Upper Basin includes Wyoming, Colorado, Utah, and New Mexico. The Lower Basin includes Nevada, California, and Arizona. The compact gave each part of the basin an equal amount of water from the Colorado River.

The Colorado River Compact said nothing about Mexico. Mexico's water users worried that there would be no water left by the time the river crossed the border. So, the United States signed a separate agreement with Mexico. In it, the United States promised to leave some water in the Colorado River for Mexico.

5. Taming the River with Dams

The Colorado River Compact gave each state the right to a portion of the river's flow. But turning that right into a constant water supply was not easy. In wet years, the river flooded its banks. In dry years, the river barely flowed.

The only way a state could get and keep its share of river water was to trap and store it by building dams. As water backs up behind a dam, it forms a **reservoir**. A reservoir is a place where water is stored for people's use.

Since the 1930s, the states have built more than 80 dams on the Colorado River and its tributaries. These dams have tamed the river. In wet years, they prevent flooding by not letting too much water flow down the river at one time. In dry years, the reservoirs provide water to farms and cities.

Most dams generate electricity. Water rushing through openings in the dam causes huge machines to spin. These machines are called turbines. The spinning turbines create electricity. This electricity is sold to help pay for the dams.

reservoir an area where water is stored for people's use

Dams provide a constant supply of water and electricity to their users. The Glen Canyon Dam holds back some of the Colorado River to form Lake Powell.

The Colorado River Basin

Legend:
- Colorado River Basin
- • City
- ⟍ Dam
- ■ Attraction

N W E S

Idaho
Wyoming
Nevada
Utah
Colorado
UPPER COLORADO BASIN
Green River
Colorado River
ROCKY
Glen Canyon Dam
Lake Powell
San Juan River
Four Corners
Las Vegas
Hoover Dam
Lake Mead
Grand Canyon National Park
LOWER COLORADO BASIN
MOUNTAINS
California
Davis Dam
Los Angeles
Colorado River
Parker Dam
Arizona
New Mexico
San Diego
Phoenix
Gila River
PACIFIC OCEAN
Gulf of California
MEXICO

0   100   200 miles
0 100 200 kilometers

6. Managing the Water

You've read how the Colorado River has been dammed to provide water and electricity for the seven compact states. But how does the water actually get to each home, business, or farm that needs it? Water has to be collected from the river, treated, stored, and then distributed. A municipal water system does all these things for you and others who use water.

A **municipality** is an agency, or business, organized by a state or city to perform a service. The service may be waste removal, fire protection, water and electricity delivery, and others. A water municipality delivers the water from the Colorado River to the people of the state. Municipalities cover a defined area, often a town, city, or even larger district. You may call your municipality the "water company."

A water company is responsible for many things. It stores and delivers the water through a system of reservoirs, pipes, pumps, or canals. And it must maintain these systems. The water company treats the water and keeps the water clean. For these services, the water company charges users a fee and, sometimes, taxes. Water companies also educate users on how to save water. By managing the water, a water municipality does its best to make sure that everyone gets the water they need now and in the future.

A water municipality delivers clean water to homes, businesses, and farms. It also helps to educate users on how save water.

> **municipality** an elected agency, or business, that performs a service for the state or city

So far, the Colorado River has met the needs of its growing number of users. Families can save water by washing only full loads of laundry.

7. The Number of Water Users Grows and Grows

The dams helped people share water from the river, but, year after year, more and more people moved to the Colorado River Basin. These people built new houses and businesses. Still, the Colorado River provided water and electricity for everyone. Who are these water users?

The largest group is made up of farmers and ranchers. A farmer uses three gallons of water to grow one tomato. A rancher uses more than 600 gallons of water to raise the beef for one hamburger.

Families are major water users, too. People need water to drink, shower, flush toilets, and wash clothes. Did you know that one load of laundry can use 30 to 40 gallons of water?

Businesses are major water users as well. A clothing company needs about 1,800 gallons of water to make one pair of jeans from cotton.

Miners are also major water users. Gold, iron, copper, coal, and uranium are found in the Colorado River Basin. Miners use large amounts of water to wash these valuable ores from the soil.

So far, the Colorado River has met the needs of these water users. But, as more people move into the basin, there may not be enough water for everyone.

8. Wildlife Water Users

People are not the only water users in the Colorado River Basin. Mammals, birds, fish, and other animals need the river, too.

The taming of the river has hurt wildlife by destroying **habitats**. A habitat is the place where a type of animal typically lives in nature. The natural habitat of fish, for example, is water.

As you know, dams built on the Colorado have turned parts of the river into reservoirs. Otters, and other animals once lived along these parts of the river. Now their habitats have changed.

Dams have also changed the water in the river. Before the dams were built, the river water was muddy and warm much of the year. The river's water level was at its high point in spring. Today, the water released from a dam is clear and cold. The water level is highest in summer. That is when farmers and cities need water and electricity the most. These changes have hurt fish and other wildlife.

Today, some dam operators try to help wildlife by releasing more water in spring. But this change means less water for people during the summer months.

Mammals, birds, fish, and other animals need the Colorado River. Dams on the river have hurt fish and other wildlife.

9. Is There Enough Water for Everyone?

The Colorado River Compact was based on the belief that about 17 million acre-feet of water flow down the river each year. An acre-foot is the amount of water it would take to cover an acre of land with one foot of water. (An acre is about the size of a football field without the end zones.)

After the United States signed an agreement with Mexico, this is how all that water was divided:

- Upper Basin states: 7 ½ million acre-feet
- Lower Basin states: 7 ½ million acre-feet
- Mexico: 1 ½ million acre-feet
- Total: 16 ½ million acre-feet

If the same amount of water flowed every year, this plan would work. But the river does not always carry this much water. In wet years, the flow may rise to more than 20 million acre-feet. In dry years, it often falls below 10 million acre-feet. And there are more dry years than wet years in the Colorado River Basin.

An acre-foot of water is about 326,000 gallons. This may sound like a lot, but it's not. A family of four uses 1 acre-foot of water each year. A farmer uses 3 acre-feet to water just one acre of land each year.

As more people settle in the Colorado River Basin, there may not be enough water for everyone.

The amount of water in the Colorado River changes if it is a wet or dry year. However, the number of water users in cities like Las Vegas keeps growing.

10. Meeting Future Water Needs: Farming

In the future, water users in the Colorado River Basin will face shortages. There are only two ways to solve this problem. One is to increase the supply of water. In the past, this was done by building dams. But most of the best places for dams have already been used. In addition, dams can hurt the natural environment.

The other solution is to use less water. This is called **conservation**. Conservation is the careful use of a resource. It sounds easy, but it is not. Using less water takes planning. It also takes new ways of thinking and new inventions.

Conservation efforts are already being made. Farmers are changing the way they irrigate their fields. Sprinkler and ditch irrigation systems lose much water to evaporation. If farmers can reduce evaporation, they can use less water. So farmers apply mulch, or a cover, to the soil and use drip systems. Irrigating at night can also help reduce evaporation.

Farmers are also changing when crops are grown and for how long. Some fields lie fallow, or unused, for a season. Cover crops, like soybeans or turnips, are planted after the main harvest. Cover crops are seeded in the remains or stems of harvested wheat or other crops. The soil is not tilled. This helps the soil hold water better and adds nutrients to the soil. Conservation efforts like these help farmers use less water.

In farming, sprinkler systems waste water to evaporation. Drip irrigation, like used here in the cornfields, helps reduce evaporation loss.

conservation the careful use of a resource

11. Meeting Future Water Needs: Cities

Turning off the water while you brush your teeth. Taking shorter showers. Only running a fully loaded dishwasher. What do these habits have in common? They are ways that you can help conserve water. Water conservation is important in homes as well as on farms. Tips like these are being followed in cities and towns of the river basin.

Conservation efforts are going beyond personal habits. For example, all new homes in the river basin are built with low-flow toilets. These toilets use less than two gallons with each flush. Older toilets use up to seven gallons per flush.

Conservation is happening outdoors. City gardeners are planting native plants to decorate their cities and reduce erosion. These plants usually don't need to be watered. Native plants are adapted to an area's climate. If you do need to water the garden, rain barrels are a way to reduce water use from a faucet. Rain barrels attached to homes or businesses capture runoff of water from roofs. This water can be used later to water gardens.

Many cities are recycling the water that goes down the drain every day. This water is called **wastewater**. Cities collect and treat wastewater so that it can be safely used again. Treated wastewater often irrigates plants in parks and grass at golf courses.

wastewater water that has been used

Water conservation can start in the home. Running only a fully loaded dishwasher is a water-saving habit.

Communities in the Southwest and all across the country are finding new ways to save water. You can help, too. Report leaky faucets at school and broken sprinklers around your community. Every little action helps. Rethinking the way you use water will help conserve it to make sure water is there when you need it.

It takes lots of water to keep a golf course green, especially in the desert. How can people conserve water in areas like this?

Lesson Summary

If John Wesley Powell could see the Colorado River today, he would be amazed. The river he explored ran free from the Rocky Mountains to the Gulf of California. Today, giant dams slow the river's rush to the sea. Those dams have changed the Colorado River in ways that Powell could never have imagined.

When Powell explored the river, few people lived on the land around it. Now, more than 25 million people rely on the Colorado River Basin. Powell would be surprised to see so many people. He would also be surprised to find farms and cities blooming in the desert.

If Powell were here today, he might issue a new report on the Colorado River Basin. Water is precious, he might tell us. It is more precious than gold. So use the river's gift of water wisely and conserve it.

Water in Your State

You just read how people in the Southwest and West depend on the Colorado River. Citizens worry there won't be enough water for the needs of a growing population.

Your state may also face a water problem. It may be a water shortage, water pollution, or flooding. You can do some research to find out your state's biggest water problem and what people are doing about it. Write these two big questions on a piece of paper:

What is the biggest water problem facing our state?
How can we help solve it?

Talk with your classmates about the best places to find answers to these two big questions. Use the library and the Internet to find sources. When you find a source, talk about who wrote the information. Does the writer want to persuade you to think a certain way? Does the writer want to only help certain businesses or groups? It is important to know that people have different opinions and want different outcomes when they suggest answers to problems.

As rain or snow runs over land that has chemicals in it, the water picks up the chemicals. It flows into streams and lakes and pollutes the water.

For example, in Iowa, one of the most important water problems is pollution in streams and lakes. Much of the pollution comes from chemicals that farmers use to fertilize their crops or kill insects. The chemicals run through the land into the water. It can hurt fish as well as people's drinking water. If you were researching solutions to this problem, it is important to hear different opinions. Farmers may want to solve the problem without hurting their business. Others may want to stop farmers from using chemicals that harm the environment.

Solving the Problem

As you research your state's water problem, write the suggested solutions on your piece of paper. Under each solution, write the author's name and the book title or Web site address. Try to find the opinions of two or more groups of people. These may include farmers, business owners, homeowners, and conservation groups.

Now write a four-paragraph presentation that you can read to your class. In the first paragraph, describe the important water problem that your state faces. Include where in the state it is happening and describe why it is a problem.

In the second and third paragraphs, write about two or more ways that people can help solve the problem. In the last paragraph, summarize your presentation and make a prediction of how the water issue may be improved if people work together.

Read your presentation to your class. Ask your classmates if they have other suggestions that might help solve the problem. With your classmates, decide on a group project to share this information with people outside of school.

These students made a poster to remind people to not waste water.

This student explains how to help keep the water clean in her state.

At Home in the Grand Canyon

For most people in the Southwest, lack of water is a problem. But the Havasupais who live in the Grand Canyon have a different challenge: flooding from Havasu Creek. How does water affect life for the Havasupais?

Chop, chop, chop. The helicopter flew through the air down into the Grand Canyon. Suddenly, the pilot saw a wall of water rushing toward Supai, the tiny village at the bottom of the canyon. Quickly, the pilot radioed an emergency warning.

Supai is the home of about 450 Havasupais, an American Indian tribe. In Supai, people soon saw the cascade of water coming from Havasu Creek. Many Havasupais ran from their homes and fled up the cliffs. Two people climbed eight feet up a tree to escape the churning water.

Lester Crooke, the tribe chairman at that time, said of the water, "It was really rushing through, bringing all kinds of big rocks and logs." Crooke and others helped people get to safety. Tourists who were hiking and camping nearby were rescued by helicopter. It was days before residents could return to the village, only to find many of their belongings destroyed.

To reach the village of Supai, you can walk or ride a mule down eight miles from the canyon rim. Or you can take a helicopter ride!

Floods in the Canyon

The flood you just read about took the Havasupais by surprise. So too had larger floods in earlier years.

Most of the time, the Havasupais have some warning about a possible flood. The floods often come after days of heavy precipitation, either rainfall or snowfall. At those times, water runs down the sides of the canyon rims filling the creeks near Supai until they overflow. The Havasupais have time to react to this danger.

Rose Marie Manakaja is an elder in the tribe. "Our parents and grandparents taught us other signs to watch out for," she explained. "For example, the animals usually know when a flood is coming. The horses and mules twitch their ears and noses in a certain way. The dogs know, too."

These are the Havasu Falls near Supai. Flooding of creeks can damage the beautiful pools near these falls.

But, sometimes, floods come unexpectedly. Then the residents of Supai are in great danger. In 1993, another surprise flood destroyed bridges, trails, and homes. This flood wrecked an irrigation system that was hundreds of years old. It washed away 43 acres of farmland and killed some of the farm animals. In all, the flood caused $2.5 million in damages.

So how *do* the Havasupais live with the threat of floods in the Grand Canyon?

The Havasupais have lived in the canyon for hundreds of years. Here, Havasupais gather in front of a schoolhouse around 1900.

Living with the Water

Manakaja explained that the residents of Supai are used to these floods that come so suddenly and unexpectedly. "We grew up here," she said. "To us, it is part of our life."

The Havasupais have lived in the canyon for hundreds of years. Their name relates to the water nearby and means "the people of the blue-green water."

Like other American Indians in the Southwest, the early Havasupais were farmers. In spring, summer, and early fall, they lived down in the canyon cultivating the land. There was plenty of water from Havasu Creek for irrigation of their fields as well as the orchards where they grew peaches.

In the Havasupai tradition, their creator Tudjupa said, "Here is the land where you will live. Go to the places where you find water. Mark off your land and live by the water."

However, in late fall and winter, the water in the canyon could become a threat to their village. When the floods came, the water could cause great destruction. So the Havasupais moved up to the canyon rim where it was sunnier and safer. Above the canyon, the Havasupais gathered food and hunted deer and elk. They roamed over thousands of acres of rich hunting grounds.

Conflict over Land

For centuries, the Havasupais lived with these cycles of nature. But the world above the canyon was changing.

By the late 1800s, thousands of Americans had moved west. Many were cattle ranchers who fenced off the land where the Havasupais hunted. Soon, conflict erupted over who had the right to use the land. In the 1880s, the U.S. government took action. It said that the Havasupais could keep only 518 acres out of the thousands of acres they had been using. All the land that was left to them was in the Grand Canyon and none at the top.

Now, without any land to escape to on the canyon rim, the Havasupais could no longer leave during flood times. So they learned to live with the water in good times and in bad.

In 1975, the government returned more than 185,000 acres of land on the canyon rim to the Havasupais. But the people of Supai stayed put. They loved their land in the canyon and wanted to live there, floods or not.

Some people think that the Havasupais should dam the creek to stop the flooding. To that, the Havasupais say no. They want to live with the natural environment rather than alter it. So they watch carefully for floods and leave their canyon when they must. The Havasupais have been at home in the Grand Canyon for many centuries and intend to stay there for many more. ◆

Today, the Havasupais live much as they did centuries ago. Here, a mule team hauls mail and other gear to Supai.

SPEED
LIMIT
25

A Van and Airplane Tour of the West

What are the features that have drawn people to the West?

Introduction

Aloha! My name is Ms. Yoshida and I will be your guide for our tour of the West. I was born and raised in Hawaii. As you probably can tell from my greeting, the word *aloha* is used for "hello" in the Hawaiian language. We also use it to say "good-bye."

I am a college student here on the mainland. My main interests are political science and government. Someday, I hope to win an election to the United States Congress and represent the people of Hawaii.

On school breaks, I work as a tour guide. It's a great job, because I get to meet all kinds of people while seeing beautiful places. We will be visiting several different states, starting in Montana and finishing in Hawaii. Whenever we visit someplace new, I want you to think about two questions: What first attracted people to this place? And why are people still coming here?

For most of our tour, we will travel in vans. But we will also fly in airplanes to two stops.

Do you hear that honk? That means it's time for us to hit the road.

> **Social Studies Vocabulary**
>
> **expedition**
>
> **geyser**
>
> **gorge**
>
> **pass**
>
> **technology**

◀ Miles of highways, like this one, allow people to travel across the Rocky Mountains.

 Civics Economics Geography History

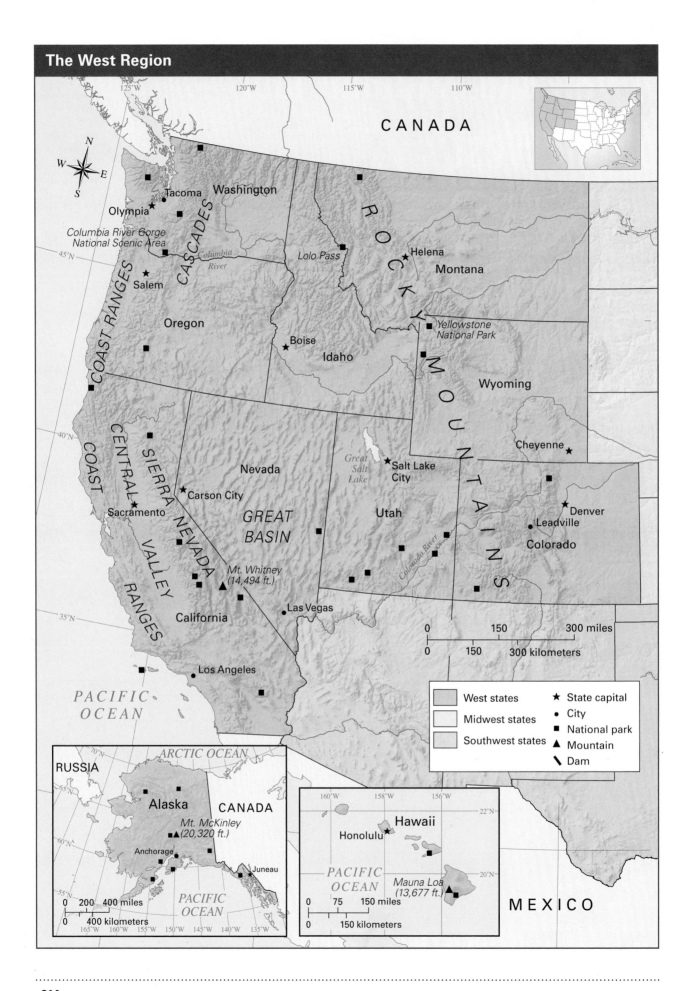

The West Region

CANADA

125°W · 120°W · 115°W · 110°W

North (compass rose)
N
W · E
S

Tacoma ■
Washington
Olympia ★
Columbia River Gorge
National Scenic Area

CASCADES

Columbia River

Lolo Pass
Helena ★
Montana

45°N

Salem ★

Oregon

Boise ★
Idaho

Yellowstone
National Park

Wyoming

40°N

COAST RANGES

CENTRAL VALLEY

SIERRA NEVADA

Nevada

Carson City ★
Sacramento ★

GREAT
BASIN

GREAT SALT LAKE
Great
Salt
Lake
Salt Lake ★
City

Utah

Colorado River

Cheyenne ★

Denver ★
Leadville ●
Colorado

COAST RANGES

Mt. Whitney ▲
(14,494 ft.)

California

35°N

Las Vegas ●

Los Angeles ●

PACIFIC
OCEAN

0   150   300 miles
0   150   300 kilometers

Legend

▮ West states	★ State capital
▯ Midwest states	● City
▨ Southwest states	■ National park
	▲ Mountain
	❭ Dam

Alaska inset

ARCTIC OCEAN
70°N
RUSSIA
65°N
Alaska
CANADA
60°N
Mt. McKinley ▲
(20,320 ft.)
Anchorage ●
Juneau ★
55°N
PACIFIC
OCEAN

0   200   400 miles
0   400 kilometers

165°W · 160°W · 155°W · 150°W · 145°W · 140°W · 135°W

Hawaii inset

160°W · 158°W · 156°W

Hawaii ★
Honolulu ●

22°N

PACIFIC
OCEAN

Mauna Loa ▲
(13,677 ft.)

20°N

0   75   150 miles
0   150 kilometers

MEXICO

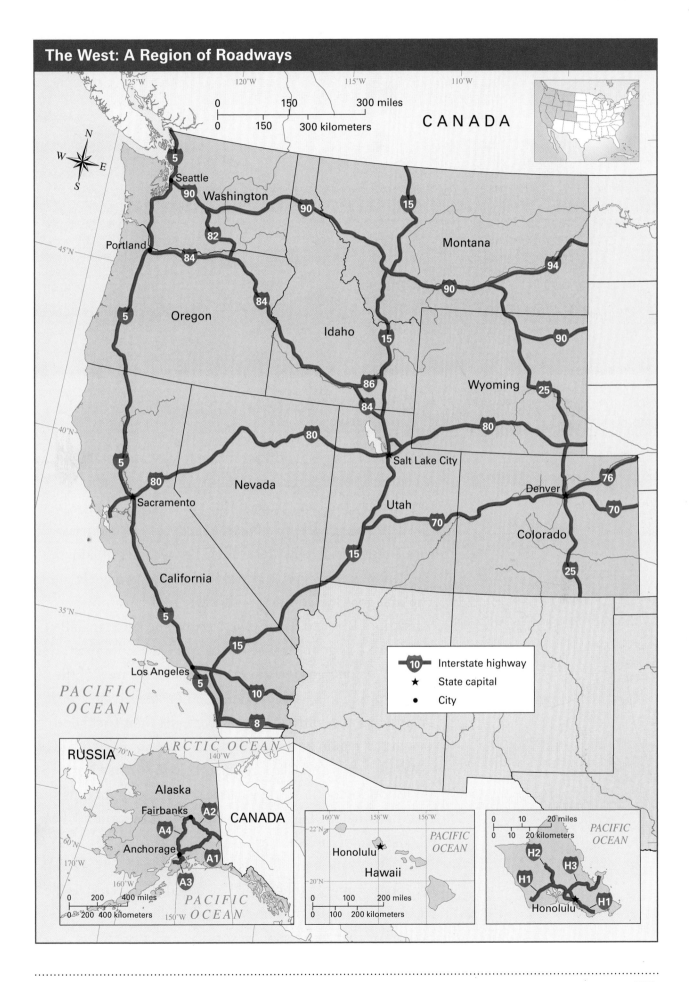

CANADA

0   150   300 miles
0   150   300 kilometers

Seattle
Washington
90

82
Portland
84
45°N

Oregon
84

5

Idaho
15

86
84
40°N

80

Nevada
Salt Lake City
5

80
Sacramento
Utah

California
70

15

35°N

Los Angeles
5

10
PACIFIC
OCEAN
8

Montana

94
90

Wyoming
90

25

80

Denver
76
70
Colorado

25

Interstate highway
State capital
City
10

ARCTIC OCEAN
RUSSIA   70°N
140°W

Alaska
Fairbanks   A2
A4
CANADA
Anchorage
A1
170°W
160°W
A3
150°W   PACIFIC
OCEAN

0   200   400 miles
0   200   400 kilometers

160°W   158°W   156°W
22°N   PACIFIC
OCEAN
Honolulu
Hawaii
20°N

0   100   200 miles
0   100   200 kilometers

0   10   20 miles
0   10   20 kilometers
PACIFIC
OCEAN

H2
H3
H1
Honolulu
H1

The Lewis and Clark National Historic Trail follows the path of the explorers and their historic trip. This old cabin lies along the Trail.

pass a route across the mountains

expedition a journey with a purpose

1. Lolo Pass, Montana: A Stop on the Lewis and Clark Trail

Our first stop is Lolo Pass in the Rocky Mountains. A **pass** is a route across mountains. In 1805, a group of 33 very hungry travelers crossed this pass.

The travelers were part of an **expedition,** or a journey with a purpose, led by Meriwether Lewis and William Clark. The Lewis and Clark expedition had two goals. The first goal was to find an all-water route from the Mississippi River to the Pacific Ocean. The travelers failed to achieve this goal because such a route does not exist.

Their second goal was to explore the lands west of the Mississippi. This goal Lewis and Clark achieved very well. Their maps and journals gave Americans their first good look at the region we now call the West.

When Lewis and Clark reached Lolo Pass, they were almost out of food. All they had left was a soup mix that everybody hated. The men survived by eating candles, bear oil, and two of their horses.

Today, people come to this part of Montana to hike and fish. Some come to follow the Lewis and Clark Trail to the Pacific. Luckily for these travelers, they don't have to eat candles or that awful soup to survive.

2. Wyoming's Yellowstone National Park

Lewis and Clark saw a lot of sights on their expedition, but they missed the **geysers** of Yellowstone National Park. A geyser is a spring that shoots hot water and steam into the air.

Geysers are like "nature's teakettles." Water is heated deep inside the Earth. When the water gets hot enough, it hisses and boils just like a teakettle on a stove. What happens when this boiling water reaches the Earth's surface? It shoots into the air.

There are about 10,000 hot springs, mud volcanoes, steam vents, and geysers in Yellowstone. A geyser named Old Faithful erupts in a cloud of steam about every 90 minutes.

Fur trappers were some of the first Americans to see Yellowstone. They told stories of steaming springs and erupting geysers. Later on, a photographer took pictures of the geysers. People were impressed with the photographs. Many people wanted to protect the geysers and the beautiful land around them from development. In 1872, the U.S. government created Yellowstone National Park to do just that. It was the first national park in the world.

Only 300 people visited Yellowstone the year it became a park. But today, the park is very popular and more than 3 million people come to Wyoming to visit Yellowstone each year. Visitors enjoy the beauty of Yellowstone's mountains and meadows.

geyser a spring that throws jets of heated water and steam into the air

Yellowstone National Park was created to protect the geysers, like Old Faithful, and land from development. This was the birth of the U.S. national park system.

Leadville, Colorado, was once a booming mining town. This wooden entrance leads to a mine under a hillside.

3. Leadville, Colorado: The West's Richest Silver Mining Town

Welcome to historic Leadville, Colorado. Look ahead and you'll see the entrance to an old mine.

Leadville sits high in the Rocky Mountains, and at nearly 10,200 feet, it is one of our country's highest cities. In the past, it was also the West's wildest and richest silver mining town.

Miners first came to this area looking for gold. They found some. Soon, however, gold became harder to find. In the 1870s, people began to take a closer look at that pesky sand that filled the area. Guess what they found? The sand was rich in both lead and silver!

The discovery of silver brought good times to Leadville. The city grew rapidly as miners flocked to the area. Then, in 1893, the silver boom ended. For a time, it looked as though Leadville would become an empty ghost town.

But Leadville was lucky because other valuable minerals were found in this area. One is molybdenum, a metal used to make high-strength steel. The town survived.

Today, Leadville is a tourist center. Some people come to learn about the history of this rich mining area. Others come to ski in winter or fish and hike in summer.

4. Sunny Southern California's Movie Industry

Watch your step! Look down at your feet and you will see stars set into the sidewalk. We are walking down Hollywood Boulevard. On this street, special movie, television, and music stars are honored with a star and their names placed in the sidewalk. We're in Los Angeles, California, and Hollywood Boulevard is one of the most famous streets in the world.

Moviemaking is a giant industry in Southern California. America's first movies were made in the Northeast. But moviemakers needed sunny days to film outdoors, and the Northeast is often cloudy and rainy. A few moviemakers found the sunshine they needed in Southern California. Others soon followed.

Today, thousands of people in Southern California work in the movie industry as writers, actors, set designers, and directors. Many more people work in jobs that help the movie industry. Some of these workers make costumes and equipment. Other workers provide important services such as transportation, food, and construction.

Each year, millions of tourists visit Southern California and enjoy its warm, sunny weather. Many of these tourists tour the movie studios, hoping to bump into a movie star!

Movie-making is a major industry in Southern California. Directors, actors, and camera operators are just some of the workers needed to make a movie.

5. California's Central Valley: America's Salad Bowl

Do you snack on raisins? Spread strawberry jam on your toast? Look around you. Those foods probably came from California's Central Valley.

The Central Valley is shaped like a long bathtub. The sides are formed by mountain ranges and the bottom is covered with deep, rich soil. Summers here are long and warm.

Does this sound like a good place to farm? It is, but there is a problem. Almost no rain falls during the growing season.

California has tried to solve this problem by building dams on rivers that flow down from the mountains. In winter, water collects behind the dams. In the summer, farmers use this water to irrigate crops.

Irrigation turned the Central Valley into what people call "America's salad bowl." Farmers here raise more than 250 crops, many of them fruits and vegetables. You probably eat some of them every day.

The Central Valley is also important for the development of farming **technology**. Technology is the use of tools and ideas to meet people's needs. Scientists here have invented many machines to help farmers pick their crops. One is a tomato-picking machine. This technology must be gentle so it won't crush the tomatoes.

technology the use of tools and ideas to meet people's needs

Two major industries of the California Central Valley are farming and the development of farming technology. Here, farmers use a machine to sort many tomatoes at one time.

6. The Columbia River Gorge National Scenic Area

We have reached the Columbia River Gorge National Scenic Area. A **gorge** is a deep, narrow valley with steep walls. The Columbia River cut this beautiful gorge out of rock.

The Columbia River begins in the Rocky Mountains in Canada. It flows 1,200 miles south and west into the Pacific Ocean. For part of its journey, the river forms the boundary between the states of Washington and Oregon.

The Columbia looks lazy here, but don't let that fool you. This is one hardworking river. Dams on the river make a lot of electricity that is used by businesses and homes. And farmers use water from the river to irrigate crops. Columbia River waters irrigate more than 5 million acres of land.

Farmers and businesspeople use the river for transportation. Many goods travel on the Columbia to shipping centers. It is one of the most traveled rivers in the country.

Putting the river to work has been good for people. Both Oregon and Washington are growing rapidly. But the use of the river has been bad for fish—especially salmon.

Since 1850, the number of salmon in the Columbia River has dropped sharply. Do you know why? You'll find out during our stop at the gorge.

The Columbia River created a beautiful gorge with steep valley walls. The river is a source of transportation and electrical power for the people of Oregon and Washington.

gorge a deep, narrow valley

The salmon population has been declining in the Columbia River since the mid-1800s.

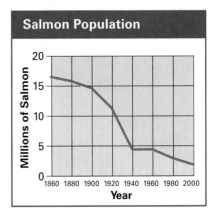

Salmon Population

The forests of Washington brought lumberjacks to the state. Demand for lumber and paper grew a wood products industry.

7. Forests of Tacoma, Washington

Welcome to Tacoma, Washington. Tacoma was founded 150 years ago as a logging town. Back then, vast forests attracted loggers and lumbermen to this region. A wood products industry quickly grew that produced lumber, cardboard, and paper. Most of these products that were used in our country came from the West.

To get lumber, you have to cut down trees. By 1880, people feared the timber companies would destroy all the forests. The U.S. government stepped in. An 1891 law set aside public land to preserve the forests in the West. These lands are called national forests.

What's the difference between a national park and a national forest? National parks preserve the land. The Forest Service manages our national forests. This can include a limited amount of activities like logging, grazing, and mining.

Together, timber companies and the government managed forests with protection in mind. As old trees were cut, new trees were planted.

The wood products industry is still important to Washington and Tacoma. And people still come to Washington because of its forests. Now they also come to enjoy the protected evergreen trees. They hike, camp, ski, and learn about nature.

Next up: Alaska! We will need to fly to this stop.

8. Anchorage, Alaska: Starting Point of the Iditarod Trail

We are in Anchorage, Alaska. Alaska is by far the largest of the 50 states, yet it has one of the lowest populations of any state. Can you guess why?

One reason is its chilly climate. Alaska is farther from the equator than any other state. This makes parts of Alaska very cold.

People have been attracted to Alaska by its resources. In 1898, gold was discovered near the town of Nome. Within two years, Nome grew to more than 20,000 people. Another rush of people came in the 1960s, when oil was discovered in northern Alaska.

The Iditarod Trail in Alaska runs between Anchorage and Nome. Mushers and their dogsled teams race this trail every year.

Today, many people come to Alaska to enjoy its open spaces and outdoor activities. A favorite sport here is dogsled racing. Alaskans used to depend on dogsleds to get around in winter. Now, they use airplanes, snowmobiles, and cars.

The most famous dogsled race is the Iditarod Trail Sled Dog Race, held each year in March. The Iditarod Trail begins right here in Anchorage and ends more than 1,000 miles away in Nome. Many teams of dogs and their mushers, or drivers, cover that distance in an amazing 9 to 12 days. No wonder Alaskans call this event the "Last Great Race on Earth."

The state of Hawaii is a series of separate islands easily seen from an airplane.

9. Honolulu, Hawaii: A Tourist Paradise

Step out of the airplane into the warm sunshine. You have just flown from our country's coldest state to one of its warmest. Hawaii lies closer to the equator than any other U.S. state. Its climate is sunny and warm all year round.

Look at beautiful Waikiki Beach in Honolulu, Hawaii. I grew up near here. My father gave me my first surfing lesson at Waikiki. Maybe I'll have a chance to teach you how to surf here.

Today, tourists from all over the world enjoy this sunny beach. Tourism is Hawaii's most important industry, but it wasn't always such a big deal.

A hundred years ago, the main industry on the Hawaiian Islands was raising sugarcane. Hawaii's sugar planters needed lots of workers for their plantations. Those workers came from China, Japan, the Philippines, Portugal, and other countries.

My great-great-grandparents came to Hawaii from Japan around 1890. They planned to work in the sugar fields for a few years and then return home. But they liked Hawaii and decided to stay.

Thousands of tourists enjoy swimming, surfing, and sailing at Waikiki Beach each year. Tourism is Hawaii's number one industry.

My grandfather remembers when jet airplanes began flying to Hawaii in the late 1950s. Before then, you had to arrive by ship. Airplanes made it easier and faster for tourists to come to Hawaii. Today, many jobs in Hawaii are related to tourism. So we are very happy that you are visiting our islands.

A hundred years ago, growing sugarcane was the main industry of the Hawaiian Islands. Sugarcane is still grown today.

Lesson Summary

What an awesome tour! We began high in the Rocky Mountains and ended up on Waikiki Beach. Along the way, we saw eight states.

Remember the questions I asked when we began: What first attracted people to the West? And why are people still coming here?

People first came to the West in search of adventure, opportunity, and sunshine. The West had beautiful places to explore. It had valuable natural resources, such as gold, silver, oil, and lumber. And, it had a climate that attracted farmers and moviemakers.

People still come to the West for adventure, opportunity, and sunshine. The adventures have changed. We now hike and ski in the region where Lewis and Clark once almost starved. The opportunities have changed, too. Today, there are many jobs in the tourism and entertainment industries.

I hope you had fun in the sun on our trip. Aloha!

Nominate Your State

We are all proud of our states. Each state has unique places to visit and special events. What is special about your state? What reasons can you give to help your state win a contest for the Best State in the Nation?

Start by learning about the most popular tourist attractions in the state. These are the places where visitors like to go. There are many Web sites and books with this information. For example, if you live in Kentucky, there is a Web site at www.KentuckyTourism.com. No matter what you are interested in, there's a place for you! There are Mammoth Cave National Park, the Louisville Slugger Museum and Factory, the Abraham Lincoln Birthplace National Historic Park, and the Muhammad Ali Center. Most tourist places have a Web site that is set up to tell you things to do and see and places to eat and stay.

Read about your state's tourist spots. Take notes about the features that excite you. If you want opinions about a place, you can look on travel-advice Web sites. These give opinions from people who have visited the places. Remember that one person may complain about a tourist attraction and another may call the same place "super fun."

Find photos of your favorite tourist spots. Paste them into a digital presentation document, or print and paste them on a blank poster.

Abraham Lincoln was born in Kentucky. A model of his family's log cabin is inside this building at the Abraham Lincoln Birthplace National Historic Park.

Kentucky State Symbols

Flag

Bird: Cardinal

Horse: Thoroughbred

Flower: Goldenrod

Celebrations and Symbols

Now find sources that talk about special celebrations in your state. In Kentucky, you might learn about a Daniel Boone Festival by searching for its Web site on the Internet. The Web site has separate pages that describe the festival's date, events, history, and location.

What special celebrations are in your state? Add photos and information about them to your presentation.

Finally, find the symbols of your state. Symbols are state birds, flowers, and other state favorites. An encyclopedia is a good source for this information. Look up the state and you will likely find pictures of the state symbols. Your state's Web site may also have this information. Once you find them, print or draw pictures of your state symbols.

Now make a presentation to your classmates about why your state deserves to be named Best State in the Nation. Include information and pictures of fun and interesting tourist spots and celebrations. Be sure to also highlight your state's symbols.

Here are some of the state symbols of Kentucky.

Exploring the Pacific Crest Trail

At one end is the Mexican border and at the other end is Canada. In between stretches the Pacific Crest Trail. The trail rambles across deserts, over mountains, and along lakeshores. What can this trail teach us about the West?

The Pacific Crest Trail runs from Mexico to Canada. The trail preserves some of the most beautiful wild areas in the western states.

In the 1930s, Clinton C. Clarke began to support an idea: building a hiking trail from Mexico to Canada. Its path would follow the Pacific Crest, a ridge of mountains running through California, Oregon, and Washington. Clarke wanted to preserve some of the beautiful wild areas of the West and help people enjoy the outdoors.

Making Clarke's idea happen was difficult. Some parts of the trail were already in place, but much of it was little more than a line on a map. The line showed the basic direction the trail would follow. But someone needed to walk and mark the trail Clarke had mapped.

The person chosen for that job was a young man named Warren Rogers. As a child, Rogers had gotten a terrible disease called polio that had harmed his legs. Though he walked with a limp, Rogers still loved hiking and climbing.

In 1935, Clarke organized hikers into teams. For the next four summers, Rogers led the teams in exploring different parts of the trail. The teams took notes on what they found, and they mapped a good route for the trail.

Rogers reached the end of the route in 1938, but it took decades of work before the trail itself was fully built. Not until 1993 did workers finally complete the Pacific Crest Trail.

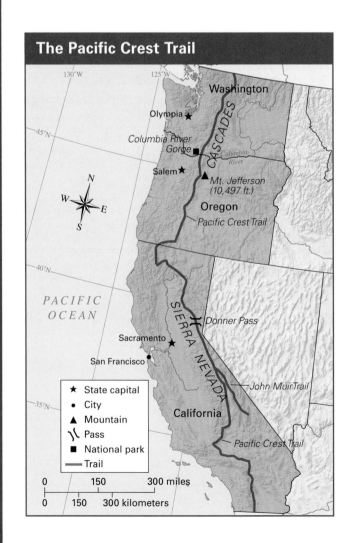

The Pacific Crest Trail

Hikers face challenging terrain at many places along the Pacific Crest Trail. Even in summer, hikers can find snow and ice.

Walking the Trail

Let's hike the Pacific Crest Trail. We will need to start in the spring and end in the fall because climbing the trail's mountains in the winter is too dangerous. We will also need to move quickly. To finish our hike we must cover about 15 miles each day.

The trail in Southern California is hot and dry, and winds through desert-like areas and over small mountains. Watch out for rattlesnakes!

The Sierra Nevada of central California is breathtaking. We are hiking between 8,000 and 13,000 feet above sea level. Brrrr! You usually find snow and ice here—even in midsummer. This stretch of trail is very wild. We might hike for 200 miles without crossing a road. Look out for coyotes, deer, and bears!

The Cascade Range will take us through Northern California, Oregon, and into Washington. These mountains were made by volcanoes. The forests here are thick and lush. The trail passes by many lakes and streams. We cross from Oregon to Washington through the beautiful Columbia River Gorge.

Get out your rain gear now because the Northern Cascades have very rainy weather. The wet climate helps rich forests grow. It also helps huckleberry bushes grow. If the time is right, we can feast on berries—a tasty end to our trip.

The Pacific Crest Trail offers hikers a dramatic view of the Cascade Range. Lewis and Clark named this peak Mount Jefferson to honor their president.

History Along the Trail

Hikers on the Pacific Crest Trail see beautiful scenery, but they also take a historical journey. The trail passes a number of key places in the history of the West.

Mount Jefferson, in the Cascades of Oregon, honors President Thomas Jefferson. In the early 1800s, it was Jefferson who picked Meriwether Lewis and William Clark to explore the nation's new territory in the West. Jefferson had purchased this land, called the Louisiana Territory, from France. Lewis and Clark mapped much of the territory, including areas along the Pacific Crest. On their trip, they named a mountain after the president.

High in the Sierra Nevada, the Pacific Crest Trail climbs through the Donner Pass. Here, in 1846, a group of settlers tried to cross the mountains as they moved west. Snowstorms forced them to spend a terrible winter in the mountains, and many of them died. The famous story of the Donner party reminds us of the challenges faced by early settlers of the West.

The trail also passes through gold country. In 1848, a man named James Marshall found gold in California. Thousands of gold-seekers flocked there to get rich. The gold rush changed the West forever. It brought new people and ideas to the region. New settlers built towns into great cities such as San Francisco and Sacramento. These settlers helped create the modern states we know today.

Walking the John Muir Trail

A special path runs near the Pacific Crest Trail in the Sierra Nevada. It is known as the John Muir Trail.

John Muir lived in the late 1800s and early 1900s. He deeply loved the outdoors and believed strongly in protecting the nation's great natural wonders. Muir was a leader of the effort to create our national parks. "Wildness," he said, "is a necessity."

Muir traveled widely. He explored parts of the United States—and beyond. But his favorite place on Earth was the Sierra Nevada, which he called the "range of light." Muir said that it was "the most divinely beautiful of all the mountain chains I have ever seen."

The John Muir Trail gives hikers a chance to experience the wilderness as John Muir did. The land around the trail looks very much as it did in the past. Hikers on this isolated trail catch a glimpse into the history of the West. They get to see the natural wonders that make this part of our country so special. ◆

John Muir believed in protecting the wilderness.

Hikers on the John Muir Trail see the Sierra Nevada much as Muir did. These mountains were one of his favorite places on Earth.

Cities of the West

What attracts people to the cities of the West?

Introduction

"Go west, young man, and grow up with the country!" An American author named Horace Greeley wrote these words. He hoped that they would inspire people to leave the big cities of the East and move westward. By the 1850s, these words were heard all over the United States.

Americans have been following this advice ever since. Americans have long viewed the West as a place to start new lives. In the 1800s, the West's wide-open spaces attracted farmers, miners, and ranchers. These pioneers loaded up their belongings in covered wagons and made the long trek west. A pioneer is someone who is among the first people to settle a region. Pioneers also went west by ship and, later, on the new transcontinental railroads. The pioneers of the West settled in the mountain ranges, near the ocean's shore, in fertile valleys, and in the vast desert. Today, the West still has mines, ranches, and lots of land. It also has lively cities that draw people from around the world.

In this lesson, you will learn about seven of these western cities. In the past, these cities were destinations or stopovers for people moving west. This caused the cities to grow and change. Today, they continue to grow. For each one, you will read about its geography, history, population, economy, and how its residents have fun. As you read, ask yourself, "What is attracting people to the West today?"

Social Studies Vocabulary

mint

Mormon

oasis

◀ Seattle, Washington, is just one of many cities attracting people to the West.

 Economics   Geography   History

Denver is one of the nation's fastest-growing cities. This capital city began as a mining town.

mint a factory where the government makes coins

1. Denver, Colorado

Denver, the capital city of Colorado, is home to a U.S. mint. A **mint** is a factory where the government makes coins such as pennies, nickels, dimes, and quarters. Back in the 1860s, miners brought their gold here. Their nuggets were melted and turned into valuable gold bars. The Mint began producing gold and silver coins in 1906. Today, the mint in Denver makes about 50 million coins every day!

Geography

Denver sits where the Great Plains meet the Rocky Mountains. It is known as the "Mile-High City." If you stand on the 13th step of the state capitol building, you'll be exactly 5,280 feet, or one mile, above sea level.

Denver has a dry, sunny climate. The city gets snow in the winter. To see how Denver's climate compares with those of other cities in the West, look at the table at the end of the lesson.

History

Denver was founded in 1858 after people discovered gold in the area. During World War II, many U.S. government offices moved to Denver. When the war ended, many of these workers decided to stay.

Population

In 2013, almost 650,000 people lived in Denver. To see how Denver's population compares with those of some other cities in the West, look at the table at the end of the lesson.

The city's population is becoming more diverse. About one-half of Denver's residents are white. More than one-third are Latino. About one-tenth of the population is African American.

Economy

Many people in Denver work for the U.S. government. Many large companies are also located in Denver.

Ways to Have Fun

Denver offers lots of opportunities to have fun. The city has more than 200 parks with trails for cycling, running, and walking. Denver even has a park where a herd of bison lives.

Denver is the center of professional sports in the Rocky Mountain region. The city's major league teams include the Denver Broncos (football), the Colorado Rockies (baseball), the Denver Nuggets (basketball), and the Colorado Avalanche (ice hockey). Every January, Denver hosts a national cattle show and rodeo.

Denver lies in the Rocky Mountains of Colorado.

Rodeo fans watch cowboys and cowgirls compete in events. These include bronco riding, calf roping, and steer wrestling.

The Wasatch Mountains tower over Salt Lake City. Mormon settlers used irrigation to bring water to this desert-like area.

Mormon a member of the Church of Jesus Christ of Latter-day Saints

2. Salt Lake City, Utah

If you stand in the center of downtown Salt Lake City, Utah, you will be in Temple Square. In front of you will be a huge white building, the Mormon Temple. Temple Square has always been the heart of Salt Lake City. The city was started by a group of people called **Mormons**. Mormons are members of the Church of Jesus Christ of Latter-day Saints. The Mormons built the city around their temple. The temple itself took 40 years to build.

Geography

Salt Lake City is in the north-central part of Utah. It is located in a high valley between the Wasatch Mountains and the Great Salt Lake Desert.

The climate in Salt Lake City is dry. The city has warm summers and some snow in the winter. (See the table at the end of the lesson.)

History

Mormons founded Salt Lake City in 1847. They wanted a place where they could freely practice their religion. When they first arrived at the site of the city, it was a desert-like area. The Mormons used irrigation to bring water to the dry valley. They turned the desert into farmland.

In the 1880s, Salt Lake City's population more than doubled because of nearby mining. The city grew again during World War II. The government needed metal for ships and planes. So more people came to work in the mines. After the war ended, many wartime workers stayed in the Salt Lake City area.

Population

In 2013, more than 190,000 people lived in Salt Lake City. (See the table at the end of the lesson.) If you include the nearby towns, more than 1 million people live in the area.

Salt Lake City's population was once almost entirely white. But it has become more diverse. Whites make up almost seven-tenths of the city's population. Latinos are the second largest group, at more than two-tenths of the population. African Americans, American Indians, Asian Americans, and Pacific Islanders make up the rest of the population.

Economy

Mining is one of Salt Lake City's most important industries. Copper, silver, lead, zinc, coal, and iron ore are all mined nearby.

Ways to Have Fun

The Wasatch Mountains tower over Salt Lake City. They are a wonderful place for hiking and skiing. Because of this, Salt Lake City was chosen as the site of the 2002 Winter Olympics. The city also has many parks.

Salt Lake City has two major league sports teams, the Utah Jazz (basketball) and Real Salt Lake (soccer).

Salt Lake City, Utah

Salt Lake City is the capital of Utah.

People of all ages enjoy skiing in the Wasatch Mountains. Hiking in these mountains is popular during the summer months.

Boise was founded as a mining town. Today the electronic industry brings people to this Idaho city.

3. Boise, Idaho

The summer is a fun time to visit Boise, Idaho. The weather is usually warm then. Some people start their day with an early-morning hot-air balloon ride. Then they might go fishing, hiking, or rafting down a nearby river.

People also walk or bike along the river that runs right through Boise. You can even float down the river in an inner tube or raft. And many families gather downtown once a week. There, people listen to live music, have picnics, and relax.

Geography

Boise is located on the Boise River in southwestern Idaho. It has a dry, sunny climate, with some snow in the winter. (See the table at the end of the lesson.)

History

Boise was founded in 1863, following the discovery of gold in the region. The U.S. government built a fort near the Boise River. The city arose next to the fort.

Boise grew rapidly as miners rushed to the goldfields. Many of the miners were immigrants from China. In 1925, the Union Pacific Railroad ran its main line through Boise. This brought even more people to the city. Boise continued to grow in the 1980s, when new electronics factories created more jobs.

Population

Between 1990 and 2013, Boise's population grew even more, from about 125,000 people to more than 214,000. (See the table at the end of the lesson.) If you include nearby towns, more than 600,000 people live in the Boise area.

Almost nine-tenths of Boise's people are white. The next largest group is Latinos. They make up close to one-tenth of the population. The rest of Boise's population includes Asian Americans, African Americans, and American Indians.

Economy

Boise provides banking, shopping, and health services for many people. Companies that make computer chips and wood and paper products are also important in Boise.

Ways to Have Fun

Many people in Boise enjoy the outdoors. There are lots of paths for walking, bicycling, skating, and jogging. In a set of parks called the Greenbelt, people picnic, play sports, watch birds, and listen to concerts. Places for skiing and whitewater rafting are within an easy drive of the city.

Sports fans in Boise can root for the city's minor league baseball and ice hockey teams.

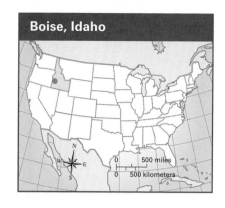

Boise is Idaho's state capital.

Visitors and residents enjoy many recreational activities in Boise. Fly-fishing is a popular sport.

Seattle is a bay city. Homes, tourist attractions, businesses, and the shipping industry compete for waterfront land.

4. Seattle, Washington

The best place to see Seattle, Washington, is from the top of the city's most famous landmark, the Space Needle. An elevator lifts you 52 stories above the ground. From there, you can look out at Seattle's skyscrapers and the ferryboats crossing Elliott Bay.

The Space Needle was built for the 1962 World's Fair. Even today, it looks like something out of the future.

Geography

Seattle is in the northwestern corner of the United States, about 100 miles south of the border with Canada. The city lies next to a large bay of the Pacific Ocean. Mountains surround it.

Seattle has a mild, rainy climate. The city is often cloudy or foggy. (See the table at the end of the lesson.)

History

Seattle was founded in 1851 by a small group of settlers. The city grew rapidly in the late 1800s with the growth of the timber industry. The discovery of gold in the Yukon Territory of Canada in 1896 transformed the city. Miners poured into Seattle on their way to the goldfields. When the gold rush ended, many of them settled in the city.

Population

In 2013, more than 650,000 people lived in Seattle. (See the table at the end of the lesson.) More than 3.5 million people live in the surrounding area. This is one of the fastest-growing areas in the United States.

Whites make up just over two-thirds of Seattle's population. The next largest groups are Asian Americans (more than one-tenth of the population), African Americans (about one-tenth), and Latinos (less than one-tenth).

Economy

Seattle is an important U.S. shipping port. From the city's ports, many goods are traded with Japan and the rest of Asia. Fishing and the lumber industry are also important to the economy of Seattle.

For many years, most jobs in Seattle were at a company that made airplanes. Today, many people work in the computer industry.

Ways to Have Fun

Seattle has more than 5,000 acres of public land. People enjoy miles of trails on which they can cycle, skate, jog, and walk. The nearby mountains offer excellent skiing, climbing, and hiking. Mount Rainier is a favorite hiking destination. And the area's many lakes make boating and fishing popular pastimes.

Seattle has three major league sports teams. They are the Mariners (baseball), the Seahawks (football), and the Sounders (soccer).

Seattle, Washington

Seattle is Washington's largest city.

Miles of paved trails make Seattle a great city for outdoor activities. On clear days, Mount Rainier is a spectacular sight.

The Willamette River winds through Portland. Goods going to California during the Gold Rush traveled via ships on the river.

5. Portland, Oregon

In spring, roses bloom in gardens all over the city of Portland, Oregon. In fact, one of Portland's biggest attractions is the International Rose Test Garden. Here you can see 10,000 rosebushes and more than 500 varieties of roses in all colors. Some people call Portland the "City of Roses."

Geography

Portland sits on the banks of the Willamette River, in northwestern Oregon. The city lies in a fertile valley between the Coast and Cascade mountain ranges.

Portland has a mild climate, with heavy rains in the late fall and winter. (See the table at the end of the lesson.)

History

Portland got its start in 1845. Settlers arrived by the thousands over the Oregon Trail. During the California gold rush, Portland grew rapidly. Settlers sold lumber and grain to miners and their families in California.

Portland continued to grow at a steady pace. In 1905, a world's fair brought 3 million visitors to the city. Many of them decided to stay. In the 1930s, dams on the Columbia and Willamette rivers provided cheap electricity. This brought a number of industries to Portland. During World War II, thousands of workers arrived in the city to build ships for the United States Navy.

Population

In 2013, Portland's population was more than 600,000 people. (See the table at the end of the lesson.) More than 2 million people live in the city and its surrounding areas.

About three-fourths of Portland's residents are white. Most of the rest of the population is divided equally among Latinos, African Americans, and Asian Americans.

Economy

People in Portland work for many different kinds of companies. Some companies make paper. Others make clothing and shoes. Portland also has new businesses, such as computer software companies. The city's busy harbor has been home to shipping companies for many years.

Ways to Have Fun

Portland has many parks and open spaces. Forest Park covers nearly 5,000 acres. It is one of the largest natural areas inside a U.S. city. Mount Hood, located less than 50 miles away from Portland, is a great place for skiing and other winter sports. Portland has two major league sports teams, the Portland Trail Blazers (basketball) and Timbers (soccer).

Portland, Oregon

Portland lies on the border separating Oregon and Washington.

People of all ages enjoy walking and hiking in Portland's many parks. From Mount Tabor Park, you can see the downtown center.

San Jose is the largest city in Northern California. It has more than 2,000 miles of streets.

6. San Jose, California

People often call San Jose, California, the "Capital of Silicon Valley." Silicon Valley is a nickname for the area between the cities of San Jose and San Francisco. Silicon is a material used to make computers. The first computer companies began in Silicon Valley in the 1970s.

Geography

San Jose lies near the southern tip of San Francisco Bay. The city has a mild to warm climate. (See the table at the end of the lesson.)

History

Spanish settlers founded San Jose in 1777. For many years, the area was home to vineyards and orchards. World War II brought new businesses and people to the city. By 1980, the city had grown to almost ten times the size it was in 1950.

Population

San Jose's population was almost 1 million by the year 2013. (See the table at the end of the lesson.)

The population is very diverse. About one-third of the people are white, one-third are Latinos, and one-third are Asian Americans. African Americans and American Indians also live in San Jose.

Economy

The San Jose region is famous for its technology companies. Silicon Valley is home to some of the most successful technology companies in the world. Thousands of computer and engineering students attend San Jose State University and other area schools. Many of them work in San Jose's technology companies after graduation.

Ways to Have Fun

San Jose has about 75 parks and playgrounds. The largest park is Alum Rock Park. It has miles of trails for hiking and horseback riding. Fans of thrill rides can go to amusement parks in nearby Santa Clara and Santa Cruz.

San Jose has two major league sports teams, the Sharks (ice hockey) and the Earthquakes (soccer).

San Jose, California

San Jose is a center of technology in California.

Many people in San Jose work in the technology field. San Jose is part of California's Silicon Valley.

Las Vegas is the largest city in Nevada. Its hotels rise above the desert landscape.

7. Las Vegas, Nevada

If you drive into Las Vegas, Nevada, you will see a sign that reads, "Welcome to Fabulous Las Vegas, Nevada." And fabulous is certainly the word for this city of bright lights and hotels. All around, colorful signs advertise music, comedy, and magic shows. It's no wonder many people call Las Vegas the "Entertainment Capital of the World."

Geography

Las Vegas is near the southern tip of Nevada. It sits in a desert valley surrounded by mountains.

Las Vegas has a dry climate. Winters are warm, and summers are hot. (See table at the end of the lesson.)

History

Las Vegas lies in one of the few places in a desert that has water and trees. Such a place is called an **oasis**. American Indian tribes roamed the area thousands of years ago. In the late 1820s, Spanish explorers came upon the oasis. Settlers soon followed.

oasis a place in the desert that has water and trees

Las Vegas remained a small town until the 1930s. Then construction began on the nearby Hoover Dam. The dam project created thousands of new jobs. Many of the workers stayed to settle in Las Vegas.

After World War II, Las Vegas grew rapidly as many hotels were built. Today, almost 40 million visitors come to Las Vegas every year.

Las Vegas, Nevada

Las Vegas sits on the southern tip of Nevada.

Population

In 2013, more than 600,000 people lived in Las Vegas. (See the table at the end of the lesson.) Half of the city's people are white. The next largest group is Latinos, who make up one-third of the population. African Americans are more than one-tenth of the population, and Asian Americans are less than one-tenth.

Economy

Tourism is a big business in Las Vegas. The city's restaurants, hotels, and shops provide thousands of jobs. There is also great demand for home building and landscaping.

Ways to Have Fun

Las Vegas is famous for its shows. Many popular singers, dancers, and comics perform there. Championship boxing matches are often held in the city.

People in Las Vegas also enjoy outdoor activities. They can hike and camp. They can fish and boat on nearby lakes. And the Grand Canyon is only a five-hour drive from the city.

The entertainment industry draws tourists and residents alike to Las Vegas. The building of new hotels and other structures creates many construction jobs.

8. Research for More Information

Did you notice as you read this lesson that the information about each city was organized the same way? You read about the geography, history, population, economy, and different ways to have fun in each city. This organization makes it easy for you to find information, and then compare and contrast the cities. For example, in the geography subsections, you read about each city's climate. Five of the cities have dry climates and two have wet ones. But what if you want to know more? How would you find specific temperatures for each city? You can research!

Perhaps you want to visit a city in the spring, but you don't like the cold. Think of a question that you can answer with research, such as: What city is warmest in April? Once you know your question, you can pick the best reference material for finding the answer. To get weather information, you can use almanacs, weather databases, city Web sites, and some atlases.

When you find the information, take notes from the resource in your own words. It helps to organize the information using a graphic organizer: table, outline, concept map, or timeline. Besides noting what you learn, write or copy the name of the source and page number or URL so you can find it again. Web sites change. So it is also good to save the Web page or take a picture of it for later use. Last, create a source list or bibliography.

Denver has warm summers and cold winters. You can research to find specific temperatures for the city.

City Temperatures and Populations

City	Average January Temperature	Average July Temperature	Population*
Boise	37.8°F	91.2°F	214,237
Denver	44.0°F	89.4°F	649,495
Las Vegas	58.0°F	104.2°F	603,488
Portland	47.0°F	80.6°F	609,456
Salt Lake City	37.4°F	92.6°F	191,180
San Jose	59.8°F	83.4°F	998,537
Seattle	47.2°F	75.7°F	652,405

*U.S. Census 2013 population estimates

Suppose you looked up information about the temperatures of the seven western cities. You might organize the information in a table like the one shown. The table makes it easy to compare similar information. You will not need to flip pages back and forth looking for information. Look at the table: City Temperatures and Populations. What does the data tell you? Which city has the warmest weather during the winter?

A table organizes information in a visual way. This table makes it easy to compare the temperatures and populations of the western cities.

Lesson Summary

For more than 200 years, Americans have been moving west to start new lives. Today, the West still attracts people from all around the world. Of course, they don't arrive in covered wagons. And few will start a farm or a ranch. Instead, many are settling down in the West's thriving cities.

Have you discovered what attracts newcomers to the West today? Here are some attractions:

- scenery
- climate
- diverse populations
- new businesses and industries
- recreational opportunities

To find out more about each city, you can research using a geographer's tools and sources. What do you think you might like in the cities of the West?

Outdoor Fun in Your State

You just read about fun things to do in some cities in the West. Now it's time for you to investigate fun activities in your state. Specifically, focus on this question: What are the best places for outdoor fun in your state?

Do your research in books about your state or on the Internet, and make a list of places for outdoor fun. Your list might include mountains, lakes, amusement parks, and outdoor sports games. For example, if you lived in the state of New York, you might list the Statue of Liberty, Yankee Stadium, Hunter Mountain, and Niagara Falls.

As you find places, record notes about where each place is located and fun activities to do there. You may also wish to write down interesting facts about the place you choose. Your notes might look similar to those shown here.

Pick your favorite place so that you can tell others about it and encourage them to visit it. There are many ways for you to present this information. You could give a speech, create an ad for social media, or design a photo brochure. For this lesson, you will go through the steps to prepare a Web site.

Here are one student's notes about fun places in New York.

Place	Statue of Liberty	Yankee Stadium	Hunter Mountain	Niagara Falls
Location	New York Harbor	Bronx, NY	Hunter, NY	NY/Canada border
Fun Activities	Climb 377 steps to the crown, take photos of New York City	Watch a major league baseball game	Ski, hike, zipline	Take a boat ride by the falls, see a light show at night

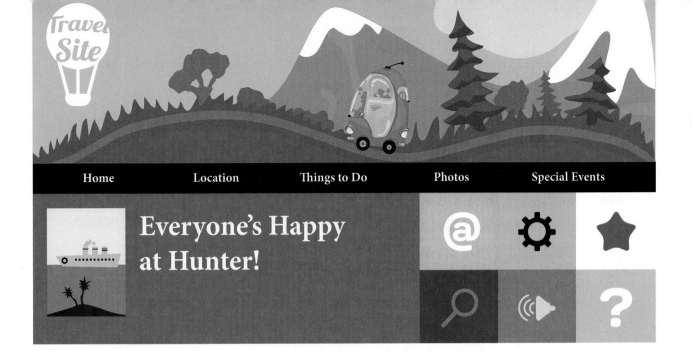

Home   Location   Things to Do   Photos   Special Events

Everyone's Happy
at Hunter!

Spread the Word!

Are you ready to plan a Web site for your favorite outdoor place? First, lay out your site by writing text and pasting photos on separate document pages. Later, you can ask for help in posting the text and photos on a real Web site.

Think of features that you like to see on a Web site. Start with the "Home Page." Find an exciting photo of the place, and write a catchy slogan. For example, a Home Page for Hunter Mountain in New York could have a photo of a skier. The slogan above the photo might be "Everyone's Happy at Hunter!"

Next, decide on the other pages to include on your site. You can show tabs to these pages at the top of your home page. You might include: "Location," "Things to Do," and "Interesting Facts." What other pages do you want to include?

Now write the information you want to include on each page. Keep your sentences simple and easy for your readers to understand. Everything you write should be in an excited tone to convince others to visit the place. Add photos to each page. If you could add music, what would it sound like?

Show your Web site plan to your teacher and classmates. Watch your classmates' presentations and talk about why your outdoor place is the best in the state. Support your opinion with strong reasons. Listen to your classmates' opinions, and see if they persuade you to change your mind.

Here's one student's Web site. What words and pictures will you use on your Web site?

Tourists at Niagara Falls love the excitement of a boat ride beside the falls.

Portland, Oregon: Green and Clean

Portland, Oregon, has always been a beautiful place. That was true when the first white settlers chose the spot in the 1840s. As the city has grown, it has found ways to add more beauty—and to help keep Earth clean. What features help make Portland a city known for being green and clean?

It is not hard to imagine why people were first drawn to the area that is now Portland. In the distance rises magnificent Mount Hood. Covered with snow year round, the great peak stands like a guard over the surrounding land. It is truly an impressive sight.

Then there are the rivers. Portland sits where the Columbia and Willamette rivers come together. These rivers add to Portland's beauty. They provided resources such as water and fish. They were a transportation route for steamers to carry supplies into, and goods out of, the city. The rivers helped make Portland an inviting place to settle.

And people did settle in Portland. After its founding, thousands of people moved in and established lives in the new town. Many came to make their living by fishing. Others came to harvest trees from the rich forests. Some came to grow crops in the surrounding area. Still others came as part of the many gold rushes in the West. For a time it was the largest settlement in the Northwest.

Portland's Washington Park offers breathtaking views of the city and Mount Hood. The area's natural resources brought early settlers to the city.

The people of Portland live in a place of natural beauty, and they work to keep it that way. Portland's many roses are a colorful example of this. These flowers earned Portland the nickname "City of Roses."

Roses have probably grown on the West Coast since before Portland was founded. Settlers brought bushes from the East. The people of Portland found that their climate and soil were perfect for growing roses.

Georgiana Pittock was a rose grower in Portland. In 1888, she started the Portland Rose Society. Its purpose was to get more people to grow and display roses. The society was the first group of its kind in the country.

The Rose Society was a success as more and more residents grew roses. By 1905, thousands of roses were planted in Portland, and there were over 200 miles of road lined with flowers. Then, in 1907, Portland held a Rose Festival that included a spectacular rose parade. Thousands of people celebrated the city's love for roses.

Portland still holds its Rose Festival every June. Over one million people come to the city to take part!

While in town, many visitors stop at the International Rose Test Garden. Since 1917, growers have been sending roses there to be observed for characteristics such as color, fragrance, and disease resistance. This magnificent garden helps the city live up to its nickname.

The International Rose Test Garden is a beautiful place in Portland for a walk or picnic. But the garden is a serious "laboratory" for growing new roses.

The people of Portland do not stop at filling their city with flowers. They have a long tradition of keeping their city green.

From its earliest days, Portland has set aside land for parks. The settlers built a bustling city, but they wanted to make sure they had natural places, too.

Including natural places in a city can be a hard task. After all, a modern city needs highways for people and businesses to use. It needs buildings and parking lots. In Portland, people have put firm limits on this.

For example, in the 1970s, a wide highway ran along Portland's riverfront, separating the city from the river. The city decided to dig it up. In its place, they put a park where people can enjoy the outdoors and the beauty of the river.

Portland has many other parks, too. In fact, more than one out of every ten acres in the city is part of a park. There are also miles and miles of trails for people to wander. Portland is proud of the many outdoor recreation opportunities it offers.

One special Portland site is a huge wilderness area called Forest Park. A million people visit this park each year, hiking on nearly 70 miles of trails. They view interesting and unusual plants and birds. The park helps people escape from the busy city life for a time.

Portland has many parks for its residents and visitors to enjoy. Waterfront Park along the Willamette River was once a wide highway.

People in Portland want to keep their city clean as well as green. They are known worldwide for their work to protect the environment.

Look at the city's miles of bike paths, for example. These paths make it easy for people to bike through all parts of the city. Portlanders ride their bikes to work, to shop, and to play, in sunshine and in rain. Since cars cause air pollution, riding bikes instead of driving helps keep the air clean. In 2012, more than 18,000 riders cycled through the city each day.

Portland is also a leader in recycling. The city, along with the rest of Oregon, was the first place to require people to pay a small fee for each beverage bottle they buy. Buyers get the money back when they return the empty bottle for recycling. Many other states now use this program.

Portland composts yard debris and most food scraps from businesses, restaurants, and homes. Compost carts are picked up once a week while garbage is only picked up every other week. This reduces the waste that goes to landfills.

Portland was the first city to take action against greenhouse gases. Many scientists think these gases may harm the environment. In 1993, Portland made a plan to cut greenhouse gases. The plan worked, and Portland now produces less greenhouse gas than it used to.

Portland is a city that believes in being green and clean. This is a big draw for people looking to visit—or live—in the Northwest. ◆

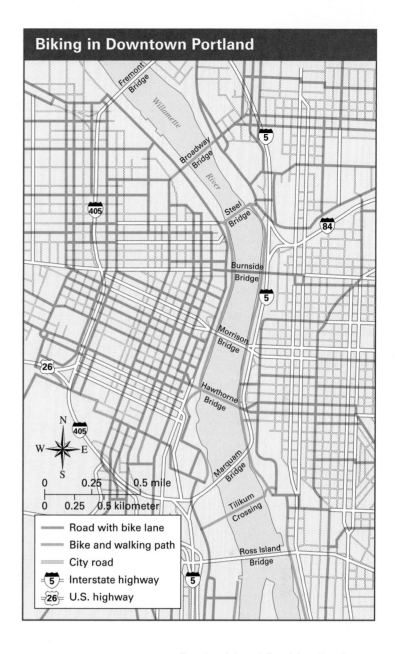

Biking in Downtown Portland

Road with bike lane
Bike and walking path
City road
Interstate highway
U.S. highway

Portland is a bike friendly city. It has miles of bike paths that make it easy for residents to get around.

The Geography of Your State

How has geography influenced life in your state?

Introduction

Suppose that you are flying in an airplane over your state. When you look down, what do you see? Do you see mountains or flat plains, a desert or a sandy coast? Are there lots of trees, lakes, and rivers? Is it cloudy, or is the sun shining brightly on your state? These features of land, water, and sky are all part of your state's physical geography.

Studying the physical geography of a place is very important. It helps us understand why and how people live in a place. Geographers may use maps, tables, graphs, and other tools to study the physical geography of a place.

What else do you see when you look out of your plane's window? You may also see cities and towns, roads and highways, bridges and dams. Geography includes the study of human features as well. Human geography explores how people have altered, or changed, their environment to make life more comfortable. Geographers use tools to study human geography, too.

Now suppose that you are a geographer. What can you find out about the physical and human geography of your state? What tools will you use to study the geography of your state? And how do you think geography has influenced life in your state? Answering these questions will help you better understand the geography in your state.

> **Social Studies Vocabulary**
>
> demographics
>
> geographic inquiry process

◄ You can see the physical and human geography of an area by looking down from an airplane. A geographer's job is to study these different features and learn how they affect life in your state.

Geography

1. Tools Geographers Use

Geographers use many tools to learn about places and the people who live there. These tools, such as maps, tables, and graphs, help organize facts and information. Physical, political, and special-purpose maps may help you discover facts about your state's geography. What could you learn about your state from a physical map or a political map? What could you discover from a special-purpose map that shows the growing seasons in different areas of your state?

You can also get interesting facts from tables and graphs. A table might give information about industries in your state. These facts might give you clues about the natural resources in your area. Or you might find a graph showing the average monthly temperatures and rainfall in your state. What could these facts tell you about how people work and play in your state?

The facts you can study about a group of people are called **demographics**. Such facts might include the average age of people in a state. They might compare the number of men to the number of women living in a state. This information often appears on tables and graphs, too.

demographics the facts you can study about a certain group of people, such as their ages, genders, or jobs

Geographers use tables and graphs to organize information. What do these tools tell you about Indiana?

Major Products of Indiana	
Manufactured Products	**Farm Product**
Transportation equipment	Corn
Metals and metal goods	Soybeans
Plastics	Hogs
Food processing	Eggs
Machinery	Dairy
	Cattle

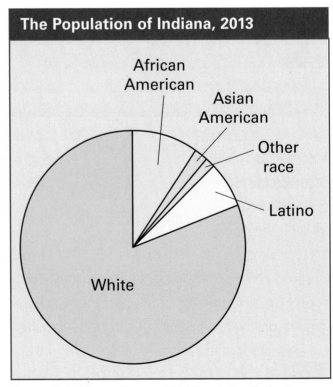

The Population of Indiana, 2013

African American

Asian American

Other race

Latino

White

Source: U.S. Census Bureau, 2013 Population Estimates

The Arch at St. Louis, Missouri, is a monument to western expansion. The Missouri and Mississippi Rivers near St. Louis were, and still are, important transportation routes.

2. Connecting Geography and History

When you study geography, you unlock lots of information. The history of a place is closely linked to its geography. The land and its features help tell the story of a place. The physical geography of a place shapes how people live and how communities grow. Think about Jamestown. This was the first permanent English settlement in America. The site that the Jamestown settlers chose caused problems. The land was swampy, and many people got sick and died. But the land and climate were good for growing tobacco. Growing this crop helped the colony survive.

Consider the Southeast's coastal plain where the edge of the Piedmont drops sharply and rivers form waterfalls. Ships navigating rivers at this point must stop at the fall line. As English settlement spread, many settlers chose this point to live. They used falling water to power mills and set up trading posts for farmers. Over time, cities were built along the fall line.

The land shaped the history of other parts of the country, too. St. Louis, Missouri, was founded near where two great rivers meet. This spot was a good departure point for western pioneers.

The history of the Southwest follows the path of the Colorado River. This waterway supported the region's first people and helped attract modern-day settlers. People still depend on the river. What is the physical geography of your state? How might the land have helped shape your state's history?

Some industries develop in unlikely places. In dry parts of Utah, sprinklers move in a circle to water fields.

3. Connecting Geography and Economics

Geography also helps us understand economics. Geography helps explain how certain industries have grown as well as how and why people work the way they do. Think about the Midwest, for example. This region is perfect for farming because the land is very flat and the soil is fertile. Rivers help farmers ship crops to market. It is no surprise that agriculture is a major industry there.

Some parts of the country are rich in resources such as coal, oil, or silver. Others have pleasant climates or scenery. In the Northeast, harbors provide access to the sea. No wonder people use these resources to make a living or that these industries help define these regions.

Geographers also study how people change the land. For example, people in Michigan built the Soo Locks to connect two of the Great Lakes. The locks allow ships to carry goods from one lake to another. Elsewhere, people built canals and constructed dams. These modifications have changed the way people live and work.

Think about the geography of your state. What natural features exist? How have people made changes to the land? What does the human geography tell you about the economy there?

4. Finding Out About the Geography of Your State

There are many ways to research the geography of your state. Try these sources of information:

Atlases and encyclopedias. An atlas is a book of maps. An encyclopedia is a book of facts about all kinds of topics. Find a map of your state in an atlas. Look up your state in an encyclopedia.

The Internet. The Internet is a fast way to find information. First, connect to the Internet on a computer. Then, type in the name of your state plus a word such as *geography* or *climate*. Read the list of Web sites that appears on the screen and click on any that sound interesting.

Libraries. Start your research in the reference section of the library. Look for books, newspaper and magazine articles, journals, and diaries about your state. Maps, drawings, and photographs might be interesting, too. Ask a librarian for help.

Chambers of commerce. Most cities and towns have an office called the chamber of commerce. You can visit yours to find brochures, maps, postcards, and books about your state's geography and attractions.

State departments of tourism. Try writing to your state's department of tourism for information or visiting its Web site on the Internet. The state department of tourism has information about your state's parks, cities, and attractions.

These students use the Internet to research the geography of their state. You can also find information at libraries as well as city or state offices.

5. Using the Geographic Inquiry Process

Knowing good sources of information can help you learn about your state. It also helps to have a process, or a set of steps, you can follow to achieve a goal. By following the **geographic inquiry process,** you can enjoy a more rewarding study of your state.

Step 1 is asking geographic questions. These are questions about what your state and its people are like. Say you live in Pennsylvania. You could ask: Where do people live in my state? Why do people live there?

Step 2 is acquiring geographic information. Once you have asked geographic questions, you need to look for information that will give you answers. Using a geographer's tools and sources of information like maps, atlases, the Internet, and libraries will help.

Step 3 is organizing geographic information. You have collected data about your state. Now you need to put it into a useful form.

Tables and maps are ways of organizing information. Suppose you found information about Pennsylvania's largest cities. You might make a table and then use your table to make a population map.

Step 4 is analyzing geographic information. The goal is to find patterns in what you have organized. Suppose you are making a map to show Pennsylvania's cities. You would see that many large ones are along waterways: rivers or Lake Erie.

geographic inquiry process a five-step process that helps answer geographic questions

How can you learn more about your state? Asking geographic questions is the first step.

Step 5 is answering geographic questions. Let's say you had asked, "Where do people live in my state?" By following Steps 1–4, you will find your answer. For Pennsylvania, you would find that many people live near waterways.

This is the end of the inquiry process. However, one answer will often lead to new questions. Next you may wonder why so many cities were built along the coast. The process of learning never ends.

Many of Pennsylvania's largest cities are on waterways. Why do you think that people want to live there?

Lesson Summary

Geography helps explain the history and economy of a place. Geographers use many tools and good sources of information to learn about a place and its people.

You can act like a geographer to study your state by following the geographic inquiry process:

1. Ask a geographic question.
2. Acquire geographic information.
3. Organize the geographic information.
4. Analyze the geographic information.
5. Answer your geographic question.

Answers to one question may lead to more questions. And the process starts over again!

Changing the Environment in Your State

What did your state look like before settlers moved in to build their homes and businesses? Was it covered with trees? Were there miles of flat land or desert? In every state, people have changed the environment. Usually this was done to create economic opportunities -- perhaps to build farms, homes, stores, or factories.

Let's look at a place in New Jersey for example. For thousands of years, the Passaic River has flowed through the northern part of the state. Early Native Americans, the Lenape, built dams on the river to create pools for trapping fish. This was an early way that people changed the environment. In the 1790s, when the United States was newly formed, businesspeople decided to use the river's power as it rushed over the Great Falls. They wanted power to run factories to make goods. This would allow Americans to stop buying goods from Britain. For the next 150 years, factories in Paterson, New Jersey, produced cotton, silk, paper, railroad locomotives, and airplane engines.

Factory workers needed homes. Factory owners needed canals and railroads to transport their goods to customers. So, the environment along the Passaic River changed.

The Great Falls of the Passaic River have existed for thousands of years. People started building factories by the falls in the 1790s. What human-made additions do you see in this photo?

Changes Over Time

There are probably places near your home that have
been changed over time. People may have cut down trees,
dug lakes, canals, or reservoirs. They may have built
bridges, dams, and buildings.

Take photos of natural settings, such as parks, rivers,
forests, and farms. Be sure the photos give you an idea of
what the land looked like before people changed it, as well
as show human-made structures that are there now. If you
can't take your own photos, print photos or satellite images
from Internet sources. Display two or three photos on
poster board.

Research and write an explanation for each photograph.
Explain how you think people changed the natural
environment. Tell why the changes were made. Perhaps it
was to solve a problem or create faster transportation or
opportunities for jobs. Include why the location made this
a good place for these changes. Also tell if there were any
problems created by the changes. Display your posters and
explanations outside your classroom.

What human-made changes
do you see in this photo of
the Shrewsbury River in New
Jersey? Why do you think the
changes were made?

Uncovering the Secrets of Ozette

Students are not the only ones who research the geography of their states. Archaeologists in the state of Washington spent years learning about a village called Ozette. How did physical and human geography help them?

The Makahs live at the tip of a stretch of land called the Olympic Peninsula. The area has both forests and coastal land.

Long before Europeans came to North America, an American Indian tribe lived in the forests and along the coast of what is now Washington. They were the Makahs. The Makahs had five villages. One village was Ozette, where Makahs lived for thousands of years. But at some point, the village disappeared. Makah legend says that it was buried in an enormous mudslide several hundred years ago.

In the 1960s, an archaeologist named Richard Daugherty became interested in Ozette. He had compelling questions. What happened to Ozette? Where had it been located? To find the answers, Daugherty got permission to dig in the Makah reservation from the Makah leader. Daugherty then found some evidence of Ozette. But he didn't have the time or money to continue digging.

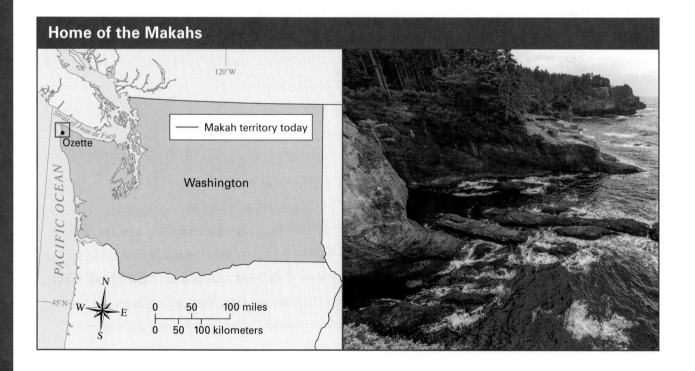

Home of the Makahs

120°W

Strait of Juan de Fuca

Ozette

Makah territory today

PACIFIC OCEAN

Washington

N
W   E
S

45°N

0   50   100 miles

0   50   100 kilometers

This mudslide in Washington has moved huge amounts of rock and soil down a mountain. It has uprooted tall trees. A mudslide 300 years ago covered Ozette in deep mud.

Geographic Research Solves a Mystery

In 1970, a huge storm hit Washington. Winds, rain, and waves from the Pacific Ocean pounded the coast. When the storm finally ended, people found old wooden items, such as canoe paddles, parts of homes, and fishing tools. Daugherty felt sure they were from Ozette.

Daugherty had always wanted to return to Ozette. Now, it seemed his chance had come. With a team of scientists and students, he spent the next 11 years investigating Ozette. Each new discovery they made answered some questions—and raised others.

When the team uncovered a village buried under ten feet of mud, they knew the Makah legend was true. But where had the mud come from? And when exactly had the mudslide happened? Answers to these supporting questions would help Daugherty's research into why Ozette disappeared.

To learn about weather patterns hundreds of years ago, the team looked at books and other written records. They learned that in January of 1700, a powerful earthquake had occurred on the coast of Washington. It shook the nearby hills of Ozette and caused a huge mudslide. Mud swept down and buried the village.

Ten feet of mud covered Ozette for almost 300 years. Deep in that mud, the village was preserved just as it had once been. A wealth of information was waiting to be examined.

This old photograph shows Makah hunters catching a whale. The Makahs used whales for food and whale oil to light lamps.

These Makah rock carvings of a whale, sun, and moon were made more than 300 years ago.

Daugherty's team learned a lot about the Makahs of the past. They studied the physical geography of Ozette. They studied the constructed features found under the mud. Their discoveries gave us a detailed picture of Makah life long ago.

The sea and richly forested lands near Ozette offered the early Makahs a wealth of natural resources. They used these for food, shelter, and clothing. They knew where to hunt and gather the food and materials that helped them survive the cold and stormy coastal winters.

Many discoveries at the site showed how important the sea was to the people of Ozette. Various fish and sea animals—such as seals, otters, and whales—served as staple foods for the Makahs.

Huge cedar trees grow around the Ozette site. The people of Ozette relied heavily on cedars. They made their houses and boats from cedar wood. They pounded cedar bark into a soft material and made clothes from it. They also built a number of types of canoes from cedar wood. They used different canoes for war, hunting whales, hunting seals, fishing, and carrying large loads of goods for trade. They even made smaller canoes for children to use.

More than 55,000 artifacts have been uncovered at Ozette, making it one of the richest archaeological finds in the world. Daugherty's team uncovered artifacts from all aspects of life. There were beautifully carved boards from houses and a riding saddle made of whalebone. There were baskets and boxes. There were toys, cradleboards for carrying babies, and ceremonial items. There were metal tools, fishing and whaling equipment, and other items.

The team recognized much of what they found. But sometimes they could not identify an artifact. What was that piece of carved wood or shaped stone used for, they wondered?

They turned to the modern-day Makahs for answers. Perhaps some Makahs had seen something like it when they were young. Maybe they had heard about it from their grandparents.

The discoveries at Ozette have helped answer many questions about early coastal life. Now we know how close to the ocean people lived. We know what their houses looked like. We know how they cut down the giant trees and built their boats.

A Makah elder called the storm that uncovered Ozette "a gift from the past." For geographers, too, the site is a gift. It continues to provide details about how people have lived in the state of Washington for hundreds of years. ◆

Today, you can see some of the treasures found at Ozette at the Makah Cultural and Research Center. These artifacts give us an understanding of what life was like long ago.

The History of Your State

How can you learn about your state's history?

Introduction

What is your state like? How did it get to be that way? Who settled your state? Who built its towns, cities, and farms? Why did these people choose your state as a place to live? Questions like these are what history is all about.

Studying history is like solving a mystery, and historians are like detectives. When you study history, you use all kinds of clues to determine what happened in the past. As you find clues, you find out more and more about history.

These clues can be written records, like journals, newspapers, and letters. People may have seen or taken part in the events described in these written records. Sometimes, they write these events down to share with other people. Historians also investigate the things you see around you, like old buildings, cemeteries, and bridges. These places show us how people in the past lived. Each of these has a story to tell you about the past. These clues help you to understand the connections between people and the events they experienced.

Discovering these clues and finding out about your state's history can help you appreciate the place where you live. It can help you understand why your state is the way it is today. It can even help you predict what your state might be like in the future.

Social Studies Vocabulary

primary source

secondary source

◄ Clues to your state's history can be found in old buildings, newspapers, and photographs. In Boston, the historic Old State House is dwarfed by modern buildings. But the Old State House is an important part of the state's history.

History

1. How We Explore the Past

The clues historians use come in many forms. You must use many types of clues to build a clear understanding of the past. You can find clues in letters, journals, newspapers, and photographs. These are all **primary sources**. Primary sources are sources created by people who have seen or taken part in the events they describe. Suppose your state's first governor made a speech about his hopes for the state. That is a primary source. When you read the speech, you learn about the past from someone who was there.

You can also use **secondary sources**. Secondary sources are created by people who have not experienced the events described. This book is a secondary source. It has information about history, but its writers did not witness that history.

A secondary source may include primary sources and describe their importance. For example, a secondary source might explain why your state's first governor gave that speech. It might tell how people reacted to it.

Primary and secondary sources are both useful. They each give different types of information. A primary source may have rich detail, but it gives just one opinion. A good secondary source draws information from many sources. It can help explain how different views and opinions fit together. Use both types of sources when you study the past.

primary source a source created by someone who has seen or taken part in the events described

secondary source a source created by someone who has not seen or taken part in the events described

A primary source gives a witness's account of a past event. This newspaper and photo both tell a story about the 1906 earthquake in San Francisco, California.

Primary sources include personal records, such as family photos. These records help historians understand connections between people and the events they experienced.

2. Why We Study the Past

Why do we live where we do? Who were the people who came before us and what events did they live through? How did those events shape their actions? How did those events shape what they believed? By studying history, we can find the answers to questions like these. We can see that events did not happen by accident and that past events have shaped our lives today. We can even find clues about how the future may unfold.

History can teach us a great deal. If we understand our history, we can better understand who we are.

Think about yourself for a moment. How would you help someone understand who you are? You might describe your family members, like your parents, grandparents, aunts, and uncles. You might say where they came from and how they came to live where they do. Or you might discuss your goals and all the things you want to do in your life.

Who you are is the result of things that happened long ago. What happens in your future depends on what you do today. Historians think about those connections. Studying history helps historians understand who we all are.

The Cliff Palace in Colorado is the largest cliff dwelling in North America. Pueblo peoples lived in the area for 700 years.

3. The Settlement of a State

Learning about your state's history can help you appreciate where you live. So, start at the beginning.

The first people to live in most of our states were American Indians. They probably came looking for a good place to hunt or to grow food. Your state, community, or street may have an American Indian name. Names are often clues to a place's past.

In the early 1500s, Europeans began to settle in North America. Some hoped to find riches or natural resources, and others came here in search of religious or political freedom. You can find out when and why settlers came to your state.

In many areas, the new settlers drove the American Indians off of their land. The settlers brought their own ways of living and introduced new languages, including English and Spanish. They built towns and farms, and they formed governments. Many of us live in or near the towns the settlers built. We use a system of government these people created.

You can find many details about the settlement of your state. Then you will begin to know the story of your state.

4. The Expanding United States

Do you live in one of the original 13 states? If so, you may know about the rich history of these states. Many contain battle sites from the American Revolution and historic towns and buildings. There are monuments to many great events and people from our country's early history. You can learn a lot about these states by visiting or reading about such sites.

Other stories unfolded in states that joined the country later. After its founding, the United States expanded to the west and began adding new states. Many of these states were created as the result of a law called the Northwest Ordinance of 1787. You can still read this law today. The document tells how states near the Great Lakes area were formed. If you live in one of those states, this primary source might interest you.

The United States also acquired lands from other countries. Can you find these lands on the map? In 1803, the United States almost doubled in size when it bought territory from France with the Louisiana Purchase. You can read primary and secondary sources about that purchase. These resources would help you learn how Louisiana and other states northwest of it were formed.

When it was still just a new nation, the United States began expanding west. It bought lands from foreign countries and acquired land through war and cession.

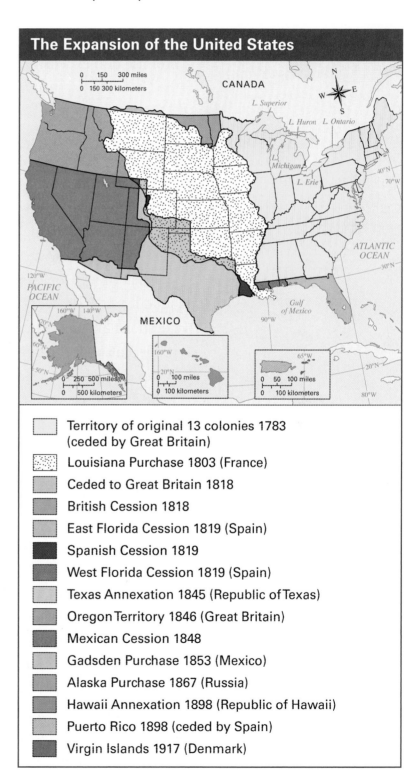

The Expansion of the United States

Territory of original 13 colonies 1783 (ceded by Great Britain)
Louisiana Purchase 1803 (France)
Ceded to Great Britain 1818
British Cession 1818
East Florida Cession 1819 (Spain)
Spanish Cession 1819
West Florida Cession 1819 (Spain)
Texas Annexation 1845 (Republic of Texas)
Oregon Territory 1846 (Great Britain)
Mexican Cession 1848
Gadsden Purchase 1853 (Mexico)
Alaska Purchase 1867 (Russia)
Hawaii Annexation 1898 (Republic of Hawaii)
Puerto Rico 1898 (ceded by Spain)
Virgin Islands 1917 (Denmark)

During the Gold Rush, miners helped California's population grow rapidly.

5. Westward, Ho!

The United States continued to expand west. As the population grew, new states were established.

Settlers in the West arrived from other countries and the eastern states. What did these settlers come to find? In the 1800s, many people were looking for land and open space. They wanted to get as far away from other settlements as they could. Many people moved west because of the promise of inexpensive land. Farmers settled many states of the Great Plains, such as Kansas and Nebraska.

Some people who traveled west followed the Oregon Trail to the Pacific coast. They settled in what would become the states of Oregon and Washington. Some of them were drawn by dreams of finding riches. In 1848, a mill worker discovered gold in the West. Tens of thousands of people came looking to strike it rich and many stayed. They formed a new state—California.

What drew people to your state? How did people build lives there? Every state has its own history. Asking questions like these and researching the answers can help you learn about the unique history of your state.

Settlers started farms on the Great Plains in the 1800s. These settlers could get large tracts of land for little money.

In the late 1850s, thousands of miners traveled west to seek gold in California. The city of San Francisco grew as people found work providing miners with clothing and transportation.

6. The Growth and Development of a State

The settling of your state is just part of its history. It continues to grow and develop today. People still come to the United States from all around the world. In addition, many Americans move from state to state. The new arrivals add to the history of your state.

The states in our country are alike in many ways and are different in others. Each is special in its own way.

In some states, towns and cities crowd together. Other states have miles and miles of open space. Some states have lots of businesses and factories. Others are mostly farmland.

States developed in different ways because of their natural resources. States also differ because of the people who settled them. What can you find out about how your state has grown and developed?

Lesson Summary

Learning about the history of your state can help you appreciate it and understand why the state is the way it is. You can act like a historian to learn about your state's past. Historians find clues to the past in primary and secondary sources. These records help a historian understand connections between people and the events they experienced.

To learn about your state, find out about its earliest settlers. Then, find out how your state fit in the expansion of the United States. Was your state one of the original 13 states or part of the westward expansion? Why did people settle there? Each state has its own story. By asking questions and researching the answers you can learn the unique history of your state.

Your State's History

Your state has a long history! Long before the word "state" was ever used, the land was home to American Indians. Over time, many events brought changes.

In this activity, you will answer this essential question: What was the most important event in our state's history? Not everyone will agree on an answer. People have different opinions. It is your job to find sources you can trust, gather information, and form your own opinion. Here's how to start:

Find an encyclopedia article that breaks down your state's history into eras, or time periods. If you live in Michigan, the beginning of the list might include: *American Indian days, French exploration, British control, Territory, Statehood, Birth of auto industry.*

Write all the eras of your state on a piece of paper. Then choose one that you think may include the state's most important event. Begin to research the important events of this era. You can start with encyclopedia articles and then use the Internet and library to find primary sources, such as newspaper articles or letters from the time period. Remember that primary sources give just one opinion. You can also use secondary sources that have drawn information from many sources. Record key events from this era on a table like the example shown here for Michigan.

A student in Michigan created this table to show the important events in the era called Birth of the Auto Industry.

Era: Birth of the Auto Industry	
Historical Event	**Why It Was Important**
1899 – Ransom E. Olds builds first auto factory in Detroit.	Cars changed how Americans travel and where they live.
1913 – The Ford Motor Company begins assembly line production of cars.	Detroit became the center of the nation's auto industry. The state population grew as people moved to MIchigan to work in factories.
1917 – Car factories begin to build trucks and airplane engines during World War I.	This helped the United States win the war.

When Ford Motor Company began making cars on an assembly line, this was an important event in Michigan history. It created jobs and caused cities to grow.

Present Your Opinion!

Is there an event on the table that you believe is the most important event in your state's history? If not, create another table for a different era. When you've chosen your important event, prepare an argument to convince your classmates.

Start with a statement that names the most important event. Then support your statement with evidence that you found in your research. You could tell what happened in the event, when it happened, and where it happened. Tell about some of the important people involved in the event. All of this evidence should support your opinion that this event was very important. To do this, explain how your state changed after that event. Did more people come to the state, or did people leave the state? Did the state become famous to people in other parts of the country or world? To convince others, it will help to present information for your research. Try to include a quote by a well-respected person who agrees that this was an important event.

Make a presentation to your classmates. Then listen as they make their presentations. Tell them if you think they made a good argument. Did they support their opinions with strong information? Did they persuade you to agree with them?

History

Lost and Found

Philadelphia is a city with a *lot* of history. Historian Ed Lawler is proud to know that history well. Yet one day he found a history mystery right in front of him. How did he uncover clues about the past?

Ed Lawler loves to show people around his hometown of Philadelphia, Pennsylvania. The city has many historical sights to see, and Lawler knows a lot about them. One day, however, a cousin asked him a question he could not answer. Lawler had just explained that Philadelphia was once the capital of our nation. He showed his cousin the buildings where Congress had met and where the Supreme Court had gathered. "Where did the president live?" his cousin asked. Lawler didn't know.

Lawler set out to find the answer. He quickly discovered that no one was sure exactly where the first presidents had lived!

As a historian, Lawler knows how to do research. He's curious, and he's a good detective. So he got right to work to learn about the President's House. He wanted to know where it was, what it looked like, who lived there, and what happened there.

Philadelphia was the capital of the United States from 1790 to 1800. Congress met in Congress Hall (left). The Supreme Court met in Old City Hall (right). But where did the president live?

This memorial at Independence Mall is an open-air footprint of the original President's House. You can see where the front door and windows would have been.

Asking Questions

Lawler began by reading many books. Historians agreed that Presidents George Washington and John Adams had lived in the President's House. They also agreed that the house was razed, or no longer stood.

The agreement stopped there. Historians said different things about where the house had been and how it looked. So Lawler started to ask some questions.

First, he wanted to know who owned the house. Lawler went to the **archives** of the city of Philadelphia. At the archives, he found the deed to the President's House that told who owned the house in the 1780s. After more searching, he found a newspaper advertisement that answered another question— where was the house? The ad gave the location on Market Street, one block north of Independence Hall.

But what did the house look like? At the Library of Congress, Lawler found another copy of the deed that included a drawing of the house's layout. Lawler figured that people in Philadelphia in the 1700s would have bought insurance for their homes. So he searched in a collection of old insurance records. Sure enough, there were papers describing the house. Lawler learned how large the rooms were and where the stairs were located. He found out how many fireplaces the house had and what the house looked like.

archives a collection of historical documents and records

Words Tell a Story

What went on inside the house? Lawler wanted to know, so he looked at other kinds of records. He read books, letters, and diaries. In them, he found many stories about life in the President's House.

Lawler read about fancy dinners that George and Martha Washington held on Thursdays. He also learned that every Tuesday President Washington had an open house when people could drop in and visit. One primary source explained, "Washington received his guests, standing between the windows in his back drawing room."

John Adams was the next president. He and his wife Abigail lived in the house until they moved to the new White House in Washington, D.C. Mrs. Adams is famous for the many letters she wrote. In one, she stated, "I feel more at home here [in the President's House] than I should any where else in the city."

The Adams' son, John Quincy Adams, also told stories about the house. In the room where Washington had his open houses, the Adams children once rolled up the rugs and held a dance for their friends.

As Lawler read these old documents, he could feel the President's House come alive. He could picture the Washingtons living there. He could almost hear the Adams family talking to him.

At parties like this one, people could meet President and Mrs. Washington. The President lived in Philadelphia during most of his presidency.

Other Voices

Lawler found other voices from the past, too. He realized that there was an untold story about the building. During President Washington's time, it was the home of nine enslaved African Americans.

What were the stories of these nine men and women? Lawler uncovered them. From the writings of Martha Washington's grandson, he learned about Hercules. This man was the chief cook for the house. Lawler read that "the whole household, treated the chief cook with such respect, as well for his valuable services as for his general good character and pleasing manners."

Lawler also found stories about a woman named Moll. She cared for the Washington children and grandchildren. He read about Oney Judge, who was Mrs. Washington's personal servant. Little by little, he learned about all the African Americans who lived and worked in the President's House.

For Lawler, it has been rewarding to learn about the lives of these African Americans. "In the past, they've been largely a list of names," he said. "I've tried to gather personal anecdotes and biographical information to help turn them back into real people."

Today, Lawler is still asking questions about history and finding answers. Because of his detective work with primary and secondary sources, historians can now tell the story of the President's House and the people who lived there. ◆

The names of Hercules and Moll appear on this 1788 list of Washington's property.

Visitors at the President's House can learn its history through colorful panels, timelines, and videos. One goal of the memorial is to tell the story of the slaves that served there during Washington's presidency.

Researching Your State's Economy

What do you need to know to understand your state's economy?

Introduction

What kind of job would you like to have when you grow up? Would you like to work with other people? Perhaps you will become a teacher, a salesperson, or a lawyer. Would you like to create new things? Maybe you will choose to design clothes or create computer programs. Would you like to work with your hands? You might choose to be a carpenter or a mechanic.

Thousands of jobs like these are a part of your state's economy. An economy is made up of all the ways in which people make, sell, and buy different goods and services. Goods are physical objects that can be bought, sold, or traded, such as food, clothing, and cars. Services are things that we pay others to do for us. For example, restaurant workers provide a service by saving people the trouble of cooking, and travel agents help people plan their next vacation or business trip.

Studying your state's economy, as well as the goods and services it produces, is necessary for you to understand how people live and work in your state. It can also help you learn what kinds of jobs you might have in the future. As you read this section and learn more about your state's economy, think about how the economy affects your life.

> **Social Studies Vocabulary**
>
> budget
>
> factors of production
>
> market
>
> scarcity
>
> tax

◀ People in your state have many different jobs. What jobs are available in your state?

$ Economics

This girl wants to buy a toy robot. The resources that are used to make it are limited, however.

1. The Basics of Economics

Economists study the choices people make, but why are our choices so important? There are some things we all need in order to survive, including food and shelter. But there are also things we want. A new bike or an MP3 player would be nice to have, but we could survive without them.

Economists know that people cannot always get everything they want, and they describe this fact of life as **scarcity**. Scarcity means that the things people want, and the resources used to make them, are limited. Because resources are limited, people cannot get all the things that they want.

All people face choices about the things that they want because of scarcity. The ways in which people make these choices shape an economy.

Your state has its own economy that is made up of the actions of people, businesses, and governments. Together, these people and groups use their actions to answer three basic questions:

1. What goods and services should be produced?
2. How should goods and services be produced?
3. Who will consume these goods and services?

2. Understanding Markets

Economists have a word for a place where economic activity occurs. They call this place a **market**. You may have been shopping at a market like a grocery store. But to an economist, the word *market* describes any place where buyers and sellers trade things.

A market can be an actual place, such as a store, but it does not have to be. In today's world, markets exist on computer networks and telephone systems. Some markets cover an entire state, the entire country, or even the entire world.

Markets are the center of our economy. In the marketplace, people work out answers to the three economic questions. There, buyers look to meet their wants, and sellers seek to provide goods and services that buyers want.

Both buyers and sellers are interested in the prices of goods and services. When the price of a good or service is high, sellers tend to produce more of it. But high prices discourage buyers. Buyers are more likely to make a purchase as prices drop.

What happens when there is more than one seller in a marketplace? The result is competition, which means that sellers will compete for consumers. One seller may try to offer a better product while another seller may offer a lower price. Competition is good for the buyer.

When people shop, they make choices about what goods and services to buy. They can also choose where to buy their goods, like at a farmers' market or a mall.

3. Workers in Your State

Before a seller sells a good, a worker must make it. These workers are also called producers. What is a producer's role in the economy?

To make a product, businesses use what economists call the three **factors of production**. One factor is land. This includes raw materials—things that are found in nature and are used to make goods. Another factor is *capital*. Capital means tools, machines, and buildings that are used to make goods. The third factor is labor, or workers.

Businesses attract workers by paying them money. The higher the wage or salary offered, the more likely that people will be willing to work for that price.

Workers use their pay to meet their wants. When workers spend their money on products, they also help sellers. You can see, then, why jobs are important to an economy. More and better jobs help everyone because jobs enable workers to buy what they want, which helps sellers earn money, too.

Workers also pay **taxes** on their earnings. Taxes support the government and pay for services that the government provides to people. For example, salaried firefighters work for the government, and taxpayer money pays for their wages.

factors of production the resources, including land, capital, and workers, used to create a good or service

tax the money that people and businesses pay to the government to support its functions

Here, you see three of the factors of production: land (the natural metal material), capital (the torch and machines), and labor (the workers).

My Budget for the Month

Money I Will Earn

Washing our car: $5

Sweeping outside our house: $5

Mowing lawns: $15

Carrying groceries for neighbors: $15

Walking dogs for neighbors: $15

Total: $5 + $5 + $15 + $15 + $15 = $55

Money I Will Spend

Going to a movie: $7

Buying music: $10

Buying a birthday gift: $10

Riding the bus: $8

Total: $7 + $10 + $10 + $8 = $35

Money I Will Save

$55 - $35 = $20

4. The Role of the Consumer

When a worker spends money to buy something, that producer becomes a consumer. Consumers are people that buy the goods and services that producers make, and they play a key role in the economy.

You are a consumer. And you can learn to be smart consumer. Being a smart consumer will help keep your state's economy strong, and it will also help you plan how much money you need. As you know, money is what we trade for goods and services to meet our wants.

You can be a smart consumer by spending wisely. To do so, you can make a **budget**. A budget details how much money you expect to have in a given time period and how you will spend that money. Following a budget helps you avoid spending more than you have.

You can also be a smart consumer by saving some of your money. Many people save money by putting it in the bank. Saving your money helps ensure that you will always have a way of meeting your needs. Savings also helps the economy because banks then have a supply of money to loan out that can help different businesses start and grow.

You can write a budget for any length of time. You can list what you will earn and spend, as well as what you plan to save.

budget a plan for how you will spend the money you expect to have

5. Types of Jobs in Our States

Each state has many types of industries and jobs. Here are some that you may find in your state as you research its economy. Can you think of others?

Agriculture. The agriculture industry is made up of businesses that grow food. Farm workers and ranchers work in agriculture. Scientists and businesspeople do, too.

Manufacturing. Any business that makes goods is part of the manufacturing industry. Factory workers, scientists, and engineers are just a few of the people who work in manufacturing.

Retail. Stores that sell goods to consumers make up the retail industry. Supermarkets, video stores, and car dealerships are all retail businesses. Two of the main jobs in retail are salesclerk and store manager.

Government. Millions of people work for federal, state, and local governments. Governments need many kinds of workers. Many teachers, firefighters, and police officers work for governments.

Service. Many people work in service businesses. Hair stylists, dry cleaners, mechanics, waiters, and security guards all provide services in a state.

Workers in your state have many different jobs. This man works in agriculture while this woman works in retail.

Many cities in Florida rely on tourism. Orlando, Florida, attracts many tourists each year.

6. A State's Economy Grows and Develops

Each state's economy grows and develops in different ways. A state's natural resources and climate can affect what producers choose to make and sell.

In Florida, the first big industry was agriculture because of the state's rich soil and warm, sunny, wet climate. Farmers could grow valuable crops, like sugarcane, that cannot be grown easily in most other states.

People saw another way to develop Florida's economy. The warm, sunny climate attracted tourists, so people built hotels, shops, and amusement parks. Today, tourism is one of Florida's most important industries.

As you research your state's economy, look for the ways in which it is linked to other economies. Many people in your state may do business throughout the country or throughout the world. They may also compete with businesses around the globe.

Lesson Summary

Learning about the economy of your state helps you understand the types of jobs that can be found in your state. Studying scarcity and the three basic questions allows you to understand why and how goods and services are produced in your state. Understanding markets helps you see the role that consumers and producers have with the economy. Finally, you need to know what types of jobs that your state has.

To learn about your state's economy, you first need to understand what different resources shape your state's economy. What is the weather like in your state? What goods or services does your state produce?

The Economy of Your State

In the early days of your state, people made their own clothing, food, and furniture. But today, people and companies often specialize in just one kind of product and service. Then they sell their goods and services to one another.

This trading goes beyond your state boundaries. The paper you write on, the bus you ride, and the cereal you eat may have come from across the country or even around the world. Your state may make products that are sold in other places. What are the most important products made in your state? To answer this question you will need to search for information about the businesses that provide many jobs in your state and the top products made or grown in the state.

If you live in Washington, for example, you might learn that your state earns more money from apples than any other state. It grows more than half the apples in the nation. Washington's economy also depends on the aerospace industry. It has more aircraft workers than any other state. More than 130,000 workers help make jet planes and other equipment for countries all over the world.

You can learn about your state's economy from several Web sites. Your state's Department of Commerce is a good source. Online news articles also may be helpful. Find information on your state's top five products, and make a graphic organizer like the one shown here for each.

Research the top products made in your state. As you research, also record why these products are made in your state and where they are often shipped.

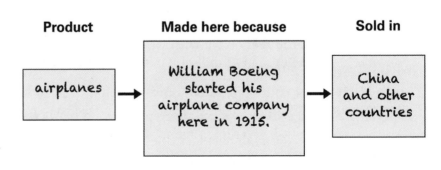

Product	Made here because	Sold in
airplanes	William Boeing started his airplane company here in 1915.	China and other countries

Making a Business Decision

Business leaders want to make smart decisions so that their businesses stay strong. Should they spend money on new equipment? Should they stop making a product to save money? They must weigh the cost of their choice with the possible benefits.

Choose one of the products from your state. Then make the following business decision: If you were a business owner, would you want to sell your products to other countries? There are many things to consider. For example, how will you get people in other countries to know about and buy your product? How will you transport the goods there, and how much will it cost? Should you build a factory there?

Use what you learned about your product and the economy to decide whether you want to sell to other countries or not. Then construct an argument to convince others. List reasons, and support them with facts that you found in your research. Show that you compared the costs and benefits.

Present your argument to your classmates. Does anyone have an argument against your decision? Listen to his or her reasons, and see if you can come to an agreement.

Aircraft is a top product that Washington ships to other places. Washington sells more planes to China than to any other country.

Doing Real Work in the Real World

What is it like to do jobs that adults usually do? Students across the country answer that question as they participate in real-world work projects. What do they learn about work?

Students can become community organizers to solve problems, such as fixing up schools like this one.

In 2004, the Robert E. Byrd Academy School was a crumbling building in a run-down part of Chicago. In winter, it was so cold that students had to wear coats in class because the building had no heat. The bathrooms had no soap dispensers, and the floors were wet from leaking pipes.

Teacher Brian Shultz asked his fifth graders what community project they wanted to work on. They answered "our school." They knew they couldn't make the repairs themselves, but they also knew they could build public support for solving their school's problems. In the adult world, community organizers work to educate the public and elected officials about a specific issue. In effect, the students became junior community organizers to win supporters and get official solutions.

For five months, the students worked to bring attention to the problems in the school building. They made lists of projects that needed to be done, and they researched the costs for these projects. They looked at the school department's budget to find where the money might come from. They even wrote letters and e-mails to school and city officials about their school's problems.

Students saw their hard work pay off. Officials listened to their arguments, and workers fixed many problems. They even put soap dispensers in the bathrooms. "The students were so excited," said Mr. Shultz. "They were coming out of the bathrooms with their hands full of bubbles, yelling, 'We've got soap!'"

4-H members learn real-world skills by working at home and in their community. This boy is feeding a calf as part of a 4-H program.

Learn by Doing

"Learn by doing" is the official saying of 4-H. 4-H is an organization of clubs for children and teenagers. (The four "H"s stand for Head, Heart, Hands, and Health.) Learning by doing has been the focus of 4-H since its beginning. Kids learn practical skills by doing real work projects.

4-H had an interesting beginning. It was created in the early 1900s so that kids could teach adults about new farming discoveries. Teachers working at agricultural colleges discovered that many adults in the farming community did not easily accept new technologies. Kids, however, were happy to experiment with these new ideas and then share their experiences and successes with adults.

For many years, 4-H clubs were mostly agricultural clubs for boys and girls. With help from adult experts, kids learned new ways to raise animals, grow crops, and preserve food.

Today, the goal of 4-H is to help kids develop citizenship, leadership, and life skills. The clubs still focus on hands-on learning, and club member do projects that teach them skills and help their community. They raise and train seeing-eye dogs or care for endangered animals. They learn first aid and work as camp counselors.

This girl is writing a check. Students used checkbooks like this to buy what they wanted in the Enterprise City stores.

Running Businesses, Being Smart Consumers

In many schools, students learn about business by running their own. At Central Middle School in Burlington, Illinois, students run a school store called "Nibbles and Scribbles." The store is run out of a math classroom at the school, and it is stocked with items such as pens, pencils, notebooks, and folders. The students who run the store order supplies, stock shelves, wait on customers, and run the cash register.

At Canyon Creek Elementary School in Richardson, Texas, groups of students take turns running Enterprise City for a day. Enterprise City has 16 businesses, including a city hall and a bank. Students become shop owners, managers, accountants, and salespeople. They run the radio station and the newspaper. They act as police officers, judges, and the mayor.

At Enterprise City, students are "paid" for their work and learn how to be smart consumers. Using checkbooks, students buy what they need and want in the Enterprise City stores. They have to pay attention, though, to make sure that they do not spend more than they have earned.

"I learned how to check how much money I had, and not to spend it all!" one student explained.

Working for Your Community

Look around your own community. Can you find kids who are doing real-world work? Some kids run farmers markets or work in stores. Some work with children or older people in schools, hospitals, and senior centers. Others work in parks or in playgrounds.

What real-world work projects could you and your friends do? Look around your school, your neighborhood, your community. Do you see any problems? Are there things your community needs?

What skills and interests do you have to share? Do you love animals? Are there animals that need to be cared for in your community? Do you love being outside? Are there parks or rivers that need cleaning and tending?

Here are some steps to take to do a real-world work project of your own:

1. Identify a problem and decide on a project.
2. Find other kids who want to help.
3. Get help from adult experts.
4. Make a plan.
5. Do it!

You can find problems and solve them in your community. ◆

In many places, kids plan, plant, and tend community gardens. Some kids even help distribute the food they grow to food pantries.

Researching Your State's Government

How does your state's government work?

Introduction

Do you see things that you would like to change in your state? Perhaps you would like to see schools get more money to fix their buildings. Maybe you would like to see somebody take better care of your state parks. Or maybe you would like to see your government support more small businesses and make your community a safer place to live.

There are always problems to worry about. Governments try to solve problems that are bigger than people can solve on their own. When our country was created, its founders had a deep fear of governments being too powerful. The country had just won independence from the too-powerful British king. The founders favored a government with limited power, so they chose a system where power would rest with different levels of government, not just one. This led to the creation of state governments, like your own.

You can have a big effect on what your state government does. But first you need to know how your state government works. In this lesson, you will learn about how power is divided within your state government and who leads our government. You will also learn how laws are created as well as rights and responsibilities that you have in your state.

> **Social Studies Vocabulary**
> bill
> citizen
> federal government
> legislator
> local government
> republic
> state constitution
> state government
> system of checks and balances

◀ The state capitol building is home to your state's government. This building is the state capitol building of Texas.

 Civics

Local governments provide many different services. Fire protection is one service that protects the community

federal government our national government that deals with issues that affect the entire country

state government the government of an individual state that deals with issues that affect that state

local government city, town, and county governments

1. The Federal System

Citizens of individual states are also citizens of the United States. That is because we have a federal system of government. In this system, the power of government is divided between different levels. The federal system is set up to protect our rights. It ensures that no level of government gains too much power over the people.

Our national government is called the **federal government**. It is concerned with problems that affect the whole country. The federal government makes laws for the entire United States. **State governments** deal with problems that affect their state. Your state government makes laws for your state. It also makes sure people obey these laws. In the federal system, the federal government holds some powers while the state governments hold most of the rest.

The United States has one other level of government. This is **local government**. Your city, town, or county government is your local government. State governments create local governments to meet local needs. For example, local governments run schools. They pick up trash or run garbage dumps. They offer fire protection. They provide police services to help protect people and property. They do many things for the people in their community.

2. The Separation of Powers

State governments work the same way as the federal government. They are divided into three parts, or branches. The legislative branch writes the laws. Just as Congress makes laws for the United States, your state legislature makes laws for your state. Most state legislatures have two houses. What are the houses called in your state?

The executive branch carries out the laws. In the federal government, the president is in charge of the executive branch. In each state, the governor is in charge of the executive branch. Who is the governor of your state?

The judicial branch makes sure that justice is done, or that people are treated fairly. In the federal government, this branch includes the Supreme Court and other federal courts. In the states, the judicial branch is made up of state courts and judges.

Having three branches creates a separation of powers. The **system of checks and balances** makes sure no branch will have too much power. Each branch's power is limited by the other two branches. For example, the governor of a state may veto, or stop, a law passed by the legislature. But in most states, two-thirds of the members of the legislature can agree to overrule the veto and pass the law.

> **system of checks and balances** a system set up in the U.S. Constitution to allow each branch of government ways to limit the power of the other two branches

Your government is broken up into three different branches. Each branch has different responsibilities.

The Three Branches of State Government

Executive	Legislative	Judicial

• The executive branch enforces state laws. • The leader of the executive branch is the governor.	• The state legislature makes the laws. • Most state legislatures have two houses.	• The judicial branch makes sure people are treated fairly. • The judicial branch includes the state courts and judges.

3. The Importance of Leadership

republic a type of government in which people choose leaders to act for them

A governor leads the executive branch. This man became the governor of the state of California in 2011.

The United States is influenced by the democratic form of government. The word *democracy* means "rule by the people." This means that in our country, and in our states, the people rule. The people have the power, and the government serves the people.

Even though the people rule, they do not typically create or write laws themselves. They also do not directly decide what the government will do about many everyday decisions. This is because the United States is a republic. In a **republic,** people choose leaders to act for them. These men and women do the day-to-day work of government.

The leaders in our states have many important responsibilities.

A good leader sets examples for others to follow and inspires people. He or she helps people put aside differences to solve problems together and also helps people make decisions. A good leader also makes decisions that benefit the most people.

We have leaders in the federal government who act on our behalf. The president, members of Congress, and federal judges represent us. Each leader in the federal government has an important job to do.

The state government works the same way. Have you heard your governor speak? Do you know who represents you in the state legislature? These are some of your state's leaders.

Candidates campaigning for office meet voters at rallies like this one. Here, this man is running for senator of Pennsylvania.

4. Choosing Our Leaders

We use elections to choose many of our leaders. In an election, citizens choose by voting.

In elections in the United States, a **citizen,** or a person who by law has a right to live in a community, chooses candidates based on many factors. Voters want a fair and honest leader whose views they agree with. They often vote for candidates who have shown wisdom or courage. To learn about candidates, people can listen to what the candidates say—in person, on the radio, on television, or on the Internet. People can also read about candidates' views, and listen to what others say about the candidates. What would you look for in a leader?

Voters in your state elect leaders to the federal government. They can vote to elect the president and representatives to Congress. Voters in your state can also vote for your governor and elect representatives to the state legislature. In some states, citizens vote on judges for some courts. When is the next election in your state?

Voting is a key part of being a citizen. Elections let the people have their say. They allow us to choose leaders to settle conflicts and make decisions. Are people happy with their leaders? Do they want new ones? On Election Day, we find out.

citizen a person who is born in a country or who chooses to become a member of that country by law

5. How Ideas Become Laws

Most laws begin in the legislature. Laws are made to protect people's rights and the common good. Suppose you have an idea for a new state law. How could you make your law a reality?

The first step is to get other people's support. When many people get behind an idea, state governments will listen to them. That is because citizens elect their governors and state **legislators**.

There are many ways to get people's support. For example, you could hang posters around town, or you could write letters to the newspaper. You could even speak at town meetings or call up television or radio talk shows. You could also organize rallies and raise support on the Internet.

For an idea to become law, a state legislator must write it up as a **bill**. The entire legislature then debates the bill and often makes changes to it. Finally, the legislature votes on the bill. If the legislature approves the bill, the governor must agree to sign it. Otherwise, the bill does not become a law.

Sometimes people believe that a state law is unfair. When that happens, they might ask state courts to take a look at the law. Courts can overrule a law if it disagrees with the U.S. Constitution or with the **state constitution**.

---

legislator a member of the branch of government that makes laws

bill a proposal for a new law

state constitution a written statement of a plan for a state government

There are many steps in the process of a bill becoming a law.

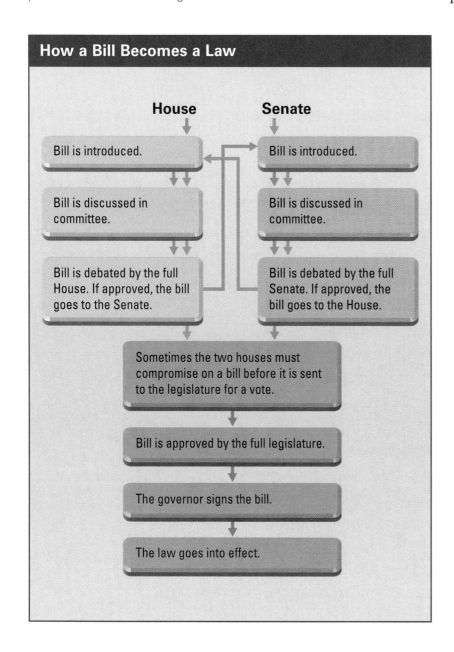

How a Bill Becomes a Law

House | Senate

- Bill is introduced. | Bill is introduced.
- Bill is discussed in committee. | Bill is discussed in committee.
- Bill is debated by the full House. If approved, the bill goes to the Senate. | Bill is debated by the full Senate. If approved, the bill goes to the House.
- Sometimes the two houses must compromise on a bill before it is sent to the legislature for a vote.
- Bill is approved by the full legislature.
- The governor signs the bill.
- The law goes into effect.

Voting in elections is a right and responsibility of citizenship. Citizens vote for leaders to represent them.

6. The Rights and Responsibilities of Citizenship

Citizens have many rights and responsibilities. One right is freedom of speech. All citizens are entitled to these and other rights. The government cannot take away a citizen's rights without a very good reason.

Citizens have responsibilities, too. These are things you must do to help support the government. One responsibility is paying taxes. Another is being on a jury. Most adult citizens share these responsibilities.

There are also many ways to be a good citizen before you become an adult. You can obey the laws of the country and your state. You can show respect for the rights of others. You can develop leadership traits, such as courage, honesty, fairness, and wisdom. You can learn to recognize these traits in others.

Lesson Summary

Learning about the government of your state helps you understand how laws are created and problems are solved. Understanding the federal system allows you to understand your state government's role within the United States. It is also important for you to understand how power is separated between the three branches of government.

To learn about your state's government, you first need to find out who the leaders in your state are. Who are your state's governor and state legislators? You will also need to learn about new laws and how they are created. You should also learn about your rights and responsibilities as a citizen. What rights do you have in your state?

Your State's Government

You've just learned that state governments make and carry out laws. Laws help keep our nation, state, and communities running smoothly. You can compare laws to rules. When you play sports, there are rules you must follow so that players are safe and the game runs smoothly. These rules are like laws that governments create for similar reasons. There are laws at work all around you. For example, some laws control the way people drive cars and the materials people use to build homes.

Sometimes state legislators make laws that directly affect you and your classmates. For example in 2005, the Illinois legislature passed a law saying that children in kindergarten, second, and sixth grades must have a dental check-up.

As you learned, your state government is based on the democratic idea of "rule by the people." It is important for you to know who makes the laws for your state. Search the Internet to find out: Who is your governor? Who are your representatives in the legislature? Where do your legislators meet to discuss laws?

Illinois lawmakers meet in this room in the state capitol. They write laws that are then voted on.

Democracy in Your Classroom

Put democracy to work in your classroom. Create a new rule for your class or school. Make your decisions by following the democratic steps described below.

First, decide on a problem you want to solve. For example, some students want the teacher to set aside a time every day for "free reading" so they can read anything they like. Other students want to change a safety rule that forbids students from riding their bicycles to school. Make suggestions for a topic to your classmates. Support your suggestion with reasons. Take a vote and find out if most students want to move forward with this rule. If not, talk about what changes might make more people agree with you.

Once you decide on a topic, write the rule carefully. Then ask a few classmates if the rule you wrote makes sense. Does it describe enough details, such as who is affected, how, and when?

Once your rule is clearly written, take a vote in your class. Do most people agree with the rule? If not, try to change people's mind with a strong argument or by rewriting parts of the rule. If the class votes in favor of the rule, then it is time to get the approval from your teacher, principal, or other person in charge. Good luck!

These students are using the democratic process to vote on a new class rule. The rule that has the most votes wins.

Student Citizens Help Make Laws

In Franklin, Massachusetts, Ms. Johnson's students were discussing state symbols, like the state flag. During their discussion, they thought of a new symbol for their state, and they used their idea to help make a law. What did the students learn about their state's government in the process?

Many states choose state symbols, like plants or animals that are found in the state. These are some of the Massachusetts state symbols.

In 1974, Palma Johnson's second grade class at John F. Kennedy Elementary School was studying the state symbols of Massachusetts. They looked at symbols like the Massachusetts flag and the state seal. Ms. Johnson explained to the class that Massachusetts also had a state bird (the chickadee), a state tree (the American Elm), and even a state fish (the Atlantic cod).

"What about a state bug?" one student asked. "Do we have one?" Ms. Johnson told that class that Massachusetts did not have a state bug.

"I think Massachusetts should have a state bug," said one student. The rest of the class agreed, and one student suggested the ladybug. Ladybugs are found in yards and parks all over Massachusetts, so they believed it would make a good state symbol.

"Every citizen of Massachusetts has the right to suggest new laws for our state," Ms. Johnson told her class. "Maybe our class can make the ladybug the state bug. Maybe we can make it a law."

Petitioning the Massachusetts Legislature

Ms. Johnson's class agreed to try to turn their idea into law. But before they could begin, the class had to first find out how they could propose a law to the government.

As citizens of Massachusetts, they had the right to give their legislators ideas for new laws. This right is called the **right of free petition**. The first step was to write to the State House in Boston where the state's legislators work and ask for a petition form.

When the petition form arrived, the class filled it out carefully. In the petition, the class explained why they proposed the ladybug as the state bug.

Next, they had to find a legislator to sign the petition. Any petition for a new law needs the support of a legislator. The class decided to ask Representative Robert Ficco to help them. Mr. Ficco represented Franklin, the town where the students lived, in the Massachusetts state legislature. The class wrote to ask him to sign their petition, and he wrote back to say he would be glad to help.

After he signed the petition, Mr. Ficco sent it to the Massachusetts House of Representatives. The ladybug idea was on its way.

The Massachusetts legislature works in the state capitol building in Boston. The students sent their petition form here.

right of free petition the right of the people to give legislators ideas for new laws

From a Petition to a Bill

Representative Ficco sent the ladybug petition to Boston, but it was not a law yet. It had only just started the long journey to becoming a state law.

Before the petition could become a law, it needed to become a bill. To do this, the House Clerk for the House of Representatives had it give the petition a number. The students' petition was given the number H.5155. Next, the House Clerk assigned it to a committee. Different committees are responsible for different issues. The Clerk also sent copies of the bill to all the legislators on this committee, and they started to study and talk about the bill.

The students hoped to go to Boston when anything important happened with their bill, and one event they did not want to miss was the public hearing the committee would hold on their bill. The students knew that they needed to show that the bill had support.

On the day of the hearing, Ms. Johnson's class dressed in ladybug costumes that they had made and rode the school bus to Boston. At the hearing, the students were allowed to speak, and they explained why the bill was important to them.

The committee listened carefully. Afterward, they told the House of Representatives that the ladybug bill should be passed into law. This was a good start. But there was still a long way to go.

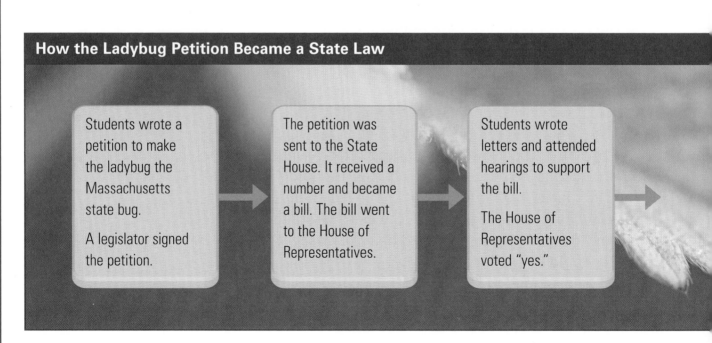

How the Ladybug Petition Became a State Law

Students wrote a petition to make the ladybug the Massachusetts state bug.

A legislator signed the petition.

The petition was sent to the State House. It received a number and became a bill. The bill went to the House of Representatives.

Students wrote letters and attended hearings to support the bill.

The House of Representatives voted "yes."

From a Bill into Law

Over the next few weeks, the class went back to hearings at the state capitol several times. The representatives in the House discussed the class's bill on three different occasions. Between hearings, the students wrote letters to representatives to convince them to vote for their bill, and some also talked to representatives in person. In the end, the House of Representatives voted "yes" on the bill.

Next, the bill went to the other house of the legislature, the Senate. It was the Senate's turn to read, discuss, and vote on the bill. When the Senate voted "yes" on the bill, the students cheered.

The bill was almost a law, but not quite. After it was printed on special paper, all the legislators voted together to enact the bill meaning that the bill could become law.

The governor of Massachusetts was the final person who had to say "yes." When he signed the bill, it officially became a state law. Ms. Johnson's students attended the signing ceremony. The students' hard work had paid off, and the ladybug was now the state bug of Massachusetts.

Ms. Johnson was happy, too. "I wanted my students to know how important it is to be active in our public life," she said. "After all, no voice is too small to be heard." ◆

The Lady Bug bill had a long journey before it could become a law. The chart below shows the different steps the Lady Bug bill had to go through.

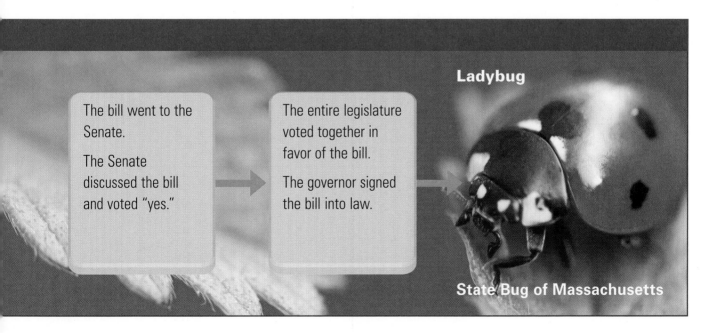

The bill went to the Senate.

The Senate discussed the bill and voted "yes."

The entire legislature voted together in favor of the bill.

The governor signed the bill into law.

Ladybug

State Bug of Massachusetts

Ideas That Unite Us as Americans

Each person in the United States is different and special. What connects Americans are shared ideals. Ideals are ideas that seem very good and worth trying to achieve.

Our country is based on ideas about freedom and equality for everyone. These ideals were shaped by our early leaders and written down so no one would forget them. The ideas of freedom and equality are still important today for all Americans.

 Civics   Economics   Geography   History

The Declaration of Independence: Creating a New Country

Although people have lived in our land for thousands of years, the United States is less than 250 years old. It was founded in 1776.

At that time, our country was a group of 13 colonies. The colonies belonged to a country called Great Britain, which was ruled by the British king.

Many colonists grew unhappy with British rule. They felt the British did not treat them fairly and they had little say in their own government.

In 1775, colonial leaders met in Philadelphia, Pennsylvania. This group was called the Second Continental Congress. For over a year, they discussed what to do about the conflict with Great Britain. In July 1776, they decided the colonies should form their own country. They declared independence from Great Britain.

This was a huge step. It was a crime to be disloyal to the British king, but the colonists believed in something more powerful than British law. They believed that they had basic rights and that no government or king could take these rights away.

A man named Thomas Jefferson explained this thinking. He did so in the Declaration of Independence.

Colonial leaders vote for independence from Great Britain.

From the Declaration of Independence

We hold these truths to be self-evident, that all men are created equal, that they are endowed by their Creator with certain unalienable Rights, that among these are Life, Liberty, and the pursuit of Happiness.

American Ideals

The Declaration of Independence describes the ideals of the new country.

Thomas Jefferson wrote, "All men are created equal." This was a new idea in 1776. In most countries, people were not born equal. But the United States was founded on the ideal of equality.

It has taken time to live up to this promise. Until 1865, most African Americans lived in slavery, and women could not vote until 1920.

Jefferson also wrote that all people have basic rights. These rights are "unalienable." This means they cannot be taken away.

Our basic rights include the right to life, liberty, and the pursuit of happiness. Liberty is another word for freedom. We believe in the freedom to make choices. We decide what we will do for a living, and we choose how we will worship. We make other basic choices. We are free to pursue happiness.

Jefferson believed that government should get its power "from the consent of the governed." In other words, power belongs to the people. They can choose to let the government use it. The United States is a republic. We choose our leaders. We give them the power to make laws. Over time, our republic has grown. More and more people have been invited to take part. Today, nearly all citizens aged 18 or older can vote.

Thomas Jefferson wrote the Declaration of Independence.

The Constitution of the United States: Creating a Government

The Declaration of Independence listed the ideals that would guide the nation. But it did not create a government.

In 1787, a group of leaders again met in Philadelphia to create a plan for the new government. The plan they wrote is called the Constitution of the United States of America.

The Constitution begins with a special paragraph. We call this the Preamble. The words make clear that "we the people" are forming the government. It exists to serve us. The words also tell the purposes of our government. These are to:

- create a more perfect union
- establish justice
- insure domestic tranquility—peace among the people
- provide for the common defense
- secure the blessings of liberty.

In 1789, the states adopted the plan.

The Preamble of the Constitution tells the purposes of government.

Preamble to the United States Constitution

We the people of the United States, in order to form a more perfect union, establish justice, insure domestic tranquility, provide for the common defense, promote the general welfare, and secure the blessings of liberty to ourselves and our posterity, do ordain and establish this Constitution of the United States of America.

How Government Achieves Its Purposes

The Preamble tells us the purposes of the government. But how does the Constitution achieve them?

One way is by giving government power. The Constitution gives the federal government power to create an army. The army helps defend us and keep us safe.

The Constitution allows the federal government to coin money. With this power, government helps people do business. It helps them build better lives.

The Constitution gives the federal government the power to tax. Taxes are how government raises money. Money allows government to offer important services. For example, government helps give people medicine. It helps the needy. Government helps keep our air and water clean. Such services promote our welfare.

The Constitution meets the purposes of the Preamble by putting limits on government power, too. One way it does this is with elections. The people can change leaders if they do not like the ones they have. This gives the people great power.

The Constitution also gives power to the states. For example, states make their own laws. They run schools and build roads. The states and federal governments both have power, but neither has too much.

The Constitution gives and limits powers to the government, states, and citizens.

The Bill of Rights guarantees certain freedoms and rights.

The Bill of Rights: Protecting the Rights of Individuals

The Constitution achieves the purposes of the Preamble in another way. It promises to protect people's rights. It does so in the first ten amendments to the Constitution. Together, these amendments are called the Bill of Rights.

What rights does the Bill of Rights guarantee? They include:

- *The freedom of speech and freedom of the press*
  Government cannot stop us from sharing our ideas and views. We can even criticize the government.
- *The freedom of religion*
  This means we can worship in any way we want.
- *The right to bear arms*
  People are allowed to own guns.
- *The right not to be searched or arrested without good reason*
  Government must follow certain rules.
- *The right to a speedy public trial in front of a jury*
  Everyone who is arrested has the right to a trial.

However, rights have limits. For example, we do not have the freedom to say things that might create danger. We cannot shout out "Fire!" in a crowded place and cause a panic. We cannot put hurtful lies about a person in a newspaper.

With our rights come responsibilities. We hear the ideas of different candidates in an election. We must choose wisely when we vote. We are free to practice any religion we like. We are responsible for respecting other people's choices.

Four Freedoms

Americans believe in freedom. We also believe in helping others enjoy freedom and equality. Sometimes, this is not easy. Sometimes, we must fight for freedom. We must resist those who would take freedom away.

The United States faced this kind of challenge in 1940. The country was about to go to war—World War II. Our enemies were dictators. In a dictatorship, people have no freedom.

Our president was Franklin Roosevelt. He gave a speech called the Four Freedoms speech to help prepare the country for the challenge ahead.

Roosevelt reminded Americans of their own freedom. He challenged them to spread American ideals. "In the future days, which we seek to make secure, we look forward to a world founded upon four essential human freedoms."

These four freedoms included the freedoms of speech and religion. Roosevelt also named two other freedoms. One he called the "freedom from want." People should be free to work and earn a good living.

The fourth freedom was "freedom from fear." This was the fear of one country taking away the freedom of another.

Roosevelt's ideas still ring true today. Americans want their freedom. They want freedom for the people of the world.

Franklin D. Roosevelt reminded Americans of their freedoms in his Four Freedoms speech.

Respect for the Flag

The flag should never be displayed with the union (the blue portion) down, except as a signal of dire distress.

The flag should never touch anything beneath it, such as the ground.

The flag should never be carried flat or horizontally, but aloft and free.

The flag should not be used as wearing apparel, bedding, or drapery.

The flag should never be fastened, used, displayed, or stored in a way that would allow for easy tearing, soiling, or damage.

The flag should never be used to cover the ceiling.

The flag should never have placed upon it any mark, letter, word, figure, design, picture, or drawing of any nature.

The flag should never be used as a container for receiving, holding, or carrying anything.

The flag should never be used for advertising or printed on anything designed to be thrown away.

No part of the flag should ever be used as a costume or athletic uniform.

When a flag is in such condition that it is no longer fit for display, it should be destroyed in a dignified way, such as by burning.

Fourth graders recite the pledge each morning.

The Pledge of Allegiance

I pledge allegiance to the flag
of the United States of America,
and to the Republic
for which it stands,
one nation under God, indivisible,
with liberty and justice for all.

Symbols of the United States of America

France gave the Statue of Liberty to the United States in the 1800s as a sign of friendship. The world has come to see the statue as a symbol of freedom and democracy. It has welcomed millions of people to the United States.

The bald eagle became a national symbol in 1782. The powerful bird was chosen because it was found only in North America. To our early leaders, the bird stood for strength, courage, and freedom.

The Great Seal of the United States shows the main ideas of the nation's founding. The colors come from the American flag. The eagle represents strength, freedom, and courage. The 13 arrows and the olive branch show the power of war and peace. The cluster of stars in the sky stand for a new nation taking its place among the other nations. The motto *E Pluribus Unum* means "from many, one." It means that we are one people made up of many different types.

The pyramid stands for strength. The eye over the pyramid stands for a greater power watching over people. Latin words celebrate the start of a new time in history. The letters on the pyramid's base are Roman numerals for 1776, the year of the nation's founding.

American Symbols

Statue of Liberty

Bald Eagle

Great Seal (front)

Great Seal (back)

These symbols represent different ideals of the United States. They are symbols of freedom, courage, and our country's history.

Some National Holidays in the United States

Presidents' Day

In February, the country notes the birthdays of two of our greatest presidents: George Washington and Abraham Lincoln. Americans today honor both of these great leaders with the celebration of President's Day. It takes place on the third Monday in February.

Memorial Day

Americans remember the men and women who died in the service of our country on Memorial Day. The holiday began in the years following the Civil War. It was called Decoration Day, after the practice of placing flowers on the graves of the war dead. Today, it is celebrated on the last Monday in May.

Flag Day

The first Flag Day was in 1877. It honored the adoption of the American flag by the Continental Congress. That took place 100 years earlier, on June 14. Now, each year on that date, we honor the great symbol of our nation.

Fourth of July—Independence Day

This holiday celebrates the day that the Continental Congress approved the Declaration of Independence. It is celebrated across the United States with picnics, parades—and, of course—fireworks.

Labor Day

On the first Monday in September, Americans celebrate the contributions of the American worker.

Constitution Day

Constitution Day falls on September 17. It celebrates the signing of the United States Constitution on that day in 1787.

Thanksgiving

In 1621, the Pilgrims of the Plymouth colony and local American Indians celebrated the harvest. Presidents Washington and Lincoln later called for national days of thanksgiving. Today, we hold this celebration on the fourth Thursday in November.

Thanksgiving dinners often feature roast turkey.

Martin Luther King Jr.'s "I Have a Dream" speech inspired a nation.

I Have a Dream

Martin Luther King Jr. fought hard for equality for all Americans. On August 28, 1963, he spoke before a huge crowd in Washington, D.C., about his dream for our country. This speech is remembered today as the "I Have a Dream" speech. Here are some parts of that speech.

I say to you today, my friends, so even though we face the difficulties of today and tomorrow, I still have a dream. It is a dream deeply rooted in the American dream.

I have a dream that one day this nation will rise up and live out the true meaning of its creed: "We hold these truths to be self-evident: that all men are created equal."

I have a dream that my four little children will one day live in a nation where they will not be judged by the color of their skin but by the content of their character.

I have a dream today.

I have a dream that one day . . . little black boys and black girls will be able to join hands with little white boys and white girls as sisters and brothers.

I have a dream today.

And if America is to be a great nation, this must become true . . . Let freedom ring . . . from every mountainside, let freedom ring.

World Political Map

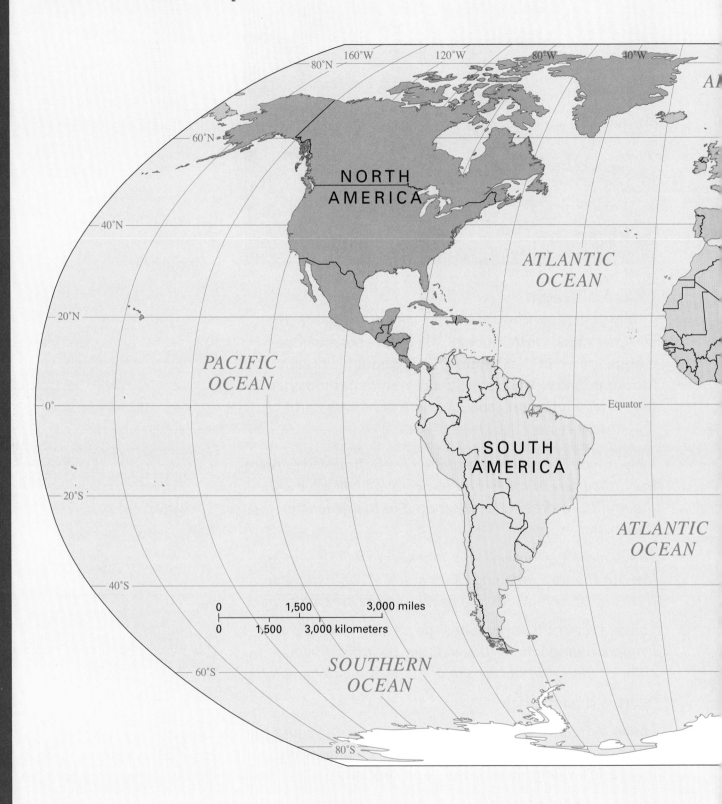

80°N

160°W   120°W   80°W   40°W

A

60°N

NORTH
AMERICA

40°N

ATLANTIC
OCEAN

20°N

PACIFIC
OCEAN

0°

Equator

SOUTH
AMERICA

20°S

ATLANTIC
OCEAN

40°S

| 0 | 1,500 | 3,000 miles |
| 0 | 1,500 | 3,000 kilometers |

60°S

SOUTHERN
OCEAN

80°S

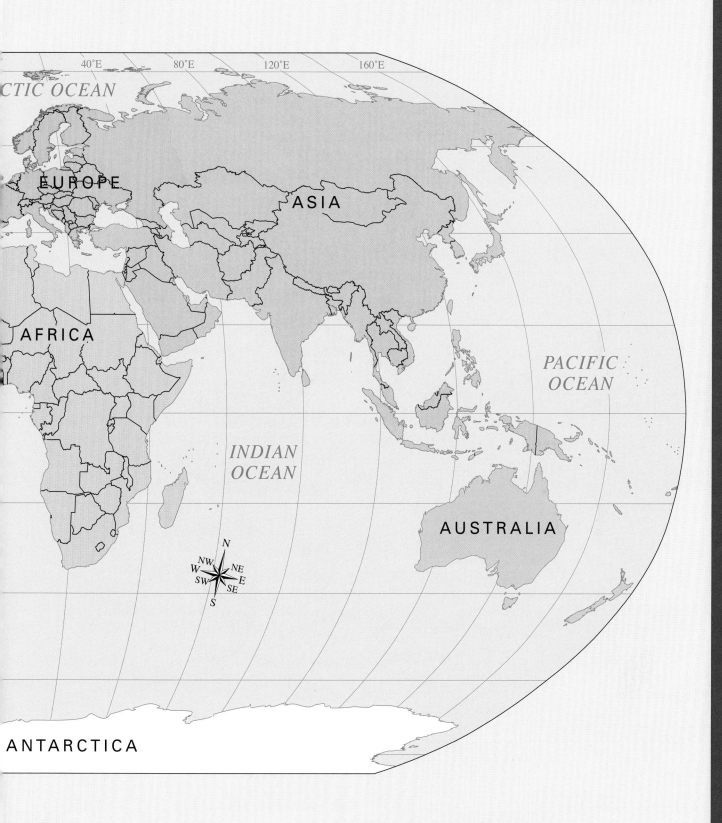

40°E   80°E   120°E   160°E

CTIC OCEAN

EUROPE

ASIA

AFRICA

PACIFIC
OCEAN

INDIAN
OCEAN

AUSTRALIA

N
NW   NE
W   E
SW   SE
S

ANTARCTICA

World Physical Map

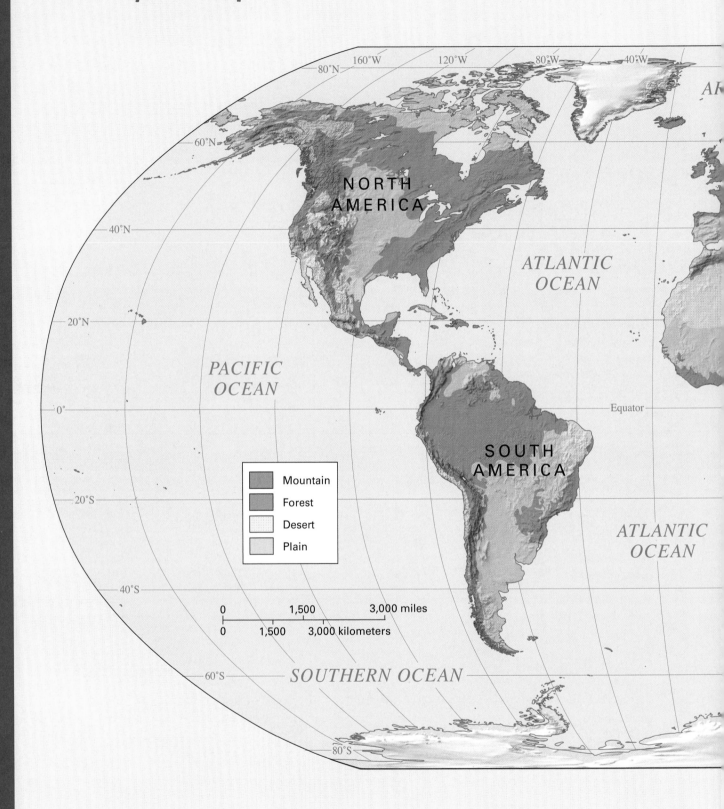

80°N
60°N
40°N
20°N
0°
20°S
40°S
60°S
80°S

160°W   120°W   80°W   40°W

NORTH AMERICA

ATLANTIC OCEAN

PACIFIC OCEAN

Equator

SOUTH AMERICA

ATLANTIC OCEAN

SOUTHERN OCEAN

AR

	Mountain
	Forest
	Desert
	Plain

0   1,500   3,000 miles
0   1,500   3,000 kilometers

World Physical Map

United States Political Map

CANADA

Washington
★ Olympia

★ Salem

Oregon

Helena ★
Montana

North
Dakota

Bismarck ★

South
Dakota

Pierre ★

45°N

★ Boise
Idaho

Wyoming

Cheyenne
★

125°W
40°N

Sacramento
★

★ Carson City
Nevada

Salt Lake
★ City

Utah

★ Denver

Colorado

Nebraska

California

35°N

Arizona

★ Phoenix

★ Santa Fe

New Mexico

Kansas

Oklahoma
City ★

PACIFIC
OCEAN

120°W

Texas

Austin ★

70°N
ARCTIC OCEAN

Alaska

60°N
170°W

PACIFIC
OCEAN

Juneau ★

150°W

140°W

160°W

0   400 miles

0   400 kilometers

160°W
Hawaii
Kauai

Niihau

Honolulu

Oahu

Molokai

Lanai
Kahoolawe

Maui

PACIFIC
OCEAN

20°N

Hawaii

0   150 miles

0   150 kilometers

MEXICO

0 250 500 miles
0 250 500 kilometers

N
NW NE
W E
SW SE
S

Minnesota
St. Paul ★

Wisconsin
Madison ★

Michigan
Lansing ★

New Hampshire
Vermont
Montpelier ★
Maine
Augusta ★
Concord ★
Boston ★
Albany ★ Massachusetts
New York
Hartford ★ Providence ★
Rhode Island
Connecticut

Iowa
Des Moines ★
Lincoln

Illinois
Springfield ★

Indiana
Indianapolis ★

Ohio
Columbus ★

Pennsylvania
Harrisburg ★
Trenton ★
New Jersey

Annapolis ★ Dover ★
Delaware
Washington, D.C. ⊛
Maryland

West Virginia
Charleston ★
Virginia
Richmond ★

Topeka ★
Jefferson City ★
Missouri

Kentucky
Frankfort ★

North Carolina
Raleigh ★

Oklahoma
Arkansas
Little Rock ★

Tennessee
Nashville ★

South Carolina
Columbia ★

Atlanta ★

Mississippi
Jackson ★

Alabama
Montgomery ★

Georgia

Louisiana

Baton Rouge ★

Tallahassee ★

Florida

ATLANTIC OCEAN

Gulf of Mexico

⊛ U.S. capital
★ State capital

70°W
70°W
75°W

95°W 90°W 85°W 80°W

United States Physical Map

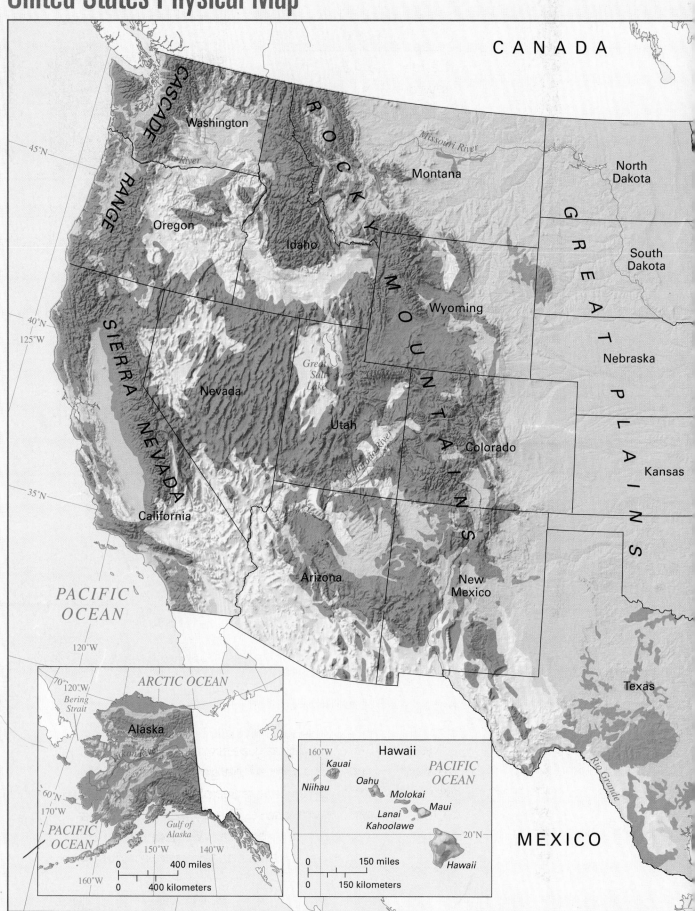

CANADA

CASCADE RANGE

Washington

Columbia River

45°N

Oregon

Idaho

ROCKY MOUNTAINS

Montana

Missouri River

North Dakota

South Dakota

SIERRA NEVADA

Nevada

Great Salt Lake

Utah

Wyoming

GREAT PLAINS

Nebraska

40°N
125°W

Colorado River

Colorado

Kansas

35°N

California

Arizona

New Mexico

PACIFIC OCEAN

120°W

Texas

Rio Grande

MEXICO

ARCTIC OCEAN

70°
120°W

Bering Strait

Alaska

Yukon River

Hawaii

160°W

Kauai

Niihau

Oahu

Molokai

Maui

PACIFIC OCEAN

60°N
170°W

PACIFIC OCEAN

Gulf of Alaska

150°W   140°W

Lanai

Kahoolawe

160°W

0   400 miles

0   400 kilometers

0   150 miles

0   150 kilometers

20°N

Hawaii

0   250   500 miles
0   250   500 kilometers

N
NW   NE
W   E
SW   SE
S

Lake Superior

Minnesota

Lake Huron

Lake Michigan

Wisconsin

Michigan

Mississippi River

St. Lawrence River

Vermont

Maine

New Hampshire

New York

Lake Ontario

Massachusetts

Lake Erie

Rhode Island

Connecticut

Pennsylvania

Iowa

Ohio

New Jersey

Indiana

Delaware

Maryland

70°W

Missouri River

West Virginia

Virginia

Missouri

Ohio River

Kentucky

North Carolina

Mississippi River

Illinois

Tennessee

Arkansas

South Carolina

Oklahoma

APPALACHIAN MOUNTAINS

Georgia

ATLANTIC OCEAN

Mississippi

Alabama

Louisiana

Florida

75°W

Gulf of Mexico

Mountain
Forest
Desert
Plain

95°W   90°W   85°W   80°W

Regional Map of the United States

Population Density Map of the United States

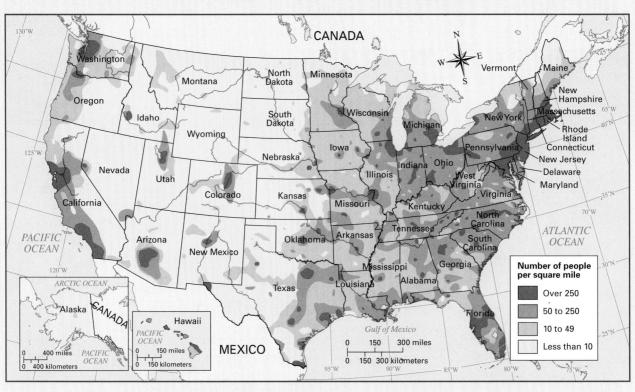

Number of people per square mile

- Over 250
- 50 to 250
- 10 to 49
- Less than 10

Elevation Map of the United States

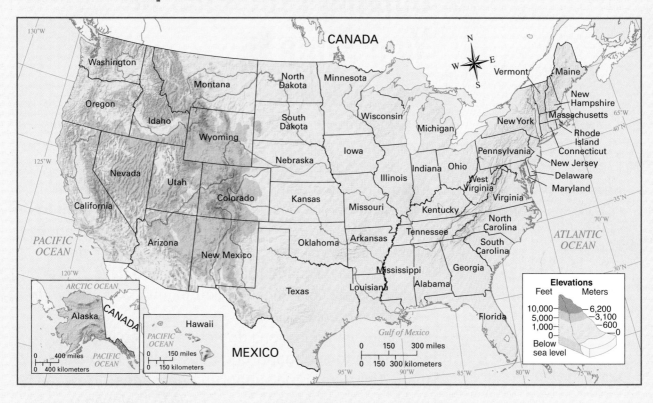

Annual Rainfall Map of the United States

Solving Problems in Your State

Asking Compelling Questions

Good citizens ask questions. They talk about their questions on television, in newspapers, and online. You can be a good citizen by asking questions, too!

Compelling questions are the questions you just need to know the answers to. They make you want to find answers. You can ask compelling questions about problems in your state. For example, you may notice that the highways and roads around you have cracks and potholes. One question you might ask is, "How do we fix the roads?"

Compelling questions do not have easy answers, so it helps to ask supporting questions to help answer them. Here are some supporting questions. "How many roads are in my state?" "Who pays to maintain roads?" "How many cars drive on roads every day?" "Are there ways to reduce damage to the roads?" "How often are roads repaired?"

compelling question
a question you just need to know the answer to

Compelling questions are interesting questions. Thinking of supporting questions will help you answer them.

Finding Helpful Sources

You answer questions by using sources. Think about your supporting questions. A Web site for your state's transportation department might be a helpful source. An expert, such as a road worker, could also be helpful. A library book about building roads might help.

A primary source of an event is an object created by someone who was there. Photos, notebooks, and letters can be primary sources. You might find a news article written about a highway that was built long ago. This could be a helpful primary source.

Knowing who wrote or made a source helps you decide if it is helpful. A person who is an expert on highways or roads is likely to have good information.

Facts and Opinions

Some sources only give **facts**. A fact is a true piece of information. A map of highways in your state contains facts. Others may mix facts with opinions. An **opinion** is what someone thinks or believes. What is your opinion about how often highways should be fixed? When you use sources, understand whether they give facts, opinions, or both.

fact a true piece of information

opinion what someone thinks or believes

You can communicate claims and evidence in many ways. One way is by giving a talk to your class.

> **evidence** the facts you use to back up your claim

Making Claims and Using Evidence

By now you have collected some facts. You have answered your supporting questions. Now you are ready to come up with an answer to your compelling question, "How do we fix the roads?"

Your answer will be a claim supported with facts. Your claim might be, "The state needs to repave our highways so we have smoother roads." The facts you use to back up your claim are called **evidence**. One fact could be that driving is safer on smoother roads. Another could be that smoother roads last longer.

Communicating Conclusions

There are many ways to present your claims and evidence. You might give a talk to your class. You can also contact your state representative. You can write a letter or e-mail with evidence supporting your claim.

You can also communicate with writing, drawings, and photos. They can be presented on a poster or a class Web page.

Taking Informed Action

Good citizens take action to help solve problems. Citizens can volunteer to help their community. They can write letters to the editor of a newspaper. They can write a petition. People who agree will sign the petition. The petition can be presented to community leaders.

Even students can make a difference. What if you wanted to find ways to fix highways in your state? You can use what you learned from helpful sources. You can share your ideas in school and outside school. What actions could you take alone? What action could you take with others?

You can take action by sharing your conclusions about a problem. How would you take action to help repair highways in your state?

State Facts

Alabama

★ Montgomery

Capital

The capital changed three times before finally becoming present-day **Montgomery** in 1847.

Famous Citizen

A group of famous Alabamans, the **Tuskegee Airmen,** were the first African Americans allowed to become military pilots and fight and fly in World War II.

Economy

Farming leads the economy with products like cotton, poultry, peanuts, and paper and other wood products. **Oil, gas,** and **coal** resources add to the economy.

Geography

Most of the state is either forested or good for farming. Rolling plains cover much of the state with mountains in the north. Beaches are popular along the coast of the **Gulf of Mexico**. Mobile is a big port city on **Mobile Bay**.

Climate: Alabama is mostly warm and sunny with a year-round temperature averaging in the 60s. Temperatures tend to be warmer near the Gulf of Mexico. It rains throughout the year. The state is prone to tropical storms.

History

During the American Revolution, parts of the South, like Alabama, were part of two British colonies that stayed loyal to the king.

Fun Facts

State Date: December 14, 1819
Motto: We Dare Maintain Our Rights
Flower: Camellia
Bird: Yellowhammer
Tree: Southern longleaf pine
Song: "Alabama"
Nicknames: Yellowhammer State (unofficial)
Web Site: www.alabama.gov

Camellia

Alaska

Juneau ★

Capital

Joseph Juneau was one of two people who found gold in Gold Creek in August of 1880. **Juneau** started as a "boomtown" along the creek beach and was named the capital of the territory in 1906.

Famous Citizen

Pop singer, **Jewel**, grew up in Homer. She attended a performing arts school, and then left the state to begin her music career.

Economy

The largest part of the state's economy is **oil** and **gas** production. **Tourism** and **fishing** are also main economic forces. Over a million tourists visit Alaska annually.

Geography

Alaska, the largest state, is bordered by the **Pacific Ocean, Bering Sea, Chukchi Sea,** and the **Arctic Ocean**. It has mountains, including North America's tallest mountain (Mt. McKinley or Denali), glaciers, three million lakes, and the **Aleutian Island** chain.

Climate: The weather inside the state can be very different from the weather along the coasts. The southern coast is especially warmer.

History

Natives have lived in the state for about 10,000 years. The United States bought Alaska from Russia in 1867.

Fun Facts

State Date: January 3, 1959
Motto: North to the Future
Flower: Forget-me-not
Bird: Willow ptarmigan
Tree: Sitka spruce
Song: "Alaska's Flag"
Nickname: The Last Frontier
Web Site: www.alaska.gov

Willow ptarmigan

Arizona

★ Phoenix

Capital

Ancient Hohokam people built irrigation canals in the **Phoenix** area. Settlers in the mid-1800s rebuilt the canals. They named the area "Phoenix" because it was built from the ruins of another.

Famous Citizen

Cochise, a Chiricahua Apache, fought with other Apaches to keep their land free of settlers. He became a chief in 1863.

Economy

The major parts of the economy are **manufacturing, mining,** and **tourism**. Tourism and the supporting services are one of the state's largest industries. People come from all over the world to see the Grand Canyon.

Geography

The state has deserts, plateaus, buttes, rushing rivers, dry washes, mountain ranges, and the amazing **Grand Canyon**. There are also **Monument Valley**, **Petrified Forest**, the **Sonoran Desert**, and **Kartchner Caverns**.

Climate: Because there are both mountains and deserts, the climate can have extremes. Temperatures can be very hot in the summer in the desert and very cold in the mountains in the winter.

History

Arizona's history is shown in its many old **American Indian** and **Spanish explorers'** sites.

Fun Facts

State Date: February 14, 1912
Motto: God Enriches
Flower: Saguaro cactus blossom
Bird: Cactus wren
Tree: Palo verde
Songs: "Arizona"; "Arizona March Song"
Nickname: Grand Canyon State
Web Site: www.az.gov

Saguaro blossom

Arkansas

Little Rock
★

Capital

Rock outcroppings along the Arkansas River gave the city its name of **Little Rock**.

Famous Citizen

William Jefferson "Bill" Clinton, the 42nd President of the United States, was born in Hope and grew up in Hot Springs. He served two terms in office from 1992–2000. His presidential library is in Little Rock.

Economy

While Arkansas is mostly **agricultural**, the mining of petroleum, natural gas, and bromine are also important. Bromine is a chemical found as a mineral salt in rock. Mining of precious and semi-precious stones has helped give the state its nickname "the gem state."

Geography

The **Missouri River** is in the north, and to the east is the **Mississippi River**. The rivers provide the state with fertile plains and lowlands, while highlands and the **Ozark plateau** cover the rest. Lakes, rivers, springs, and some low mountains also dot the state.

Climate: The climate is mild with generous rainfall.

History

The first European to visit Arkansas was Hernando **de Soto** in 1541. The first permanent settlement was built in 1686. Settlers came because of good land and precious gems.

Fun Facts

State Date: June 15, 1836
Motto: The People Rule
Flower: Apple blossom
Bird: Mockingbird
Tree: Pine
Songs: "Arkansas"
Nicknames: Land of Opportunity; Wonder State
Web Site: www.arkansas.gov

Mockingbird

California

Capital

Sacramento became the capital in 1854 but had to pay the state one million dollars for that honor!

Famous Citizen

Cesar Chavez was born in Arizona, but he spent much of his adult life living and working in California. He worked to improve the civil rights of farm workers.

Economy

California has millions of acres of **farmland**, and it leads the United States in agricultural production. Top products include **dairy**, **nursery products**, **almonds**, and **grapes**.

Geography

California has many different landforms. Its **Pacific Ocean coastline** is 800 miles long. The highest and lowest points in the lower 48 states are located within 100 miles of each other. **Mt. Whitney** is 14,505 feet, and **Badwater Basin** in Death Valley is 282 feet below sea level.

Climate: Southern California has a warm and often hot and dry climate. The north has more rain along the coast and snow in the mountains.

History

California became a state due to the gold rush of 1848. **Hollywood** became famous around the world in the 1920s for its movie studios.

Fun Facts

State Date: September 9, 1850
Motto: I Have Found It
Flower: Golden poppy
Bird: California Valley quail
Tree: California redwood
Song: "I Love You, California"
Nickname: The Golden State
Web Site: www.ca.gov

California Valley quail

Colorado

Capital

Denver is known as the "Mile High City" because the 13th step on the west side of the capitol building is exactly one mile, or 5,280 feet, above sea level.

Famous Citizen

Condoleezza Rice attended high school and college in Denver. She was the first African American woman to be Secretary of State of the United States.

Economy

Colorado generates most of its money through **service industries**, although **agriculture** is in the eastern part of the state. The western half, covered by the Rocky Mountains, has many recreation areas as well as **oil** and **gas deposits**.

Geography

Colorado is a land-locked state that is flat in the east, where it is part of the **Great Plains**. Further west, it is covered with the **Rocky Mountains** and the **Colorado Plateau**.

Climate: The climate is mild but varies because of the plains and the mountains. There is often snow and colder temperatures in the mountains, while the plains are drier and warmer.

History

When **gold** was discovered in 1858, many new settlers arrived.

Fun Facts

State Date: August 1, 1876
Motto: Nothing Without Providence
Flower: Rocky Mountain columbine
Bird: Lark bunting
Tree: Colorado blue spruce
Songs: "Where the Columbines Grow"; "Rocky Mountain High"
Nickname: Centennial State
Web Site: www.colorado.gov

Rocky Mountain columbine

Connecticut

★ Hartford

Capital

The first Boys and Girls Club was started in **Hartford** in 1860. It was a place for children to go instead of hanging around the streets.

Famous Citizen

Noah Webster was born in West Hartford. He published the first American English dictionary in 1783. He helped make the spelling of words the same, or standard, everywhere.

Economy

Industry is the main basis for the economy. The manufacture of textiles, electronics, computer equipment, helicopters, and submarines are important. The service industries of tourism and insurance are also important parts of the economy.

Geography

The southerly flow of the Connecticut River roughly divides the state into the **eastern** and **western highlands**. About two thirds of the state is open land. There is also a **coastal plain** in the south along **Long Island Sound**, a popular summer resort area.

Climate: The coast has warmer winters and cooler summers than the inner parts of the state.

History

The state was settled by **English Puritans** in 1633.

Fun Facts

State Date: January 9, 1788
Motto: He Who Transplanted Still Sustains
Flower: Mountain laurel
Bird: American robin
Tree: White oak
Song: "Yankee Doodle"
Nicknames: Constitution State; Nutmeg State
Web Site: www.ct.gov

American robin

Delaware

★ Dover

Capital

Every year, two NASCAR races in **Dover** bring so many tourists the population of the city grows from 30,000 people to more than 200,000 the weeks of the races.

Famous Citizen

Henry Heimlich, surgeon, was born in Wilmington. In 1974, he told about a new way to stop people from choking, now known as the "Heimlich maneuver."

Economy

Most of Delaware's economy counts on service industries like **finance**, **insurance**, and **real estate**. **Industrial chemicals**, **drugs**, and **plastics** are important products made in the state.

Geography

Delaware is nearly surrounded by water with the **Atlantic Ocean** on the east and **Delaware Bay** on the west. The majority of the state is in the **Atlantic Coastal Plain**, which means that the state is low and flat. The southern part of Delaware is 30,000 acres of swampland!

Climate: The climate on the coast is milder, with winters being 10 degrees warmer and summers being 10 degrees cooler than the inland areas of the state.

History

Henry Hudson discovered Delaware Bay, opening the area for European settlement in 1609.

Fun Facts

State Date: December 7, 1787
Motto: Liberty and Independence
Flower: Peach blossom
Bird: Blue hen chicken
Tree: American holly
Song: "Our Delaware"
Nicknames: First State; Diamond State
Web Site: www.de.gov

American holly

Florida

★ Tallahassee

Capital

South of **Tallahassee** are huge underground sinkholes, many filled with water. Miles of underground passageways lead from the sinkholes to a famous tourist spot, Wakulla Springs.

Famous Citizen

Sidney Poitier was born in 1927 in Miami. He was the first African American to receive an Academy Award for Best Actor in 1964.

Economy

With over 87 million visitors annually, Florida is the top travel destination in the world. The **service industry**, which supports **tourism**, is a multi-billion dollar addition to the state's economy. The **space industry** and **farming**, especially of oranges, are also important to the state's economy.

Geography

With the **Atlantic Ocean** on the east and the **Gulf of Mexico** on the west, most of Florida's **peninsula** is coastal plain. **Big Cypress Swamp** and the **Everglades** are unique swamp areas in the state.

Climate: Florida is known for its warm, mild winters and very hot and humid summers with thunderstorms.

History

In the mid-1500s, Florida stretched from the Atlantic Ocean to the Mississippi River.

Fun Facts

State Date: March 3, 1845
Motto: In God We Trust
Flower: Orange blossom
Bird: Mockingbird
Tree: Sabal palm
Song: "Old Folks at Home"
Nickname: Sunshine State
Web Site: myflorida.com

Orange blossom

Georgia

★ Atlanta

Capital

While **Atlanta** has been the capital since 1868, it was not the first capital. In fact, there have been five capitals of Georgia!

Famous Citizen

Martin Luther King Jr. was born in Atlanta in 1929. He was a Baptist minister and an important Civil Rights activist and leader. He promoted non-violent activism as a way to get change.

Economy

Georgia leads the country in the farming of **pecans**, **peanuts**, and **peaches**. However, most of Georgia's money comes from the manufacture of **petroleum products** and **transportation equipment**.

Geography

Georgia is the largest state east of the Mississippi River. It has some of the **Blue Ridge Mountains** in the north and gets flatter closer to the **Atlantic Ocean**. The land is good for agriculture and forestry.

Climate: The climate in Georgia varies because of the geography. The summers in the east are warm, but in the middle of the state, it is even hotter. It hardly ever snows in any part of Georgia.

History

Georgia was named for **King George II**.

Fun Facts

State Date: January 2, 1788
Motto: Wisdom, Justice, Moderation
Flower: Cherokee rose
Bird: Brown thrasher
Tree: Live oak
Song: "Georgia on My Mind"
Nicknames: Empire State of the South; The Peach State
Web Site: www.georgia.gov

Pecans

Hawaii

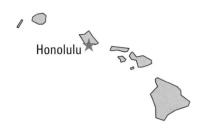

Honolulu

Capital

Honolulu was first named Kou, but the name was later changed to Honolulu. In the Hawaiian language it means "sheltered harbor."

Famous Citizen

Liliuokalani was the first woman to sit on the Hawaiian throne. She became queen in 1891. She was asked to give up her throne and did in 1895.

Economy

Tourism and service industries like **health care**, **restaurants**, and **law offices** provide the most money for the state. Hawaii is also a leading state for growing pineapples and sugar cane.

Geography

Hawaii is the **southernmost** state in the United States. It is the only state that is made up of just **islands**. The Hawaiian Islands are the world's longest island chain. **Coral** and **volcanoes** formed the islands. They continue to shape and reshape them today.

Climate: The state's climate is warm all year round. It is usually warm and sunny, although there is snow at the top of some of the mountains. **Trade winds** blow year round.

History

Hawaii was an important harbor and base for the United States in World War II.

Fun Facts

State Date: August 21, 1959
Motto: The Life of the Land Is Perpetuated in Righteousness
Flower: Yellow hibiscus
Bird: Hawaiian goose
Tree: Candlenut
Song: "Hawaii Pono'i"
Nickname: The Aloha State
Web Site: www.hawaii.gov

Yellow hibiscus

Idaho

★ Boise

Capital

The capitol building in **Boise** is the only U.S. capitol to be heated by geothermal water from 3,000 feet below the surface.

Famous Citizen

Sacajawea was born in what is now eastern Idaho around 1790. She was the Shoshone guide and interpreter for explorers Lewis and Clark starting in 1804.

Economy

Major industries include **manufacturing**, **tourism**, **agriculture**, **timber**, and **mining**. Idaho leads the country in production of **potatoes**, **trout**, **Austrian winter peas**, and **lentils**. **Mining** includes 72 types of precious and semi-precious stones, some found only in the state.

Geography

Idaho is home to **Hells Canyon**, a **river gorge** that is deeper even than the Grand Canyon. The state is **landlocked** and is bordered by six other states and Canada.

Climate: Despite being in the north, Idaho has a moderate climate, especially in the plains, which are quite dry. The mountains have plenty of snow and cold winters.

History

The Louisiana Purchase in 1803 included the Idaho territory. The discovery of gold in 1852 brought new settlers.

Fun Facts

State Date: July 3, 1890
Motto: Let It Be Perpetual
Flower: Syringa
Bird: Mountain bluebird
Tree: Western white pine
Song: "Here We Have Idaho"
Nickname: Gem State
Web Site: www.idaho.gov

Potatoes

Illinois

★ Springfield

Capital

The first European settler to arrive at the prairie site that is now **Springfield** was Elisha Kelly who came in 1819.

Famous Citizen

Illinois's most famous citizen is probably **Abraham Lincoln**. He lived and worked in both New Salem and Springfield prior to becoming president and leading the country through the Civil War.

Economy

Much of the northern part of the state around Chicago is urban and a leader in **manufacturing** and **service industry** jobs. Chicago is considered the financial capital of the Midwest. The central part of the state has farming. The southern part of the state has important **coal** deposits.

Geography

Illinois is located in the center of the Midwest. It is on **Lake Michigan** and is bordered by the **Mississippi, Wabash,** and **Ohio rivers**. The **Fox, Rock,** and **Illinois rivers** run through the state. The land has **fertile, rich soil,** common in the plains states.

Climate: Illinois has four distinct seasons with hot summers and cold winters.

History

Congress purposefully drew the state's border to include **Chicago**.

Fun Facts

State Date: December 3, 1818
Motto: State Sovereignty, National Union
Flower: Violet
Bird: Cardinal
Tree: White oak
Song: "Illinois"
Nicknames: The Prairie State; The Land of Lincoln
Web Site: www.illinois.gov

Violet

Indiana

★ Indianapolis

Capital

Indianapolis is referred to as "Indy" by the local residents. The city is the home of the Indianapolis Motor Speedway, which was built in 1909.

Famous Citizen

Macon Bolling Allen (1925–2005) was the first African American to be licensed to practice law in the United States. He was born in Indiana.

Economy

The northern part of the state, close to Chicago and Lake Michigan, used to be famous for its steel production. However, many of those jobs are now gone, and most of Indiana's jobs and income comes from service industries such as **wholesale and retail trade, health care,** and **financial services**. Indiana is also a leading **agricultural state**. It grows corn, soybeans, and dairy products.

Geography

Indiana is almost all **fertile plains**. The state's borders include **Lake Michigan** in the northwest and the **Ohio and Wabash rivers** in the south and southwest.

Climate: The climate is typical for the Midwest with hot summers and cold winters. The area just south of Lake Michigan receives a lot more snow in the winter because of the lake.

History

Built in the center of the state, Indianapolis became a crossroads for roads and trains.

Fun Facts

State Date: December 11, 1816
Motto: The Crossroads of America
Flower: Peony
Bird: Cardinal
Tree: Yellow tulip poplar
Song: "On the Banks of the Wabash"
Nickname: Hoosier State
Web Site: www.in.gov

Peony

Iowa

Des Moines

Capital

Originally a military outpost, the name **Des Moines** comes from an American Indian word for the Indian burial mounds that were near the cities' rivers.

Famous Citizen

Johnny Carson, (1925–2005) late night TV host, was born in Corning, Iowa. He is best known as the host of "The Tonight Show" for 30 years.

Economy

Primarily an agricultural state, Iowa is the U.S. leader in **hog** and **corn production**. Farms also produce **milk**, **eggs**, and **soybeans**. The leading manufacturing industry is **food processing**.

Geography

Iowa is a "bridge" state, joining the forests of the East and the plains of the West. The **Mississippi** and **Missouri rivers** border the state on the east and the west, providing very **fertile land** in between. Ideal for farming, this land is mostly rolling plains.

Climate: Iowa has four distinct seasons with very cold winters and warm and humid summers. Rain can fall heavily in the summer causing floods.

History

Iowa played an important role in the **Underground Railroad** during the **Civil War**.

Fun Facts

State Date: December 28, 1846
Motto: Our Liberties We Prize, and Our Rights We Will Maintain
Flower: Wild prairie rose
Bird: Eastern goldfinch
Tree: Oak
Song: "The Song of Iowa"
Nickname: Hawkeye State
Web Site: www.iowa.gov

Oak

Kansas

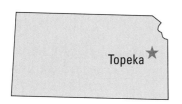

Topeka

Capital

Three French Canadians settled in the **Topeka** area and set up a ferry service over the Kansas (Kaw) River in 1842. The Oregon Trail crossed the river at Topeka. The site became the capital in 1861.

Famous Citizen

Amelia Earhart was born in 1897 in Atchison. She was the first woman to fly over the Atlantic Ocean in 1928.

Economy

Kansas has expanded from an **agriculture** economy to a diverse mix of industries. While agriculture is still important (Kansas ranks first in the United States for wheat production), **aviation** in the Wichita area, **wind energy**, and **food processing**, provide important revenue for the state.

Geography

Kansas is a Midwestern state almost entirely made up of **plains**. The eastern half of the state has some **hills** and **forests**, but the western portion is flat. The soil is fertile and ideal for farming.

Climate: Kansas generally has a moderate climate, but there are large extremes in temperatures between winter and summer.

History

After many bloody battles, Kansas chose to enter the Union as a free state in 1861.

Fun Facts

State Date: January 29, 1861
Motto: To the Stars Through Difficulties
Flower: Wild native sunflower
Bird: Western meadowlark
Tree: Cottonwood
Song: "Home on the Range"
Nickname: Sunflower State
Web Site: www.kansas.gov

Wild native sunflower

Kentucky

Frankfort

Capital

Originally known as Frank's Ford, **Frankfort** was one of several fords, or places to cross, on the Kentucky River. It was named for Stephen Frank, a settler who died at or near the site in 1780.

Famous Citizen

Helen Thomas (1920–2013) was born in Winchester. She was a journalist known for her coverage of the White House. She broke barriers for women reporters.

Economy

Kentucky's economy includes **manufacturing**, **service industries**, **mining**, **real estate**, **farming**, **forestry**, and **fisheries**. **Horses** are the leading source of farm income with famous thoroughbred farms.

Geography

Lying just west of the Appalachian Mountains, Kentucky has more running water than any other state except Alaska. It is bordered by the **Ohio River** to the north and west. Other important rivers include the **Mississippi**, **Cumberland**, **Green**, and **Kentucky**.

Climate: It is generally mild to moderate with warm summers, somewhat cold winters, and plenty of rainfall.

History

The electric light bulb was first introduced by **Thomas Edison** in 1883 in Louisville.

Fun Facts

State Date: June 1, 1792
Motto: United We Stand, Divided We Fall
Flower: Goldenrod
Bird: Cardinal
Tree: Tulip poplar
Song: "My Old Kentucky Home"
Nickname: Bluegrass State
Web Site: www.kentucky.gov

Horse

Louisiana

Baton Rouge

Capital

Baton Rouge is the farthest inland deep water port on the Mississippi. Because ocean-going vessels can get to Baton Rouge, it has become a major center for commerce and industry.

Famous Citizen

Noted jazz musician, **Louis Armstrong**, was born in 1901 in New Orleans, the birthplace of jazz.

Economy

Coastal **oil** and **gas production**, as well as **mining** of **sulfur**, **lime**, and **salt** are the mainstays of the economy. **Tourism** is the second most important industry, especially in New Orleans, the state's largest city. **Forestry**, **agriculture**, and **commercial fishing** also play large roles.

Geography

Much of southern Louisiana is **lowland** or **swamps**, home to rice fields and alligators. Two large rivers, the Mississippi and Sabine, form the eastern and western borders. The interior is **forest** and **agricultural land**.

Climate: The state's climate is almost tropical. It has hot, humid summers and mild winters. Rain is frequent throughout the year.

History

The state was governed by Spain, France, and Great Britain before it became part of the United States.

Fun Facts

State Date: April 30, 1812
Motto: Union, Justice, Confidence
Flower: Magnolia
Bird: Eastern brown pelican
Tree: Bald cypress
Songs: "Give Me Louisiana"; "You Are My Sunshine"
Nickname: Pelican State
Web Site: www.louisiana.gov

Brown pelican

Maine

★ Augusta

Capital

Old Western Fort was the first building on the site of what would become the city of **Augusta**. This 1754 fort is the oldest surviving wooden fort in New England.

Famous Citizen

E.B. White (1899–1985) lived most of his adult life in North Brooklin, Maine. He is best known for his children's books, *Stuart Little* and *Charlotte's Web*.

Economy

Maine's economy is strong in **timber**, **boat building**, **tourism**, and **agriculture.** Blueberries, maple syrup, and apples are the state's best known agricultural products. The seafood industry is important, with lobster catchers catching millions of pounds of lobster each year for visitors and locals alike.

Geography

Glaciers helped create more than 2,000 **lakes** in Maine's heavily forested interior. The state also has a **rocky coast** along the Atlantic Ocean.

Climate: Maine has a northern climate of warm summers and cold, snowy winters. Temperatures along the Atlantic coast are a bit warmer in the winter and cooler in the summer.

History

The first Veterans' Hospital in the United States was built in Togus, Maine.

Fun Facts

State Date: March 15, 1820
Motto: I Lead
Flower: White pine cone and tassel
Bird: Chickadee
Tree: Eastern white pine
Song: "State of Maine Song"
Nickname: Pine Tree State
Web Site: www.maine.gov

Chickadee

Maryland

Annapolis ★

Capital

As a colonial city, **Annapolis** was known as the "Athens of America" because of its many cultural activities.

Famous Citizen

Thurgood Marshall was born in Baltimore in 1908. He studied law at Howard University. He was the first African American to sit on the U.S. Supreme Court, serving from 1967–1991.

Economy

Information technology, telecommunications, aerospace, and **defense** industries lead the state's economic growth. Because of Chesapeake Bay, ocean-going ships are able to **export** its goods to other countries.

Geography

Maryland is partially bordered by the **Atlantic Ocean** and is divided by **Chesapeake Bay**, with the two sections referred to as the **East Shore** and the **West Shore**. Maryland also has the **Atlantic Coastal Plain**, the **Blue Ridge region**, and the **Appalachian ridge** and **plateau**.

Climate: The East Shore has a warm, moist climate. The West Shore has cold winters and hot summers.

History

George Calvert received a royal charter for a colony from English king **Charles I**, so he named it Maryland in honor of the queen.

Fun Facts

State Date: April 28, 1788
Motto: Manly Deeds, Womanly Words
Flower: Black-eyed Susan
Bird: Baltimore oriole
Tree: White oak
Song: "Maryland, My Maryland"
Nicknames: Old Line State; Free State
Web Site: www.maryland.gov

Baltimore oriole

Massachusetts

Boston ★

Capital

Firsts for **Boston** include the first subway system in the United States built in 1897. The Boston Common became the first U.S. public park in 1634.

Famous Citizen

Squanto, an American Indian of the Patuset tribe, acted as interpreter and guide for the Pilgrims at Plymouth during their first winter.

Economy

Besides agricultural income found in **dairy**, **nursery products**, **cranberries**, and **fruit**, the state has considerable industry. **Defense technology**, **biotechnology**, **financial services**, a growing **film industry**, and **manufacturing** are important economic contributors.

Geography

Once totally forested except for the **Atlantic Coast** and **Cape Cod**, Massachusetts now has farms in the fertile **Connecticut River Valley**. The coastal areas are a mix of **rocky shores**, **sandy beaches**, and **salt marshes**.

Climate: The climate is moderate, with cold and snowy weather inland in the winter and hot summers. The coast is milder.

History

Pilgrims arrived in Massachusetts in 1620.

Fun Facts

State Date: February 6, 1788
Motto: By the Sword We Seek Peace, but Peace Only Under Liberty
Flower: Mayflower
Bird: Black-capped chickadee
Tree: American elm
Song: "All Hail to Massachusetts"
Nicknames: Bay State; Old Colony State
Web Site: www.mass.gov

American elm

Michigan

Lansing ★

Capital

The area of **Lansing** was wilderness when two brothers from Lansing, New York, settled the area in 1835 and called it "Biddle Town."

Famous Citizen

Henry Ford was born near Dearborn, Michigan, in 1863. He introduced the Model A in 1908. He is best known for developing the moving assembly line.

Economy

Mining is a big part of Michigan's economy. The world's largest limestone quarries are in the state. Michigan ranks second in the production of iron ore. Surrounded by four of the Great Lakes, **fishing** is also important. The state is also famous for its **production of transportation parts** and **vehicles**.

Geography

Michigan is unique because it is made up of two separate **peninsulas** (land that sticks out into water on three sides): the Upper and Lower.

Climate: The Great Lakes help to give Michigan a more moderate climate than other northern states. The Upper Peninsula is cooler than the Lower Peninsula.

History

All of the car plants made military equipment during **World War II**.

Fun Facts

State Date: January 26, 1837
Motto: If You Seek a Pleasant Peninsula, Look About You
Flower: Apple blossom
Bird: American robin
Tree: White pine
Song: "My Michigan"
Nicknames: Great Lakes State; Wolverine State
Web Site: www.michigan.gov

Apple blossom

Minnesota

★ St. Paul

Capital

St. Paul, the capital, and its neighbor, Minneapolis, are known as the "Twin Cities." The Twin Cities, with their suburbs, hold over half the state's population!

Famous Citizen

Charles M. Schulz, creator of the *Peanuts* cartoons and characters, was born in Minneapolis in 1922. He launched the *Peanuts* comic strip in 1950.

Economy

Minnesota has a strong economy with much of it centered in the Minneapolis/St. Paul area. This urban area is home to major **national and international corporations. Agriculture** adds to the economy with livestock, dairy products, corn, and soybeans.

Geography

Most of Minnesota is gently rolling **plains** well suited for agriculture. There are more than 10,000 **lakes** dotting the landscape. Major bodies of water include **Lake Superior**, the **St. Croix River**, **Mississippi River**, and the **Red River of the North**.

Climate: The climate has four distinct seasons with warm to hot summers and very cold and snowy winters.

History

Between 1830 and 1900, large numbers of **German and Scandinavian immigrants** settled in the state.

Fun Facts

State Date: May 11, 1858
Motto: The Star of the North
Flower: Pink and white lady's slipper
Bird: Common loon
Tree: Red pine
Song: "Hail! Minnesota"
Nicknames: North Star State
Web Site: www.mn.gov

Common loon

Mississippi

★ Jackson

Capital

Originally known as LeFleur's Bluff, **Jackson** was renamed honoring Major General Andrew Jackson who later became the 7th President of the United States.

Famous Citizen

Oprah Winfrey, actress and talk show host, was born in Kosciusko, Mississippi, in 1954. She has donated millions of dollars to educational causes.

Economy

Lumbering, **wood products**, **manufacturing**, **farming**, **oil production**, and **tourism** are common in Mississippi's economy. Cotton, soybeans, and farm-raised catfish are important agricultural products. Tourists are especially drawn to Civil War sites and to the Gulf Coast.

Geography

The **Mississippi River** forms the western boundary of the state and gave it its name. The **Gulf of Mexico** is to the south. Much of the state is coastal plain. The state has lots of southern pine forests and farmland.

Climate: The warm, humid climate is good for growing crops. The summers are long and hot, and the winters are short and mild.

History

While hunting in 1902, President Teddy Roosevelt refused to shoot a captured bear. This kindness inspired the "Teddy Bear" toy.

Fun Facts

State Date: December 10, 1817
Motto: By Valor and Arms
Flower: Magnolia
Bird: Mockingbird
Tree: Magnolia
Song: "Go, Mississippi"
Nickname: Magnolia State
Web Site: www.ms.gov

Magnolia

Missouri

Jefferson City

Capital

Jefferson City was created in 1821 specifically to serve as the state's capital. It was named for Thomas Jefferson, 3rd President of the United States.

Famous Citizen

Mark Twain was born as Samuel Langhorne Clemens in 1835 in Florida, Missouri. He is best known for his novels, including *The Adventures of Tom Sawyer*.

Economy

Missouri has a mixed economy and is a leader in the **manufacture of transportation equipment**. **Service industries** are also important, and the cities of St. Louis and Kansas City are among the Midwest's leading financial cities.

Geography

Much of the state is covered by **plains**. The northern and western plains are fertile and particularly good for growing crops. The area near the **Mississippi River** was once swampy, but is now drained. It has rich soil good for growing crops as well.

Climate: The state has a "continental" climate, which means there are four distinct seasons.

History

So many settlers began their treks west from Missouri, it earned the name **"Gateway to the West."**

Fun Facts

State Date: August 10, 1821
Motto: The Welfare of the People Shall Be the Supreme Law
Flower: White hawthorn blossom
Bird: Eastern bluebird
Tree: Flowering dogwood
Song: "Missouri Waltz"
Nickname: Show Me State
Web Site: www.mo.gov

Eastern bluebird

Montana

Helena

Capital

Helena started as a boomtown after gold was discovered in the nearby creek, Last Chance Gulch.

Famous Citizen

Evel Knievel was born in 1938 in Butte, Montana. He was a stunt motorcycle rider. He drove through firewalls, and jumped over buses and a canyon. During his career, he broke almost 40 bones.

Economy

The wide open spaces of Montana are good for raising **livestock**. In fact, some of the country's biggest cattle ranches are in the state. Montana's largest industries are agriculture (almost half just in livestock), tourism, timber, and mining (copper, gold, and silver).

Geography

The land can be roughly divided into two regions. The eastern part of Montana is part of the **Great Plains.** The western portion of the state includes the **Rocky Mountain** region.

Climate: This eastern half of the state has a harsh climate with hot summers and very cold winters. The climate of the western part is milder with warm summers and cool winters.

History

The discovery of **gold** at Grasshopper Creek in 1862 brought prospectors to the state.

Fun Facts

State Date: November 8, 1889
Motto: Gold and Silver
Flower: Bitterroot
Bird: Western meadowlark
Tree: Ponderosa pine
Song: "Montana"
Nicknames: Treasure State; Big Sky Country
Web Site: www.mt.gov

Ponderosa pine

Nebraska

Capital

The state's first capital was in Omaha, the most populous city. It was moved to Lancaster and renamed "**Lincoln**" to honor the former president.

Famous Citizen

Warren Buffett, born in Omaha in 1930, is one of the wealthiest and most respected businessmen in the world. He has donated billions to worthy causes.

Economy

Agriculture is the main economic force in Nebraska with **cattle**, **hogs**, **corn**, and **wheat** being raised. Nebraska has always been a major food-producing state. In fact, food processing is an important manufacturing industry.

Geography

Nebraska is part of the **Great Plains** with fertile farmland crisscrossed by numerous **rivers**. The western part of the state contains the bottom of the **Rocky Mountains** and is considered to be semiarid, or desert-like.

Climate: All of the state can have major changes in temperatures, with very hot summers and cold winters. Snow and rain amounts, especially in the eastern half of the state can be heavy.

History

American Indians hunted bison, an abundant animal in Nebraska's early history.

Fun Facts

State Date: March 1, 1867
Motto: Equality Before the Law
Flower: Goldenrod
Bird: Western meadowlark
Tree: Cottonwood
Song: "Beautiful Nebraska"
Nicknames: Cornhusker State; Beef State
Web Site: www.nebraska.gov

Western meadowlark

Nevada

Capital

Carson City was named for Kit Carson, the famous frontiersman and scout, who explored much of the American West.

Famous Citizen

Velma Bronn Johnston (1912–1977) was a rancher, wild horse advocate, and activist. Her work to protect wild horses and set up refuges earned her the nickname "Wild Horse Annie."

Economy

Nevada's economy relies heavily on **agriculture**, **mining**, and **tourism**, especially in the largest city, Las Vegas. Its agriculture industry includes cattle, hay, and dairy products.

Geography

Most of Nevada is within the **Great Basin** of the United States. This area has no drainage to any sea or ocean. The basin is surrounded by hills and mountains. Nevada has many mesas, buttes, and deserts.

Climate: Nevada is the driest state in the country. The climate is a mix. Much of the state is desert with wide temperature ranges (both daily and seasonally) and very little precipitation. Forests grow in the mountain ranges.

History

In 1859, the largest silver deposit in the United States was discovered: the **Comstock Lode**.

Fun Facts

State Date: October 31, 1864
Motto: All for Our Country
Flower: Sagebrush
Bird: Mountain bluebird
Trees: Single-leaf piñon; bristlecone pine
Song: "Home Means Nevada"
Nicknames: Battle-Born State; Sagebrush State; Silver State
Web Site: www.nv.gov

Bristlecone pine

New Hampshire

Concord ★

Capital

Concord has large amounts of granite rock near the city. Workers cut out, or quarry, the granite for use in buildings, such as those in Washington, D.C.

Famous Citizen

Alan Shepard, the first American to travel in space, was born in 1923 in Derry. He commanded *Apollo 14* in 1971 when it landed on the moon.

Economy

Mining of **granite**, **sand**, and **gravel** for roads and **concrete** are New Hampshire's leading mining products. Within manufacturing, **computer**, **electronics**, and **telephone equipment** industries take the lead. Agricultural crops include **hay** for livestock and **maple syrup**.

Geography

New Hampshire is part of the **New England** region. **Mt. Washington** of the **White Mountains** is the highest peak in the northeastern United States.

Climate: The climate in the state is changeable. Each of the four seasons vary greatly in temperature. Summers are usually warm and pleasant, and winters are snowy, cold, and long.

History

The first **American public library** was in Peterborough.

Fun Facts

State Date: June 21, 1788
Motto: Live Free or Die
Flower: Purple lilac
Bird: Purple finch
Tree: White birch
Song: "Old New Hampshire"
Nicknames: Granite State; Mother of Rivers; White Mountain State; Switzerland of America
Web Site: www.nh.gov

Purple finch

New Jersey

★ Trenton

Capital

Trenton was named for William Trent, one of its early landowners. The city was the national capital for a short time in 1784.

Famous Citizen

Judy Blume, author of numerous children's books, was born in Elizabeth, New Jersey, in 1938. *Tales of a Fourth Grade Nothing* was the first of her "Fudge" books.

Economy

New Jersey's economy is concentrated in the **finance** and **insurance** areas as well as manufacturing items such as **industrial chemicals**, **paints**, and **plastics**. The state is a leader in harvesting **clams**.

Geography

New Jersey's **Atlantic Coastal Plain** covers the southern coast of the state and includes **rolling hills**, **pine forests**, and **salt marshes**. Further inland lie the **Piedmont** and the **New England Upland**.

Climate: Being close to the Atlantic Ocean, New Jersey has a fairly moderate climate. There are cold winters and warm, humid summers. Snowfall and rainfall are considered moderate.

History

During the **American war for independence**, Americans and British fought **100 battles** in the state.

Fun Facts

State Date: December 18, 1787
Motto: Liberty and Prosperity
Flower: Violet
Bird: Eastern goldfinch
Tree: Red oak
Song: (None)
Nickname: Garden State
Web Site: www.nj.gov

Eastern goldfinch

New Mexico

Santa Fe

Capital

Spanish explorer Don Pedro de Peralta laid out a plan for **Santa Fe** in 1609 at the site of an ancient Pueblo ruin. The city's history attracts tourists each year.

Famous Citizen

In war, secret communication is important. During World War II, **Navaho marines** created a code in their Dine language. Their code saved thousands of lives.

Economy

New Mexico is a leading state in **mined oil**, **coal**, and **gas** products. The land is very dry so crops need irrigation. The largest agricultural products are **dairy**, **livestock**, **hay**, and **pecans**. **Tourism** is also important to the economy.

Geography

Eastern New Mexico is part of the **Great Plains**. This area is good for sheep and cattle. The central part of the state contains an extension of the **Rocky Mountains**. The **Sangre de Cristo**, **Nacimiento**, and **Jemez mountains** lie further to the west.

Climate: The state has a partly dry to dry climate with much sunshine and low humidity. The days in summer are usually hot, but the nights are always cool.

History

Ancient civilizations in New Mexico include the Clovis, Folsom, and Anasazi.

Fun Facts

State Date: January 6, 1912
Motto: It Grows as It Goes
Flower: Yucca
Bird: Greater roadrunner
Tree: Piñon pine
Song: "O Fair New Mexico"
Nicknames: Land of Enchantment; Sunshine State
Web Site: www.newmexico.gov

Yucca

New York

Albany ★

Capital

Albany became well known when, in 1807, Robert Fulton built a steamboat *Clermont* and traveled up the Hudson River from New York City to Albany. This was the start of regular, faster transportation by steamboat.

Famous Citizen

Sonia Sotomayor was born in the Bronx, New York, in 1954. She became the first Latina U.S. Supreme Court Justice in 2009.

Economy

Much of New York's economy is driven by New York City, the country's leading **financial center**, home to the New York Stock Exchange. Other finance, insurance, and real estate companies also have their headquarters in New York City.

Geography

New York's important water borders include the **Atlantic Ocean**, **Lake Ontario**, **Lake Erie**, and **Lake Champlain**. Its many landforms include **lowlands**, the **Appalachian highlands**, and the **Adirondack** and **Catskill Mountains**.

Climate: New York generally has a moderate climate. Summers can be hot and humid. Winters are often snowy and cold.

History

New York City was the first capital of the new United States after the ratification of the Constitution in 1789–1790.

Fun Facts

State Date: July 26, 1788
Motto: Ever Upward
Flower: Rose
Bird: Eastern bluebird
Tree: Sugar maple
Song: "I Love New York"
Nickname: Empire State
Web Site: www.ny.gov

Sugar maple

North Carolina

Raleigh ★

Capital

Raleigh is known as the City of Oaks because of its many oak trees. A large acorn sculpture is used to count down the new year in Moore Square.

Famous Citizen

Virginia Dare, born August 18, 1587, at Roanoke Island, was the first child born in the Americas to English-speaking parents. The area was part of Virginia, providing the little girl's name.

Economy

Being on the Atlantic Ocean makes services related to **tourism** a major contributor to the economy. People flock to the ocean beaches but also visit the state's western mountains.

Geography

The **Atlantic Ocean** lies to the east of the state, and the **Blue Ridge** and **Great Smoky Mountains** are on the west, along the border with Tennessee. The landforms include the **Atlantic Coastal Plain**, foothills, and the **mountains**.

Climate: The state has a warm temperate climate, but the mountains and the coastal plains can vary in temperature. The state receives moderate rainfall and a little snow.

History

The **Wright Brothers** flew their first airplane at **Kitty Hawk.**

Fun Facts

State Date: November 21, 1789
Motto: To Be Rather Than to Seem
Flower: Dogwood
Bird: Cardinal
Tree: Pine
Song: "The Old North State"
Nickname: The Old North State; The Tar Heel State
Web Site: www.nc.gov

Dogwood

North Dakota

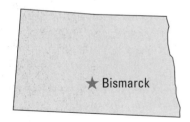
★ Bismarck

Capital

When gold was discovered in the Black Hills, **Bismarck** became a center for prospectors. The town grew from this and the railroad that arrived shortly after. The town burned down in 1898 but was quickly rebuilt.

Famous Citizen

Louis L'Amour, born in North Dakota in 1908, became famous for the popular westerns he wrote.

Economy

North Dakota has a large **agricultural economy** including livestock, wheat, barley, sugar beets, soybeans, and sunflower seeds. **Oil production** is also important to the state's economy.

Geography

The northernmost state of the **Great Plains** has very **fertile soil**. Farms cover most of the state's land area. The **Garrison Dam** on the **Missouri River** provides much needed water for crop irrigation. The western section of the state contains the **North Dakota Badlands** and **Theodore Roosevelt National Park**.

Climate: The climate of the state is moderate with hot summers and cold winters. It is often dry but does get some rain and snow.

History

Lewis and Clark wintered with the Mandan Indians in 1804–05.

Fun Facts

State Date: November 2, 1889
Motto: Liberty and Union, Now and Forever, One and Inseparable
Flower: Wild prairie rose
Bird: Western meadowlark
Tree: American elm
Song: "North Dakota Hymn"
Nicknames: Peace Garden State; Flickertail State; Roughrider State; Dakota, Sioux State
Web Site: www.nd.gov

Wild prairie rose

Ohio

★ Columbus

Capital

In 1964, Ohio native Geraldine F. Mock became the first woman to fly solo around the world. She left from **Columbus** flying the *Spirit of Columbus*.

Famous Citizen

Tecumseh, born in 1768 near Chillicothe, was a Shawnee chief. He fought with the American Indian Federation to keep settlers off American Indian lands.

Economy

Manufacturing is the most important economic activity in the state. The assembly of cars and trucks leads the sector. The largest bar **soap factory** in the country is in Cincinnati, Ohio.

Geography

To the north of the state is **Lake Erie**, and to the south lies the **Ohio River**. Both waterways are important for barge traffic and the economy. The interior contains the **Allegheny Plateau**, the **central plains**, and the **Erie lakeshore**. The plains area contains some of the most fertile farmland in the country.

Climate: Ohio has a temperate climate with cold winters and warm summers. There is moderate rain and snow during the year.

History

In 1953, President Eisenhower actually signed, and back dated, the papers to make Ohio a state.

Fun Facts

State Date: March 1, 1803
Motto: With God All Things Are Possible
Flower: Red carnation
Bird: Cardinal
Tree: Ohio buckeye
Song: "Beautiful Ohio"
Nickname: Buckeye State
Web Site: www.ohio.gov

Ohio buckeye

Oklahoma

★ Oklahoma City

Capital

Oklahoma City is nearly the same distance between New York City and Los Angeles. It has more than 130 miles of highways.

Famous Citizen

Maria Tallchief (1925–2013) was born in Fairfax. She was the first American Indian to break into ballet, and the first prima ballerina of the New York City Ballet.

Economy

Agriculture is important to Oklahoma's economy, especially the farming of cattle, wheat, and hogs. The **mining** of **petroleum** and **natural gas** as well as the manufacture of **oil field machinery** are also major aspects of Oklahoma's economy.

Geography

Flat, fertile plains and **low hills** are most common in Oklahoma. **Low mountains** exist in south central and southwestern parts of the state. Fertile soil is concentrated in the **Red River valley**.

Climate: The state has a continental, or moderate, climate with cold winters and hot summers. Oklahoma is likely to have many tornadoes.

History

In the 1800s, the U.S. government relocated more than 30 **American Indian tribes** to the area, then known as the Indian Territory.

Fun Facts

State Date: November 16, 1907
Motto: Labor Conquers All Things
Flower: Oklahoma rose
Bird: Scissor-tailed flycatcher
Tree: Redbud
Song: "Oklahoma!"
Nickname: Sooner State
Web Site: www.ok.gov

Oklahoma rose

Oregon

Salem

Capital

In 1840, missionaries came to the site where **Salem** is now located. A school, the Oregon Institute, was started there for local American Indians.

Famous Citizen

Linus Pauling was the only person to have won two unshared Nobel Prizes. He won his first in chemistry, the second for peace. He was born in Portland in 1901.

Economy

Oregon is a leading producer in the United States of **Christmas trees** and **hazelnuts**. Because of the mild climate in the Willamette River Valley, Oregon is a top producer of **berries**, **pears**, **plums**, and **cherries**.

Geography

Oregon is known for its **forests,** most of which can be found on the low level **coastal mountains** near the Pacific Ocean or on either the **Klamath** or the **Cascade Mountains**. Eastern Oregon is a **plateau** and contains wheat fields.

Climate: West of the Cascades there is heavy rainfall and moderate temperatures. East of the Cascades there is little precipitation and more extreme temperatures.

History

Pioneers came to Oregon across the plains on Conestoga wagons, or prairie schooners.

Fun Facts

State Date: February 14, 1859
Motto: She Flies with Her Own Wings
Flower: Oregon grape
Bird: Western meadowlark
Tree: Douglas fir
Song: "Oregon, My Oregon"
Nickname: Beaver State
Web Site: www.oregon.gov

Pears

Pennsylvania

Harrisburg ★

Capital

Harrisburg is the host each year for the largest indoor agricultural exposition in the United States. This immense farm show first started in 1916.

Famous Citizen

Louisa May Alcott (1832–1888) was born in Germantown. She was a best-selling author in her time. *Little Women* is a story based on herself and her sisters.

Economy

Pennsylvania has long been a leading **coal, petroleum,** and **natural gas-producing** state. The type of coal found in the state is harder and burns better than other types of coal, making it sell well since the early 1800s.

Geography

Pennsylvania has a small border on **Lake Erie**. Major rivers include the **Delaware, Susquehanna, Allegheny,** and **Ohio**. The **Allegheny Mountains** run diagonally across the state with **plateau**, **piedmont**, and **coastal plains** on the sides.

Climate: Pennsylvania has warm summers, while winters are usually freezing. Erie, Pennsylvania, is one of the snowiest cities in the country.

History

One of the 13 original colonies, Pennsylvania was founded by **William Penn**.

Fun Facts

State Date: December 12, 1787
Motto: Virtue, Liberty, and Independence
Flower: Mountain laurel
Bird: Ruffed grouse
Tree: Hemlock
Song: "Pennsylvania"
Nickname: Keystone State
Web Site: www.pa.gov

Mountain laurel

Rhode Island

Capital

During the 1800s, the eastside of **Providence** was mostly railroads, bridges, and industry. In the 1990s, rivers and railroads were moved to create Waterplace Park.

Famous Citizen

Matthew C. Perry was born in South Kingston in 1794. He led an expedition to Japan in 1853–54 that opened Japan to trade with the West.

Economy

Service industries, especially **finance**, are important to Rhode Island's economy. **Fishing** for cod, flounder, and a variety of shellfish is also important.

Geography

The southern edge of the smallest state is the **Atlantic Ocean**, and **Narragansett Bay** cuts deep into the state. Besides the lowland of **sandy beaches** and **salt marshes** along the bay and the ocean, the rest of Rhode Island is part of the **Appalachian Highlands**, a hilly plateau of forests and lakes.

Climate: The state has a humid climate with cold winters and warm summers. There have been quite a few damaging storms, floods, hurricanes, and blizzards that have affected the state.

History

Rhode Island signed the U.S. Constitution only after the **Bill of Rights** was added.

Fun Facts

State Date: May 29, 1790
Motto: Hope
Flower: Violet
Bird: Rhode Island red
Tree: Red maple
Song: "Rhode Island It's For Me!"
Nicknames: Ocean State; Little Rhody
Web Site: www.ri.gov

Rhode Island red

South Carolina

Capital

Columbia was a planned city. All of its streets and areas for the capitol and other buildings were laid out before they were built.

Famous Citizen

Mary McLeod Bethune (1875–1955), a civil rights activist, was born in Mayesville. She believed that education was the key to improving race relations. She started a school in Florida.

Economy

Trade, **services**, **manufacturing**, and **government sectors** define South Carolina's economy. **Travel** and **tourism** and **agriculture**, especially tobacco and peaches, are also important to the state's economy.

Geography

Much of eastern South Carolina is part of the **Atlantic Coastal Plain** with many rivers, rolling hills, and fertile soil. Traveling west and northwest is the **Piedmont** and the **Blue Ridge**—land that is more hilly and forested.

Climate: The state has a humid climate with warmer temperatures along the coast and cooler ones in the mountains. Summers are hot, and winters are mild with very little snow or sleet.

History

South Carolina was **one of the original 13 colonies**.

Fun Facts

State Date: May 23, 1788
Motto: Prepared in Mind and Resources; While I Breathe, I Hope
Flower: Yellow jessamine
Bird: Carolina wren
Tree: Palmetto
Songs: "Carolina"; "South Carolina on My Mind"
Nickname: Palmetto State
Web Site: www.sc.gov

Palmetto

South Dakota

★ Pierre

Capital

Pierre was selected as the state capital in 1889 when Congress divided Great Sioux Reservation into North and South Dakota.

Famous Citizen

L. Frank Baum moved to South Dakota in 1888 and lived there for three years. The description of Kansas in *The Wizard of Oz* is probably based on his time in the Dakota Territory.

Economy

The state is a leading producer of **beef**, **wheat**, **flaxseed**, **hay**, **oats**, **rye**, and **sunflower seeds**. Several large financial companies and a large computer company are located in the state.

Geography

Other than the corner of the state that contains the **Black Hills**, the balance of South Dakota is either **prairie** or **plains**, with the greatest portion being part of the **Great Plains**. The **Missouri River** runs through the center of the state providing fertile farmland to the east of the river.

Climate: The state has hot summers and very cold winters. The state also gets high winds because there are not many trees to stop the wind.

History

South Dakota is well known as the home of **Mt. Rushmore** and the **Crazy Horse Memorial**.

Fun Facts

State Date: November 2, 1889
Motto: Under God, the People Rule
Flower: Pasque
Bird: Ring-necked pheasant
Tree: Black Hills spruce
Song: "Hail, South Dakota"
Nickname: Mount Rushmore State
Web Site: www.sd.gov

Ring-necked pheasant

Tennessee

★ Nashville

Capital

Nashville has the nickname "Music City." It is famous for country music, a style of music based on songs brought by settlers.

Famous Citizen

Sequoyah was a member of the Cherokee tribe and was born about 1775 in Monroe County. He invented a written alphabet for the Cherokee language in 1821.

Economy

Farmland covers almost half of Tennessee. **Beef, chickens, dairy products, soybeans**, and **cotton** are the main farm products. But service industries such as **health care** and **business services** contribute more dollars overall.

Geography

Tennessee is a long state that allows it to have varied landforms. The **Great Smoky Mountains** lie in the east. The land flattens when moving west from **mountains** to **plateau** to a fertile **river basin** that has rich farmland. The **Tennessee, Cumberland,** and **Mississippi rivers** are important waterways.

Climate: Tennessee has warm summers, cool winters, with about 51 inches of rain each year.

History

Tennessee became popular for the push for **westward expansion** across the Appalachians.

Fun Facts

State Date: June 1, 1796
Motto: Agriculture and Commerce
Flower: Iris
Bird: Mockingbird
Tree: Tulip poplar
Songs: There are ten official state songs. Two are "My Homeland, Tennessee" and "When It's Iris Time in Tennessee."
Nickname: Volunteer State
Web Site: www.tn.gov

Iris

Texas

Austin ★

Capital

Austin is known as the "Live Music Capital of the World." Live music can be heard in grocery stores, the airport, clubs, restaurants, and at festivals, city council meetings, and countless other places throughout the city!

Famous Citizen

Buddy Holly, born in Lubbock, Texas, was an important rock singer and songwriter.

Economy

There is a big **livestock industry** as well as crops such as **cotton**, **rice**, **sugar cane**, and **fruits**. **Oil**, **gas**, **mining**, **manufacturing**, and **service industries** play a big part in the Texas economy.

Geography

Texas is so large that it has a **varied physical geography**. There are high plains, rolling prairies, pine-covered hills and swamps, dry areas, multiple fertile river valleys, and the coastal plains of the Gulf Coast.

Climate: The climate is varied. Generally, the summers are hot and the winters are short and mild. Rainfall in the eastern part of the state is around 56 inches per year, but in the western part, it is less than eight inches per year.

History

In 1836, after war with Mexico, Texas became a republic, or separate nation. Ten years later, it became part of the United States.

Fun Facts

State Date: December 29, 1845
Motto: Friendship
Flower: Bluebonnet
Bird: Mockingbird
Tree: Pecan
Song: "Texas, Our Texas"
Nickname: Lone Star State
Web Site: www.texas.gov

Livestock

Utah

★ Salt Lake City

Capital

Salt Lake City is the world headquarters of the Church of Jesus Christ of Latter Day Saints (Mormons).

Famous Citizen

Jim Bridger, American frontiersman, trapper, and trader, established an important supply fort in Utah territory. Many travelers to the West relied on supplies bought at Fort Bridger.

Economy

Mining is one of the most important parts of Utah's economy. In fact, the world's largest open pit copper mine lies just outside of Salt Lake City. The **Bingham Canyon** Mine is almost one mile deep!

Geography

From south to north, the state has a varied geography including **canyons**, **pastures**, **forests**, and **mountains**. The **Great Salt Lake** is the largest inland salt sea in the United States.

Climate: Utah's climate is very dry. Summers are usually hot and winters are mild. The mountains get about 40 inches of precipitation, but the western part of the state receives less than 5 inches.

History

The first **transcontinental railroad**, built from both east and west of the United States, met at **Promontory Summit** in 1869.

Fun Facts

State Date: January 4, 1896
Motto: Industry
Flower: Sego lily
Bird: California gull
Tree: Quaking aspen
Song: "Utah, This Is the Place"
Nickname: Beehive State
Web Site: www.utah.gov

California gull

Vermont

★Montpelier

Capital

Montpelier was selected as the state's capital in 1805 because of its central location.

Famous Citizen

Ethan Allen was born in 1738 in Connecticut. He bought land in the New Hampshire grants. Allen and other farmers started the Green Mountain Boys to protect their land. This land eventually became Vermont.

Economy

Service, electronics, and computer components industries contribute to Vermont's economy. **Granite**, **marble**, and **limestone** are all mined in the state. Vermont has the largest granite quarries in the United States. Maple products also sweeten the economy.

Geography

Lake Champlain runs along Vermont's western border. The **Green Mountains** run through the middle of the state and are primarily low and **forested**. Below the mountains are **rolling hills** and **fertile valleys** that support agriculture.

Climate: Vermont's climate has four distinct seasons and the precipitation is moderate throughout the year.

History

Vermont was an **independent republic**, or separate country, between 1777 and 1791 before it became the 14th state.

Fun Facts

State Date: March 4, 1791
Motto: Freedom and Unity
Flower: Red clover
Bird: Hermit thrush
Tree: Sugar maple
Song: "These Green Mountains"
Nickname: Green Mountain State
Web Site: www.vermont.gov

Red clover

Virginia

Richmond ★

Capital

In March of 1775, Patrick Henry delivered his famous speech, "Give me liberty or give me death," in St. John's Church in **Richmond.**

Famous Citizen

George Washington was a farmer, surveyor, commander-in-chief, and founding father. He was the first president of the United States, serving from 1789 to 1797.

Economy

Virginia's economy is a mix from the **service**, **mining**, **manufacturing**, **fishing**, and **agricultural** industries. **Crab** and **oyster** lead the fishing sector. Virginia is a leading employer of **technology** workers.

Geography

Virginia's eastern border is the **Atlantic Ocean**. Moving west, landforms include the Atlantic Coastal Plain, the piedmont, **Blue Ridge Mountains**, and the Appalachian ridge, valley, and plateau.

Climate: Virginia has a mild, humid coastal climate. Temperatures become cooler moving from the coast westward into the mountains. Yearly precipitation is about 44 inches.

History

During the **Civil War**, more than half of the battles were fought in Virginia.

Fun Facts

State Date: June 25, 1788
Motto: Thus Always to Tyrants
Flower: Dogwood
Bird: Cardinal
Tree: Dogwood
Song: "Carry Me Back to Old Virginia"
Nickname: Old Dominion
Web Site: www.virginia.gov

Crab

Washington

★ Olympia

Capital

The state's first fire engine company was established in **Olympia**. Known as Columbia Number 1, it was formed in 1865.

Famous Citizen

Born in Seattle in 1955, **Bill Gates** built one of the largest software businesses in the world, Microsoft. In the process, he became one of the world's richest people.

Economy

Washington is the leading **apple-producing** state. It produces 64% of the nation's apples. Besides agriculture, the state is a leader in the production of **aircraft, space,** and **communications equipment**.

Geography

The high mountains of the **Cascade Range** run north-south dividing the state. The western third is rainy and includes the **Olympic Peninsula** with its conifer forests and **temperate rainforest**. In contrast, the eastern two-thirds of the state has large areas of dry grassland plains.

Climate: Some areas of the coast receive more than 200 inches of rain each year! Areas in the eastern sections of the state are nearly as dry as a desert.

History

The 605-foot tall **Space Needle** is an observation tower that was built for the 1962 **World's Fair** in Seattle.

Fun Facts

State Date: November 11, 1889
Motto: Bye and Bye
Flower: Coast rhododendron
Bird: Willow goldfinch
Tree: Western hemlock
Song: "Washington, My Home"
Nickname: The Evergreen State
Web Site: www.access.wa.gov

Apple

West Virginia

★ Charleston

Capital

When West Virginia became a state, the legislature moved the capital a few times before settling on **Charleston** in 1885.

Famous Citizen

Pearl S. Buck, Pulitzer Prize and Nobel Prize winning author, was born in Hillsboro in 1892. She was the first American woman to receive both these awards.

Economy

Once a railroad was built in 1883, the coal in West Virginia could be shipped to other parts of the country. Many people came to work in the mines, but the jobs were dangerous because of accidents and explosions. Safety improvements eventually came to the mines, and West Virginia is still a leader in **coal production**.

Geography

The state is known for its **mountains, underground caverns,** and **sinkholes**. Parts of the **Appalachian Mountains** and the **Blue Ridge Mountains** run through the state.

Climate: It has a humid climate, with hot summers and cool to cold winters. Precipitation is about 44 inches per year.

History

President Lincoln issued a proclamation creating West Virginia from Virginia in 1863.

Fun Facts

State Date: June 20, 1863
Motto: Mountaineers Are Always Free
Flower: Rhododendron
Bird: Cardinal
Tree: Sugar maple
Songs: "The West Virginia Hills"; "This Is My West Virginia"; "West Virginia, My Home Sweet Home"; "Take Me Home, Country Roads"
Nickname: Mountain State
Web Site: www.wv.gov

Cardinal

Wisconsin

Capital
Madison, the "City of Lakes," has four lakes within its boundaries.

Famous Citizen
Laura Ingalls Wilder (1867–1957) was the author of what are known as the *Little House* books. She was born in a log cabin near Pepin, Wisconsin. Her memories of her first home are the basis for her first book in the series, *Little House in the Big Woods*.

Economy
Dairy farming leads agricultural activity in the state nicknamed the "Dairy State." Wisconsin is also the leading producer of **cranberries** and **paper** in the United States.

Geography
Most of Wisconsin was carved by **glaciers** thousands of years ago. They left **rich soil deposits** and more than 15,000 lakes. Important waterways include **Lake Superior, Lake Michigan, Lake Winnebago**, and the **Mississippi, Chippewa,** and **Wisconsin rivers**.

Climate: The state has four distinct seasons, with warm summers and very cold winters. Yearly precipitation is about 31 inches.

History
New miners to the state in the early 1800s lived in caves referred to as **badger dens**. This is the meaning of one state nickname.

Fun Facts
State Date: May 29, 1848
Motto: Forward
Flower: Wood violet
Bird: American robin
Tree: Sugar maple
Song: "On Wisconsin!"
Nicknames: America's Dairyland; Badger State
Web Site: www.wisconsin.gov

Dairy cow

Wyoming

Capital
Cheyenne was named for a local American Indian tribe. Settlement was so rapid that the city became known as the "Magic City of the Plains."

Famous Citizen
Nellie Tayloe Ross was the first elected woman governor to take office in the United States in 1925. She later became the first woman director of the U.S. Mint.

Economy
Wyoming is **cattle country**, resulting in strong income from livestock products. It is also a leading producer of **sheep** and **wool**. The other main portion of Wyoming's economy is from **coal, oil,** and **natural gas production**.

Geography
Wyoming is a "bridge" state where the **Great Plains** meet the **Rocky Mountains**. It is a plateau broken by mountain ranges. The **Continental Divide** runs through the state. The state is also home to **Yellowstone National Park**.

Climate: The state has a dry climate, with cold winters and warm summers. Temperatures can vary quite a bit between the mountains and the plains.

History
Wyoming is home to the world's first national park, **Yellowstone**, established in 1872.

Fun Facts
State Date: July 10, 1890
Motto: Equal Rights
Flower: Indian paintbrush
Bird: Western meadowlark
Tree: Plains cottonwood
Song: "Wyoming"
Nicknames: Big Wyoming; Equality State; Cowboy State
Web Site: www.wyo.gov

Indian paintbrush

A

abstract making use of shapes and patterns, rather than showing people or things as they actually are

adapt to change in order to survive

agribusiness farming on a large scale by big companies

agriculture the business of growing crops and raising animals

American Revolution the war in which the American colonies won independence from Great Britain

the Americas the landmasses and islands of North America and South America

aqueduct a pipe or canal for carrying water over a long distance

archaeologist a social scientist who studies the past by looking at artifacts people have left behind

archives a collection of historical documents and records

assembly line a process in which each worker assembles one part of a product before passing it on to the next worker down the line

B

basin a bowl-shaped landform that is lower than the surrounding land

bayou a stream that flows through a swamp

bill a proposal for a new law

border a boundary line that separates two places

budget a plan for how you will spend the money you expect to have

C

canal a ditch dug across land that often connects two waterways

canning preserving food by cooking and sealing it in cans or jars

canyon a deep, narrow valley with steep sides

capital a city where the government of a country or state is located

cavern a large cave

citizen a person who is born in a country or who chooses to become a member of that country by law

coastal plain low, flat land that runs along a coast

colony a settlement that is ruled by another country

combine a machine for cutting and threshing grain

compelling question a question you just need to know the answer to

conservation the careful use of a resource

culture a way of life shared by a group of people

D

dairy a farm that produces milk and milk products

dam a wall built across a river to stop the flow of water

Declaration of Independence the document that declared the United States to be free from Great Britain

delta a triangle-shaped area of land at the end of a river

democracy a form of government in which people vote for their leaders

demographics the facts you can study about a certain group of people, such as their ages, genders, or jobs

desert an area of land that receives very little rain

diverse made up of different groups of people

drought a long period of time when little or no rain falls

E

economy the way people in a community use resources to meet their needs and wants

evidence the facts you use to back up your claim

expedition a journey with a purpose

F

fact a true piece of information

factors of production the resources, including land, capital, and workers, used to create a good or service

fall line an imaginary line, marked by rapids and waterfalls, where rivers start to drop from higher land to lower land

federal government our national government that deals with issues that affect the entire country

feedlot an area or a building where livestock are kept while being fattened for slaughter

fertile able to produce good crops

fertilizer a substance added to the soil to improve plant growth

floodplain   the low, flat land along a river that may be underwater during a flood

foothills   a hilly region at the base of a mountain range

frontier   the beginning of unexplored land

G

geographic inquiry process   a five-step process that helps answer geographic questions

geography   the study of the natural and human features of Earth's surface, and its climate and life-forms

geyser   a spring that throws jets of heated water and steam into the air

global grid   the grid formed by crisscrossing lines of latitude and longitude on a map

gorge   a deep, narrow valley

H

habitat   the place where a type of animal typically lives in nature

history   the study of the past

hurricane   a storm, with heavy rains and high winds, that develops over the ocean and often moves toward land

I

immigrant   someone who comes from another place to live in a country

inland   not bordering an ocean or a large body of water by an ocean

industry   an organized economic activity connected with the production, manufacture, or construction of a particular product or range of products

irrigation   a way to bring water to dry land, using water from another location

L

legislator   a member of the branch of government that makes laws

levee   a wall typically made of dirt, built along a river to keep it from flooding

line of latitude   an imaginary line that runs east and west around the globe; also called a parallel

line of longitude   an imaginary line that runs between the North and South Poles; also called a meridian

livestock   animals that are raised on farms, such as cattle, hogs, and chickens

local government   city, town, and county governments

lock   a water elevator used to raise and lower boats

M

map key an explanation of what the symbols on a map stand for

market a place where economic activity occurs

mass production a way of making large quantities of products

meatpacking the preparing of meat for sale

megalopolis a "great city" consisting of a string of towns and cities where many people live

mesa a flat-topped hill

mill a factory in which people make products out of raw materials

mineral a natural material found in rock

mint a factory where the government makes coins

mission a Spanish settlement built to teach Christianity in North America

Mormon a member of the Church of Jesus Christ of Latter-day Saints

municipality an elected agency, or business, that performs a service for the state or city

N

natural resource a material found in nature that is useful to people

navigable deep enough and wide enough for ships to use

O

oasis a place in the desert that has water and trees

opinion what someone thinks or believes

P

pass a route across the mountains

peak the top of a mountain

pesticide a substance used on crops to kill insects and other pests

petroleum a thick, black liquid found underground

plantation a large farm, usually worked by many laborers

plateau a high, flat landform that rises steeply from the land around it

political science the study of governments and how they work

pollution any substance that makes air, water, or soil dirty or unsafe to use

population density a measure of the average number of people living in one unit of area

prairie flat or gently rolling land that is covered with tall grasses and wildflowers

primary source a source created by someone who has seen or taken part in the events described

R

reaper a machine for cutting grain

rebellion an armed fight against a government

region an area that shares similar features

republic a type of government in which people choose leaders to act for them

reservation public land set aside by the government for use by American Indians

reservoir an area where water is stored for people's use

right of free petition the right of the people to give legislators ideas for new laws

river basin the area around a river and its tributaries

S

savanna a flat grassland

scale a diagram that shows the relationship between distances on a map and real distances on Earth

scarcity the idea that the things and the resources people want are limited

secondary source a source created by someone who has not seen or taken part in the events described

segregation the separation of people because of race, religion, or gender

self-sufficient doing everything necessary to take care of yourself on your own

skyscraper a very tall building

sod a mixture of dirt and roots of grass

special-purpose map a map that shows just one kind of information such as rainfall or elevation

state constitution a written statement of a plan for a state government

state government the government of an individual state that deals with issues that affect that state

strip mine a place where minerals are scraped from the ground

swamp a low area of land that is covered by water at least part of the year

system of checks and balances a system set up in the U.S. Constitution to allow each branch of government ways to limit the power of the other two branches

T

tax the money that people and businesses pay to the government to support its functions

technology the use of tools and ideas to meet people's needs

tenement a four- to six-story building with many small apartments

tornado a violent and powerful windstorm that is shaped like a funnel

transportation hub a city that serves as a center for moving goods and people

U

United States Constitution the plan of government for the United States

W

wage a payment of money for work

wastewater water that has been used

E

Hudson, Henry, 55
Hudson River (New York), 66
Hunter Mountain (New York), 250–251
Hurricane Andrew, 102, 130–133
Hurricane Katrina, 37, 107
hurricanes, 102
    categories of, 132
    National Hurricane Center, 130
    in the Southeast, 127

I

ice age, 40, 62
Iditarod Trail, 223
Iditarod Trail Sled Dog Race, 223
Illinois
    Central Middle School (Burlington, Illinois), 296
    Champaign, 74
    Chicago, *see* Chicago, Illinois
    cities in, 74
    Monks Mound, 12–14
    Springfield, 74, 75
    "The Corn Belt," 170
    University of Illinois, 74
Illinois Capitol Building, 75
immigrants, 44
    African-American, *see* African Americans
    Asian, 48, *see also* Asian Americans
    Cambodian, 49
    Chinese, 48, 49, 224, 238
    European, 44, 274, *see also* European Americans
    French, 44
    German, 45
    Indian, 49
    Irish, 45

Italian, 56
Japanese, 48, 49, 224
Korean, 48, 49
Laotian, 49
Pacific Islanders, 49
Philippine, 48, 49, 224
Polish, 45
Portuguese, 224
Russian, 44, 56
Thai, 49
Vietnamese, 49
Independence Day (July 4, 1776), 69
Independence Hall (Philadelphia), 69, 281
Indiana
    major products of, 258
    population diversity in, 258
Indian immigrants, 49
industry, 124
    assembly line, 143
    automobile industry, 143, 278, 279
    factors of production, 288
    geography and, 260
    in Indiana, 258
    lumber industry, 222
    mass production, 68
    in Ohio, 148, 149
    in Paterson, New Jersey, 264
    in the Southeast, 124
    in Washington, 292
    workers, *see* workers
    in your state, 148–149
inland regions, 28
insecticides, 162
    crop dusters, 135, 162
International Rose Test Garden (Portland, Oregon), 253
Internet research, 187, 261
    Washington Department of Commerce, 187
inventions, 94–97

Iowa, 139
    name, meaning of, 41
    "The Corn Belt," 170
Irish Americans, 45
irrigation, 196
    in the Grand Canyon by the Havasupais, 210
Italian Americans, 45
Italian immigrants, 56

J

James River (Virginia), 104
Jamestown, Virginia, 104, 259
Japanese immigrants, 48, 49, 224
jazz, 107
Jefferson, Thomas, 72, 141, 230
Jefferson Memorial (Washington, D.C.), 72
jobs, 290, *see also* industry
    in the Northeast, 87
John F. Kennedy Elementary School (Franklin, Massachusetts), 308–311
John F. Kennedy Space Center, 103
John Muir Trail (Sierra Nevada), 231
Judge, Oney, 283
judicial branch
    federal, 71, 301
    state, 183, 301

K

Kansas
    Dodge City, 140
    golden wheat of, 140
    plains of, 140
Kennedy Space Center, 103
Kentucky, 226, 227
    celebrations in, 227
    symbols of, 227
    tourist spots in, 226

King, Martin Luther, Jr., 110
Korean immigrants, 48, 49

L

M

New York City, *see* New York City

Philadelphia, Pennsylvania, *see* Philadelphia, Pennsylvania

places to live in, 86

pollution in, 89

population density in, 84–86

population map of, 61

"train tour" of, 59–73

transportation in, 88, 96

Washington, D.C., *see* Washington, D.C.

Northern Hemisphere, 20

North Korean immigrants, 49

North Pole, 18, 20, 21

Northwest Ordinance (1787), 275

O

oasis, 246

Oglala, 141

O'Hare International Airport (Chicago, Illinois), 144

Ohio

coal mining in, 149

industry in, 148, 149

oil refineries, 108

oil rigs in the Gulf of Mexico, 108

Oklahoma

Guthrie, 184–185

land rush, 184, 185

Old City Hall (Philadelphia, Pennsylvania), 280

Old Faithful (Yellowstone National Park), 217

Old State House (Boston, Massachusetts), 65, 270, 309

opinions, 112

orange groves, 125

Oregon

Pacific Coast Trail, 228–231

Portland, *see* Portland, Oregon

Willamette Valley, 31

Oregon Trail, 242, 276

Otis, Elisha, 95

oxen-drawn plows, 157

Ozette village (Makah Indians), 266–269

P

Pacific Coast, 242

Pacific Crest Trail, 228–231

Pacific Islanders

immigrants to the U.S., 49

in Salt Lake City, Utah, 237

Pacific Ocean, 25

paper mills, 124

pass, 216

Passaic River, 264

Paterson, New Jersey, 264

peaks (mountains), 63

Pennsylvania

Hershey, 68

Leap the Dips (Altoona), 112

Philadelphia, *see* Philadelphia, Pennsylvania

pesticides, 162

crop dusters, 135, 162

petitioning the legislature, 309, 310

"petrochemicals," 108

petroleum, 108

Pettway, Arlonzia, 114, 116

Pettway, Mark, 115

Philadelphia, Pennsylvania, 69

historical events in, 280–283

Liberty Bell, 112, 113

as U.S. capital, 280

Philippine immigrants, 48, 49, 224

Phoenix, Arizona, 177

physical maps, 23

Piedmont of Southeast Coastal Plain, 120, 123, 125

Pilgrims, 64

pioneers, 138

Pittock, Georgiana, 253

plains

coastal, 26, 29, *see also* Coastal Plain

flat, 28

floodplains, 126

Great Plains, *see* Great Plains (Midwest U.S.)

of Kansas, 140

plantations

cotton plantation (Natchez, Mississippi), 109

slavery, *see* slavery

plastic (corn-based), 171

plateaus, 29

plows, 157

machine-plows, 163

steel, 160

Plymouth, Massachusetts, 64

Plymouth Harbor (Massachusetts), 64

Polish Americans, 45

political candidates, 303

political maps, 23

political science, 6

and Cahokia (American Indian city), 14

questions asked by political scientists, 9

pollution, 89

from fertilizers, 161

in the Northeast, 89

from pesticides, 161

population density and, 89

population density, 84

Denver, Colorado, 235

in the Northeast, 84–86

pollution and, 89

tables, 92

apple orchards in, 167
Jamestown, 104, 259
poultry farms in, 166
Shenandoah Valley, 166
Winchester, 167
voters and voting, 70, 303

W

Wabanoki, 62
Waikiki Beach (Honolulu), 224
Wasatch Mountains (Utah), 236
Washington, D.C., 70
    government buildings in, 70, 71
    national monuments in, 72–73
Washington, George, 72, 141, 281, 282, 283
Washington, Hercules, 283
Washington, Martha, 282, 283
Washington, Moll, 283
Washington Monument (Washington, D.C.), 72
Washington state
    Department of Commerce, 292
    economy of, 292
    Ozette village (Makah Indians), 266–269
    Pacific Coast Trail, 228–231
    Seattle, 240–241
    Tacoma, 222
wastewater, 204
water
    conservation of, 203–205
    in the Grand Canyon, 209–210
    in your state, 206–207
water company, 199
water municipality, 199
water pollution, 89
waterpower, 77
"Welcome to Fabulous Las Vegas, Nevada" sign, 246

West, 30–31
    California's Central Valley, 220
    cities of, 233–247, *see also specific city*
    Columbia River Gorge National Scenic Area, 221
    Honolulu, Hawaii, 224
    Leadville, Colorado, 218
    Lolo Pass, Montana, 216
    maps of, 29, 214, 215
    Pacific Crest Trail, 228–231
    roadways, map of, 215
    settlers in, 276
    Southern California, 219
    Tacoma, Washington, 222
    "van and airplane tour," 213–225
    Yellowstone National Park (Wyoming), 217
Western Hemisphere, 21
West Quoddy Head, Maine, 62
West Quoddy Head Lighthouse (Maine), 62
Westward expansion of the U.S., 276
wetlands, 27
whale oil, 268
wheat
    Kansas's golden wheat, 140
    in the Midwest region, 137
White, Jim, 180
White House (Washington, D.C.), 71, 72, 282
White Mountains (New Hampshire), 63
wildlife
    Colorado River, use of water in, 201
    in the Everglades National Park (Florida), 102
    habitats, 201
Willamette River, 242, 252
Willamette Valley (Oregon), 31

Willow Run Factory (Detroit, Michigan), 151–152
Willy Wonka and the Chocolate Factory (Dahl), 68
Winchester, Virginia, 167
2002 Winter Olympics, 237
Wisconsin's natural resources, 128, 129
wood products industry, 222
Woods, Granville, 96
workers, 290
    at Lowell (Massachusetts) textile mills, 78–81
    unemployment, 148, 149
    in your state, 288
World Series of 1932, 145
1962 World's Fair, 240
World War II
    Denver, Colorado during, 234
    Detroit, Michigan during, 150–153
    Las Vegas, Nevada during, 247
    Portland, Oregon during, 243
    San Jose, California during, 244
Wrigley Field (Chicago), 145
Wyoming
    Colorado River Compact, 197
    Yellowstone National Park, 217

Y

Yankee Stadium (New York City), 250
Yellowstone National Park (Wyoming), 217
Yukon Territory of Canada, 240

CREDITS

Lesson 7

118: Robert Harding Picture Library/Superstock **120 T:** Thinkstock **120 B:** Thinkstock **122:** Thinkstock **123:** Thinkstock **124 L:** iStockphoto **124 R:** Shutterstock **125 L:** Thinkstock **125 R:** Thinkstock **126:** Shutterstock **127:** Thinkstock **128:** iStockphoto **129:** iStockphoto **130:** NASA/NOAA **131:** Shutterstock **132 T:** Corbis/Superstock **133 T:** Corbis/Superstock **133 B:** Steve Starr/Corbis

Lesson 8

134: Thinkstock **138:** Thinkstock **139:** Thinkstock **140 L:** Shutterstock **140 R:** Andre Jenny/Alamy **141 T:** Thinkstock **141 B:** Cindy J. Daly/Dreamstime **142 T:** age fotostock/Superstock **143:** Library of Congress **144:** Shutterstock **145:** iStockphoto **146:** Jeff Coleman/Dreamstime **147:** Yanmingzhang/Dreamstime **149:** Thinkstock **150:** Library of Congress **151:** Bettmann/Corbis **152:** Library of Congress **153:** Bettmann/Corbis

Lesson 9

154: Kentannenbaum/Dreamstime **156:** Vladislav Gajic/Dreamstime **157:** North Wind Picture Archives/Alamy **158:** North Wind Picture Archives/Alamy **159:** Bettmann/Corbis **160:** Shutterstock **161:** Shutterstock **162:** Thinkstock **163 L:** Ilene MacDonald/Alamy **163 R:** Shutterstock **165:** Corbis

166: Purestock/Alamy **167:** Map courtesy of Virginia Agriculture in the Classroom. An online interactive version of the map as well as other resources can be found at www.AgInTheClass.org. **168:** iStockphoto **169 TR:** Shutterstock **169 TL:** Shutterstock **169 B:** Wikimedia Commons **171:** Roger Ressmeyer/Corbis

Lesson 10

172: Thinkstock **176:** Shutterstock **177:** Barry Howe/Corbis **178:** iStockphoto **180:** iStockphoto **182:** iStockphoto **183:** iStockphoto **184:** Library of Congress **185:** Justin Brotton/Dreamstime **187:** Thinkstock **188:** Bettmann/Corbis **189:** Bettmann/Corbis **190:** Shutterstock **191:** Danwatt417/Dreamstime

Lesson 11

192: Slowder1/Dreamstime **194:** Kaye Eileen Oberstar/Dreamstime **195:** Corbis **196:** Jim West/Alamy **197:** Herbert Hoover Presidential Library **198 R:** 167/David Edwards/Ocean/Corbis **199 L:** Verabutr Piriyanontana/Dreamstime **199 R:** Tokyo Space Club/Corbis **200:** Thinkstock **201:** National Geographic Image Collection/Alamy **202:** Thinkstock **203:** AgStock Images/Corbis **204:** Thinkstock **205:** Thinkstock **206:** Thinkstock **207 T:** Ted Spiegel/Corbis **207 B:** iStockphoto

208: National Geographic/SuperStock **209:** Danny Magee/Dreamstime **210:** Library of Congress **211:** Thinkstock

Lesson 12

212: Oksanaphoto/Dreamstime **216:** Macduff Everton/Corbis **217:** iStockphoto **218:** Americanspirit/Dreamstime **219:** Radekdrewek/Dreamstime **220:** Danita Delimont/Alamy **221 T:** iStockphoto **222:** George Kroll/Dreamstime **223:** Jeanninebryan/Dreamstime **224 T:** Andre Jenny/Alamy **224 B:** Thinkstock **225:** iStockphoto **226:** Thinkstock **227 TL:** Thinkstock **227 TR:** Thinkstock **227 BL:** Thinkstock **227 BR:** Thinkstock **229:** Robert Findlay/Dreamstime **230:** Troy Farr/Dreamstime **231 T:** Library of Congress **231 B:** Wyatt Shudlick/Alamy

Lesson 13

232: Thinkstock **234:** iStockphoto **235 B:** Shutterstock **236:** iStockphoto **237 B:** Erik Isakson/Tetra Images/Corbis **238:** iStockphoto **239 B:** Ben Blankenburg/Corbis **240:** Thinkstock **241 B:** iStockphoto **242:** Thinkstock **243 B:** Thinkstock **244:** Thinkstock **245 B:** Luchschen/Dreamstime **246:** Welcomia/Dreamstime **247 B:** Wojciech Kimborowicz/Dreamstime **248 L:** Ambientideas/Dreamstime

248 R: Teri Virbickis/Dreamstime
251 T: Thinkstock **251 B:** Thinkstock
252: Photodisc/Alamy **253:** George
Ostertag/Alamy **254:** Thinkstock

Lesson 14

256: Rick Moulton/Dreamstime
259: iStockphoto **260:** iStockphoto
261: iStockphoto **262:** Thinkstock
263: F11photo/Dreamstime
264: Gary718/Dreamstime
265: Thinkstock **266 R:** Thinkstock
267: Thinkstock **268 B:** iStockphoto
268 T: Library of Congress
269: WorldFoto/Alamy

Lesson 15

270: Julia Freeman-woolpert/
Dreamstime **272 L:** Shutterstock
272 R: The Granger Collection,
New York **273:** Shutterstock
274: Larry Gevert/Dreamstime
276 B: Shutterstock **276 T:** Library
of Congress **277:** Gavril Margittai/
Dreamstime **279:** Library of
Congress **280 L:** Shutterstock
280 R: Alexandre Fagundes
De Fagundes/Dreamstime
281: Aviahuismanphotography/
Dreamtime **282:** The Granger
Collection, New York
283 T: Wikimedia Commons
283 B: Aviahuismanphotography/
Dreamtime

Lesson 16

284: Thinkstock **286:** Thinkstock
287 L: Thinkstock **287 R:** Thinkstock
288: Thinkstock **290 L:** Thinkstock
290 R: Thinkstock **291:** Thinkstock
293: Thinkstock **294:** Thinkstock
295: iStockphoto **296:** Thinkstock
297: Thinkstock

Lesson 17

298: Thinkstock **300:** Thinkstock
302: Thinkstock **303:** iStockphoto
305: Thinkstock **306:** Seth Perlman/
AP/Corbis **307:** Thinkstock
308 K: Thinkstock **308 C:** iStockphoto
308 R: Lukas Blazek/Dreamstime
309: Thinkstock

Back Matter

310–311: Thinkstock
312: Shutterstock **314:** ClassicStock/
Alamy **315:** Thinkstock
316: National Archives
317 T: Thinkstock **317 C:** Hill Street
Studios/Blend Images/Corbis
317 B: iStockphoto **318:** Fotosearch
319: Library of Congress **319:**
Library of Congress **320:** 68/
Ocean/Corbis **321 TL:** iStockphoto
321 TR: Shutterstock **321 BL:** United
States Department of State
321 BR: United States Department
of State **322:** Thinkstock **323:** Bob
Adelman/Corbis **334:** Monkey
Business Images/Dreamstime
335: Hero Images Inc./Alamy
336: Thinkstock **337:** Modfos/
Dreamstime **338 T:** iStockphoto
338 B: Roman Krochuk/
Dreamstime **339 T:** Steven Love/

Dreamstime **339 B:** Thinkstock
340 T: Shutterstock **340 B:** Thinkstock
341 T: Thinkstock
341 B: Marianne Campolongo/
Dreamstime **342 T:** iStockphoto
342 B: iStockphoto
343 T: Shutterstock
343 B: Xuanmai2009/
Dreamstime **344 T:** Thinkstock
344 B: iStockphoto **345 T:** Thinkstock
345 B: Shutterstock
346 T: Shutterstock
346 B: Steve Byland/Dreamstime
347 T: Thinkstock **347 B:** iStockphoto
348 T: Thinkstock **348 B:** Le-thuy
Do/Dreamstime **349 T:** Shutterstock
349 B: iStockphoto
350 T: iStockphoto
350 B: Thinkstock **351 T:** iStockphoto
351 B: Thinkstock **352 T:** iStockphoto
352 B: Shutterstock **353 T:** Thinkstock
353 B: Thinkstock **354 T:** iStockphoto
354 B: Shutterstock **355 T:** Maria
Janicki/Alamy **355 B:** Shutterstock
356 T: Thinkstock **356 B:** iStockphoto
357 T: Steven Frame/
Dreamstime **357 B:** Scottnodine/
Dreamstime **358 T:** Shutterstock
358 B: Shutterstock
359 T: iStockphoto
359 B: iStockphoto
360 T: iStockphoto **360 B:** Feng Yu/
Dreamstime **361 T:** Shutterstock
361 B: iStockphoto
362 T: iStockphoto
362 B: Shutterstock